On the Threshold of the Apocalypse

1913-1915

The Gate of the Humble...

LÉON BLOY

Translated By Richard Robinson

Sunny Lou Publishing Company
Portland, Oregon, USA
http://www.sunnyloupublishing.com

2nd Edition: Mar 29, 2024
Original Publication Date: September 6, 2021

ISBN: 978-1-955392-65-5

* * *

This translation from French is based on
the Mercure de France edition of
Au Seuil de l'Apocalypse, Paris, 1916.

Contents

Foreword

Sed ut perspiciatis, unde omnis iste natus error sit voluptatem accusantium doloremque laudantium, totam rem aperiam eaque ipsa, quae ab illo inventore veritatis et quasi architecto beatae vitae dicta sunt, explicabo. Nemo enim ipsam voluptatem, quia voluptas sit, aspernatur aut odit aut fugit, sed quia consequuntur magni dolores eos, qui ratione voluptatem sequi nesciunt, neque porro quisquam est, qui dolorem ipsum, quia dolor sit, amet, consectetur, adipisci velit, sed quia non numquam eius modi tempora incidunt, ut labore et dolore magnam aliquam quaerat voluptatem. Ut enim ad minima veniam, quis nostrum exercitationemullam corporis suscipit laboriosam, nisi ut aliquid ex ea commodi consequatur? Quis autem vel eum iure reprehenderit, qui in ea voluptate velit esse, quam nihil molestiae consequatur, vel illum, qui dolorem eum fugiat, quo voluptas nulla pariatur? [33] At vero eos et accusamus et iusto odio dignissimos ducimus, qui blanditiis praesentium voluptatum deleniti atque corrupti, quos dolores et quas molestias excepturi sint, obcaecati cupiditate non provident, similique sunt in culpa, qui officia deserunt mollitia animi, id est laborum et dolorum fuga. Et harum quidem rerum facilis est et expedita distinctio. Nam libero tempore, cum soluta nobis est eligendi optio, cumque nihil impedit, quo minus id, quod maxime placeat, facere possimus, omnis voluptas assumenda est, omnis dolor repellendus. Temporibus autem quibusdam et aut officiis debitis aut rerum necessitatibus saepe eveniet, ut et voluptates repudiandae sint et molestiae non recusandae. Itaque earum rerum hic tenetur a sapiente delectus, ut aut reiciendis voluptatibus maiores alias consequatur aut perferendis doloribus asperiores repellat.

– Cicero, 45 BC (*de Finibus Bonorum et Malorum*)

Dedication

For Jean de la Laurencie

You are, my very dear friend, among those who cannot forget a thing. It is clearly a redoubtable grace, but a true divine grace, as it works in souls opposite to the enterprises of Death.

This book, full of the Unforgettable, ought above all to suit a wounded heart, and it is for that reason that it is dedicated to you.

Whatever our paths in life might be, you know, we are all guests of Light, Glory, and unimaginable Peace. That which one calls the Milky Way, without understanding a thing about it, is an immense river of tears whose estuary is located at Paradise.

It is there and nowhere else, my dear Jean, that I will see you again.

– LÉON BLOY.

Mévoisins, 29 September 1915.

Introduction

There happened to be, in the 19th and 20th centuries, a nation that would undertake what had never been seen before in History: THE EXTINCTION OF THE AXES. That is called *German Culture*.

To enslave, to degrade souls, – that no longer sufficed the Prince of Darkness. He needed to extinguish them and he succeeded. Prussian Germany ceased to belong to humanity. It became an enormous, ferocious brute and menaced the entire world.

In a book very anterior to the present events, to which my memories of 1870 were consigned,[1] I had tried to give a warning. I was judged excessive, intempestive, and profoundly unjust. The benumbed French soul did not sense the monster's approach.

The reawakening has been what it had to be: infinite horror and near death. Here we are for more than one year engaged in horrifying battles, not only in France, but everywhere, in order to save the poor human lamp.

May God make this book, written by an old solitary, have the power, even in the hour of death, to recomfort some souls of God, some rare and dolorous tenants of Christian Grandeur and Beauty that some want to efface!

---

[1] a book: *Sueur de sang* (*Sweating Blood*).

1913

January

1ˢᵗ. – I feel a sort of interior consolation, and even a little bit of pride, thinking that the only letter come to-day is that from a poor old man absolutely incapable of being useful to me, unless by his prayers and the acceptation of his sufferings.

2. – From Christine van der Meer to Jeanne:

> *What a nice day we had together! You have no idea what a clear impression I had of your souls which appeared beautiful, strong, and impassioned to me! How I love them, those dear souls! Your husband's is of a heroic simplicity. He is truly the monster who, with his supernatural vision, sees and judges all things and turns upside down the apparent order of the poor world. How great and dear to God he appeared to me!*

Letter from two young soldiers who came to see me, I no longer remember when. They wish me, not banally, suffering and pain for 1913. Such wishes will not be long in coming perhaps.

4. – *The Official Doctrine of the University*, by Pierre Lasserre. A book not devoid of talent, which shows the universitarian quagmire and makes it felt. Occasion of an hors-d'œuvre in a new series of the *Exegesis of Commonplaces*, my present work.

7. – Letter from P. L. reproaching me for certain pages in the *Old Man of the Mountain*, in which he finds me unjust and harsh, which is possible, but I had such a need to do away with that frightening boor!

Visit by another, no less frightening boor. He brings a horrible Holy Face, drawn and painted by himself, which he believes to be a work of art. Immediately a conference for more than two hours on the Holy Shroud of Turin, which inspired him, and which he's committed to proving to us the perfect authenticity of. Swamp of eloquence. I didn't have it in me to stop that chatterbox.

8. – Interminable letter from the same. Not content with having bored me to tears yesterday, he sends me several sentimental pages in which he talks only of himself and the dolorous state of his soul devoid of consolations. I am threatened with frequent visits and, what's more, he sends me a list of the books of mine that he possesses, desiring also to possess all the others, with *dedications*. Deliver me, O Lord, from the multitude of admirers!

10. – Infantile verses from a young Corsican of Bas-

tia. Dedication wherein I'm treated like a hero. Several pieces being addressed to great men like Haraucourt, I have the curiosity to look for my name as a hero. The young and enthusiastic poet thought that it might be compromising to name me.

12. – In *l'Univers*:

> *On the occasion of the reconvening of Chambers and in order to summon the lights and graces of the Holy Ghost on the works of Parliament and specially on the election of the President of the Republic, His Em. the Cardinal Archbishop of Chambéry has prescribed public prayers in all the churches.*

13. – The engraver Vibert has undertaken to make my portrait. Very long sitting. He is a Godless man and Genevan. He tells me that he was baptized into the church of Loyson, formerly Father Hyacinthe.[2] What kind of portrait will he be able to make?… It has to do with an exhibition of my face at the head of a beautiful edition of *The Desperate Man*[3] which Georges Crès is preparing.

---

[2]Father Hyacinthe: Charles Loyson (1827-1912), a Catholic priest who was excommunicated by the church in 1869. Married in 1872 (to an American, at Westminster Abbey), he founded his own Neo-Gallican Church in 1878.

[3]*The Desperate Man*: in English translation, Snuggly Books, 2020.

14. – To a pirate:

> *I have just received what you sent me.*
> *That renewed proof of your devotion*
> *was sweet for me after a very rough*
> *beginning of the new year. You would*
> *like to see me "installed in glory, in*
> *this life even." I fear that you will*
> *need to quit that desire or that hope.*
> *Based on the experience of my last*
> *book,* The Soul of Napoleon,[4] *it is*
> *conclusive. God* does not want it, *that*
> *much seems clear. One does not*
> *conceive of me having success, like*
> *Barrès, for example, or M. Bottom. My*
> *friends, no longer seeing me suffer,*
> *would not recognize me anymore and*
> *would be disgusted with me. Some-*
> *thing in the divine plan of things*
> *would be upset. Yesterday, I posed*
> *three or four hours for my portrait,*
> *before a sort of artist. "I am an ocean*
> *of contempt," I explained to that man,*
> *"and it is I who launched the iceberg*
> *that cut into the flanks of the Titanic."*
> *How could I become a prairie studded*
> *with flowers where the ruminants of*
> *contemporary sottishness graze?*

17. – To a religious:

> *... I imagine that the martyrs them-*
> *selves sometimes let groans escape*

---

[4]*The Soul of Napoleon*: in English translation, Sunny Lou Publishing. 2021.

when their sorrow was too terrible. God keep me from comparing myself to those great men, from comparing my very inferior sufferings to their sufferings, which, however, were sometimes quite long, much longer even than one thinks. There is in my past of thirty years ago a gulf that I have not shown, that God alone knows and that I brush aside the memory of. One day, my wife, surprised to see me suffering, said to a priest of our friends that she was afraid I lacked resignation. That priest, who is, happily, a man of wit, responded to her, "What do you know? Let him complain, it does him good and does not displease God." What's more, I know I have exactly what I asked for, formerly... How could I have written my books, if I had lived a life of delights? After that, if I lament sometimes, it is like women at delivery, because I cannot do otherwise. But my courage returns soon enough and even gaiety.

A quite unexpected circumstance brought me to Versailles at the very moment when Poincaré's[5] election was decided, the result of a beautiful parliamentary cuisine. The crowds were considerable and extremely excited. But I did not see any scenes of clashes. One is stupid and cowardly, simply.

[5]Poincaré: Raymond Poincaré (1860-1934), president of the French Third Republic from 1913-1920.

19. – To Raïssa Maritain:

*My beloved goddaughter, I was think-
ing, this morning, of the three of you,
remembering that fear you have of the
Septuagesima, of that first sigh from
the Garden of Gethsemane.* Circum-
dederunt me gemitus mortis. *If you are
really tested ordinarily at this time in
the liturgical calendar, be happy, on
the contrary. What a sign of predestination!*

*Generally, Christians capable
of love do not feel the mourning of the
Church except at the start of Ash
Wednesday or the first Sunday in Lent.
You are among the small number of
privileged people who feel more profoundly and who can give more than
others. What have you got to fear? I
am telling you that you are blessed,
and you must believe me. Did you not
feel, this morning, how amorously
Saint Paul calls you to the baptism of
our fathers* in Moses, *in the clouds
and in the sea,[6] and the delight that
was given to them to eat and drink
spiritually as happens for us, the Lord
having promised to serve us in person,
like a domestic, promise recorded in
the Gospel of Saint Luke! Isn't that the
drunkenness that was promised to us*

---

[6]baptism... in Moses: 1 Corinthians 10:1-2.

by Someone who is dead-drunk in love, each morning? Have we anything else to do in life but to get drunk like him and with him? It is why the workers of the last hour are paid as much as the others. Isn't it necessary that they should be able to go altogether to get drunk at the Son of God's cabaret, at the end of the day[7]

My truly beloved godchildren, I would like to tell you something. But I have drunk so much since morning, before having worked even, that I do not find my equilibrium of a prophet. So, I beg you charitably to suppose that I have told you something and suffer me to embrace you with the tenderness of an old drunk!

21. – Dedication for one of my books:

To my very dear... Animæ ejus conglutinata est anima mea et inivi fœdus cum eo ad dedecus et exitium apostatarum.[8]

(Broken pact. The very dear person aban-

---

[7]Editor's Note: the remainder of this passage may have been suppressed by the original censors. Thus the lack of an end stop.

[8]*Animæ... apostatarum*: Latin for "My soul is bound to his soul, and I entered into a pact with him, for the shame and destruction of apostates."

doned me soon afterwards, a women even more dear having forbidden him to see me.)

22. – A religious speaks to me about the terrible situation of priests who suffer persecution and for whom nobody prays. *Foris pugnæ, intus timores,*[9] said Saint Paul.

"Ah! ah! you are a Bonapartist!" the curate of Bourg-la-Reine said to me. That's all he saw in a copy of *The Soul of Napoleon* that I had given to him.

31. – To Philippe Raoux:

> ... *It is true that the insuccess of my book was very difficult for me. But you are right to write to me that I can bear, all the same, resplendent victories in the Invisible. The Invisible, it is composed of souls, and I know that many have been deeply touched. I have received extraordinary letters from Holland, Finland, etc. Poor and simple priests have written to me that I was their benefactor, the reading of my books having given them what nobody had given them until then. Yesterday even, at the funeral service of an unfortunate man, incredulous for a long time, for whom we had had the good fortune, my wife and I, of procuring a Christian end, the priest,*

---

[9]*Foris... timores*: Latin for "fighting without, fears within," 2 Corinthians 7:5.

an old missionary, gave an emotional speech to inform the audience that the conversion of the deceased was due to the reading of the books by Léon Bloy. Imprudent words that he could be punished for, if the Archbishop found out.

I continue to explore the Commonplaces. *When you read this new series, becoming familiar with my tribulations and my present state of troubles and disquietude, you will be surprised probably to see in me such good humor, apparent good humor at any rate. I don't understand it myself. One would have to think that there was an extraordinary double personality, my sad person and the strange preacher that God has instilled in me. But will that book be able to be published only?*

I think like you do, and for a long time now, that some terrible things are about to happen. Will the universal evil come, as always, from Germany, Austria, or Prussia? God knows, but one begins to feel it as inevitable. Have you noticed that there are almost no more gold coins [in circulation]? When one wants to change a banknote, one is bombarded with one-hundred sous pieces. The Bank has returned all the gold coin to its vaults, in prevision for some dreadful war. It's a panic. For the grace of God, and would that he might have pity on us all!

February

1st. – Embarkation, back to her village, of a little sixteen-year-old domestic, picked up, two years ago, in Périgord and who turned out to be a nightmare for us. We had to call the police to constrain her to leave. Jeanne told me that horrible and troubling thing which the miserable girl exhaled from her mouth, an appalling odor of excrement.

6. – To the Abbot Cornuau:

> *...Yes, dear friend, I work on the second in a series of my* Commonplaces, *and I assure you that it is exceedingly difficult. Already the first had caused me a great deal of trouble. But, in ten years, I have had the leisure of exasperating myself, and I want to believe that a greater intensity will be the recompense of my zeal.*

> *You have understood that it is not merely a question of flagellating the Bourgeois, which gives a certain, but insufficient satisfaction doubtless. I have principally a view, under that*

*form of irony and enormous comical-
ness, to practice a sort of apostolate,
by demonstrating the dreadful misery
and infinite ridicule of everything that
is opposed to God. But, once again, it
is an exhausting task, enough to make
all the convicts of literature tremble.
Sometimes, I keel over in the dark.*

7. – To Henri van Haastert, a young Hollander who
wrote delicious letters to me:

*... I am happy to learn that you distin-
guish me from Louis Veuillot. All the
sottishness of modern Catholics was
needed to attribute, I do not say genius, which would be too ridiculous,
but only greatness to that famous journalist whom I knew personally, forty
years ago. Several words will give you
all my thought and furnish you with, I
believe, a good answer for imbeciles.*

*In the heroic times of the Cru-
sades, there were two sorts of warriors for the conquest of the Holy Sep-
ulcher: the Knights and the Boors.
Those latter could be and were often
very intrepid. But they were boors and
Louis Veuillot was never a knight. He
had a base soul, and one can say that
he was, in that sense, the precursor of
the ignoble journalists at the Cross*

who have so vilified Christian thought.

> *I congratulate you on your having escaped that mastodon. As for me, I do not know if I can be classified among the knights, but I know that I have always wanted to fight with nobility, something that Louis Veuillot certainly did not do.*

12. – Georges Crès gives me the first proofs of his beautiful republication of *The Desperate Man*. He is impatient to republish *Sweating Blood* also. I am delighted by the goodwill and good grace of that publisher.

13. – Today, gospel reading of the Canaanite woman, irresistible for me. Would that not be a powerful prayer: *Domine, in Nomine tuo fiat mihi sicut volo?*

14. – Received from Vibert, the engraver mentioned on the 13th of January, a proof of what he calls my portrait. It's dreadful. Paul de Kock distracted by colic. I immediately decommissioned that image.

19. – To Termier:

> *I must have told you about my project to finish the second in my series of* Commonplaces *with your "Atlantis." I*

owe you for a good idea, and I hope
for a grave and sumptuous conclusion
for my new book that will not dis-
oblige you.

20. – Those who will laugh when reading my *Commonplaces*, finding in me a furious verve, will not
guess that what amuses them issued from my sadness
and often from my anguish. Some people today know
it and are surprised by it, me first.

21. – Article by Camille Lemonnier, in *Comœdia*, of
remarkable improbity. It is entitled "Literary Memories" and it is written in the style of a tale. There is
mention of Huysmans, me, Villiers, and there is perhaps not two lines that are exact.

22. – Perfect tribulation.

26. – Extraordinary dream last night. I saw Barbey
d'Aurevilly again, very distinctly. Same attention to
his toilette as before, face freshly shaven. We were, I
believe, on the edge of a water course. He had come, I
do not know how. I knew he was dead and I thought
that he was dead for someone or something. He spoke
to me seriously and softly, telling me things I had forgotten. I recall only an impression of distance between him and me. I felt him both very close and very
distant at the same time, and I saw how the dead are

powerless to manifest themselves. There were words that he could not speak, that disappeared, the word "to die," for example. I was interrogating him, but my questions bounced off him without penetrating him. All of that was inexplicable, and I cannot say any thing more about it other than that the vision was extremely precise. A sound of bells like a tolling woke me. I understood that I needed to say the office of the dead, which I did immediately with love.

March

1st. – To Termier:

> *You thought of me then on beautiful* Lætare *Sunday. As for myself, I remembered Saint Joseph, of whom today is the first day,*[10] *and I remembered also the* absent *person, whom you will find doubtless quite grown, when you see her again... later.*

> *My beloved Pierre Termier, this morning, at the same time as yours, I received another letter, quite extraordinary, from a young Hollander whom I have never met and for whom I am all that one can love in the world. I would send you those exceptional pages if I did not have to re-*

---

[10]Saint Joseph: in the Catholic Church, March is dedicated to Saint Joseph.

*spond to them, but I will have you
read them. It is overwhelming to know
that I have received such power to
gain control over the most noble souls.*

*Today's office tells the story of
the adulterous woman which is surely
the Church menaced with a stoning, as
I remarked in* The Soul of Napoleon.
*While one accuses her, Jesus "writes
with his finger in the earth." What
could he possibly write, if not a mysterious summary of the two Testaments?
As soon as he has spoken of the
"stone," before it is thrown by Him
who is without sin, the accusers go
away, one after the other, the oldest
taking off first.*

*Without knowing it, would I
not be imitating Jesus in that manner,
given that I defend the Church by writing, me also, in the dirt, and even in
the mud, and seeing them disappear,
one by one, forever, the stoners of the
Church and of myself, each going off*
in locum suum? *There is almost nothing left of this* Desperate Man *who will
reappear and whom one thought to
have been buried. As for the "stone"
that nobody, just or sinner, thinks anymore to pick up against me, would it
not be in Vaugirard?*

Very rapidly, I sketch out these

*ideas or reveries for what they are
worth, asking you nonetheless to note,
in that gospel, great like all the mountains, that the words* sine peccato et
primus[11] *can only be applied to Jesus
who refers to himself in that way.*

*Lean over that well, if you are
a bold person.*

5. – A religious asks me to help him, by my prayers,
in "the redoubtable duty of predication." He writes
this to me, probably inspired by a reading of *Blood of
the Poor*:[12]

*I am looking for where to attack doc-
trinally the abominable* deification *of
capital which makes it produce interest without ever exhausting it. One
had thought until now that that power
was reserved for God. Seeing it in
Capital, what is so surprising that one
should adore it? It is the necessity of
nourishing an ever growing capital
that clearly deducts from the price of
labor what ought to redound in large
part to the worker and would give him
shelter from misery.*

---

[11]*sine... primus*: Latin for "without sin and first." See John 8:7.
The actual phrase, in Latin, is *"Qui sine peccato est vestrum,
primus in illam lapidem mittat."*

[12]*Blood of the Poor*: for an English translation of which, see
Sunny Lou Publishing, 2021.

6. – Madeleine had been in Paris for the rehearsal of a concert that will take place tomorrow. Anxious on learning that she would return very late alone, I decided to go and wait for her at the Orléans Gate. Not having seen her before the departure of the first tramway, I waited for her there through all the departures, gnawed at by anxiety, given over to all the phantoms of my already-troubled imagination. Finally, I returned home after ten o'clock and I found all my poor little world waiting for me, it also, sorrowfully. I *relived*, at that moment, one of the cruelest evenings of my life.

10. – Letter from my friend van Bever, to whom I owe the conquest of Crès, informing me that the sad publisher Stock claims, against all verisimilitude and justice, to oppose the republication of *The Desperate Man*, which absolutely does not belong to him, having had the audacity, in 1893, to produce a nicked and defective edition of that book, act of piracy which could have cost him dearly, if I had the taste for trials. I had no difficulty demonstrating to him the inanity of anything to be afraid of in that respect.

As regards the so-called portrait of myself by Vibert, which van Bever brings up again, I tell him simply that that image is horribly botched and that I stick to my refusal. If the author is mortified by it, I cannot be but afflicted to see so vain an artist, or one so devoid of generosity. I am surprised as well that, for definitive and sumptuous editions, which are intended to honor a house of publication, M. Vibert cannot be, in certain cases, replaced by someone else.

11. – Three dedications to a religious.

Life of Mélanie: *One asks for a little pity for God.*

She Who Weeps: *One asks that someone weeps with Our Lady of Compassion.*

The Old Man of the Mountain: *One asks for a little mercy for the poor old man who suffers at the Feet of Mary on the Mountain.*

12. – To the same person, Capuchin and vaunted preacher:

> *I am indisputably a mendicant, God having wanted it for his Glory and perhaps for mine. But I grow old. In three years, I will be seventy and I am far from having accomplished my mission which you call redoubtable and that is, in fact, more than one knows. I am tasked with speaking to souls situated outside the Church and I have proof that I do not speak to them in vain. God knows that I ask only to continue, but, I repeat, I am old and more than thirty years of misery and woe have nearly destroyed my physical strength. Today, I cannot pursue my work save on the condition of working with a sense of security, without the daily torment of subsistence for me and mine. It's up to you to see*

what can be done about it. You are in a position of knowing rich people. Is it really impossible to act on those souls ordinarily incapable of understanding the perfect iniquity of their terrestrial pleasures when there are beings who suffer while working for the Glory of God?

22. – Holy Saturday. To Termier:

As you attempted, yesterday, to follow, in the Way of the Cross, "the frightening procession," – much more frightening certainly than one might think and that every attentive man could see in his own heart – did you notice, in that horrible crowd, my excellent friend Dismas, the Good Thief, whom the Church honors on March 25? It seems to me that you must have noticed him, for starters because he is different from everyone else, then also because there is something between you and him. You know that I want to finish my book through "Atlantis." Since that idea came into my head, I think a lot about Saint Dismas who provided me with the most admirable and most precious information on that lost continent. I don't say any more about it and I ask you even not to ask me about it, my being, because of it, in a sort of ecstatic state.

23. – To Léo Funtek, in Helsingfors, Finland, a poor man who sent me fifteen francs:

> *I have received with simplicity and a really touched heart the evangelical "glass of water" that our crucified Lord inspired you to send to me. Rest assured that it was not received in vain, and rejoice for having done something for a miserable writer who glories in being despised and who considers the several poor souls who come to him from the ends of the earth more precious than the diamond of friendship.*

29. – Return to Bourg-la-Reine, after a very difficult week of Easter spent in Mévoisins, near Saint-Piat, in the new habitation leased last October. The weather, ordinarily mild, in the week of the Resurrection, was horrible this time around, and we had to leave, after four days, to escape a mortal sadness.

April

3. – *The Religion of the Body.* Article in the *Journal* being offered possibly to Mgr. Gibier, apostle of Ver-

sailles and bishop of gymnastics:

> *The body holds, in modern life, the place that the soul held formerly. The body's hygiene occupies us today like the soul did in the past; one prescribes the period of a hygienic act as one used to prescribe an examination of conscience or a time of meditation. The state of cleanliness is our state of grace, and the tub our absolution.*
>
> *Gymnastics has the importance that theology had. One does one's limbering-up exercises as one used to say one's morning and evening prayers... Sports open up for us the school of new perfection. Our great sportsmen are our great saints... Everywhere one searches for the principles of bodily life as one used to define dogmas, and the congresses that give to muscles the rules of conduct play the role of our councils previously... The Fathers of Faculty succeed the Fathers of the Church... Salvation takes place here on earth in the body and for the body only, henceforth... As for transgressions to watch out for, I remember the legend of a drawing by Forain: "He just drove a stick into the tree of Liberty..."*

The most remarkable word of that article is

the word *stick*. It is most certain that, in this religion, new only for those who know nothing of barbarous antiquity, the stick must be the insignia of the supreme pontificate. Assuredly the author of that sacrilegious plagiarism of Christianity is of an unordinary sottishness. But, all the same, without knowing it, he prophesies. With the soul having been sent packing, the right of the strongest would become immediately the one and only law, as with brutes. It is perhaps the future of tomorrow, or the day after tomorrow, caught glimpse of by that imbecile.

(Germany calls its combatants: DAS MENSCHENMATERIAL, human materiel! That ignoble expression says it all. *Note from July 1915.*)

4. – Bell rings. Madeleine descends and meets on the stairs a well-dressed and greying man who entrusts her with an envelope made out to me and then takes off. In that envelope there is a 50-franc bill and this:

> *Sir, two women, friends, have read the* Ungrateful Beggar *together. They felt intensely the savors, the ironies, the passionate flights of poetry that that book is visited with. Allow them to come with simplicity and give testimony of their appreciation by a small gift, and let the veil they wish to keep assure you of the disinterestedness of their sympathy.*

Without a signature nor any other indication

[as to who they are]. The style and writing appeared to be that of a woman whom I have the sorrow of being unable to know.

Finished the tedious task of the correction of proofs for *The Desperate Man*. That attentive and complete reading of a book that I had forgotten in part, and which I feel myself very far from, made a great impression on me. It is evident, despite the errors or experimentation, that, since this beginning book, the author was already in possession of all his means and that, since then, he could acquire only the experience of the *profession*, horribly costly experience.

5. – I learn that the first edition of *The Woman Who Was Poor*, of which two thousand copies were printed in 1897, has finally sold out. It took sixteen years to obtain that result.

7. – "He who believes that there are sins that he cannot commit is not a Christian." Words of the Absolute spoken by a true priest.

10. Letter from Philippe Raoux telling me agreeably of the mendicants of Poland who "return money," with abundant benedictions.

I'm told this anecdote:

An individual, the friend of a Jewish banker,

and on the verge of going on a long voyage, comes to find him, saying: "Here are 50,000 francs that I cannot take with me. I entrust them to you until my return." The banker offers a receipt which is refused. "What's the point?" says the traveler full of confidence, "aren't you my friend?" The banker insists in vain. In the end, two bank employees are called on to be witnesses to his putting that money into the safe. In the event of the depositor's death, they can provide testimony. One year later, the return of the traveler who comes to pick up his 50,000 fr. Astonishment of the banker declaring to have no recollection of the deposit. The stunned traveler invokes the testimony of the two employees who are called on to come. "Gentlemen," the boss says to them, "here is my friend who claims to have confided 50,000 francs at such and such an epoch, of which transaction I have no recollection. He says that you were witnesses and he counts on you to refresh my memory." Energetic denial on the part of the two employees. After they leave, the financier says to his friend: "Now I will give you back your money. The little scene you just witnessed was simply to make you familiar with the fine discipline of my business."

13. – Mgr. Bolo, protonotary *apostolic*, gives lectures for high-society women. "He is the most distinguished of our fireplace prelates," says the *Journal des Débats*, "and one imagines him as some rude countryside curate, poor, making ends meet, going to visit the sick along the mountain paths leading to the Lord, across ice-covered rocks, the flock who smell of sweat." Mgr. Bolo belongs to another school altogether and reminds me of one of our bishops, fire-

place prelates, as well, who, feet in the air before a good fire and puffing on a fat cigar after a copious meal, belched, while rejoicing, a veridic word or two: "To think that we are the successors of the apostles!" Bolo is in favor of the "royalty of salons," perfumes, good food above all, estimating that gourmandise is an essentially intellectual pleasure and that "the more intelligent one is, the more one ought to be delicately nourished," which puts us rather far from the Fathers of the desert, envisaged probably like animals. Bolo is a "regenerator." Suchlike predicators are ordinarily procured on the eve of a catastrophe.

14. – End of my *Exegesis of Commonplaces* (new series). Completely worn out by that task, and to take some time off from my readers, I have decided to collect the commonplaces that still remain on my consciousness and pile them up such as they are in an impertinent *post-scriptum* for the benefit of the courageous man who would be tempted to continue my explications or my glosses.

17. – To a purchaser of *Blood of the Poor*:

> *I want to hope that this book will please you. It is a violent nourishment that few stomachs can support. Your quality as a friend of Father S. makes me think that you are not one of those modern Christians who sift through the Gospel, not wishing of the divine*

*Word but what does not bother them
and who tell the Lord to descend from
his Cross, as the Jews did before them.*

19. – To Elizabeth Joly, a printed dedication of the
Exegesis of Commonplaces that I just finished:

> A poet who was wandering in the
> cemetery was advised to knock at the
> door of a tomb. That door opened and
> it was his soul that appeared to him,
> his soul that he had never regarded, but
> which he recognised by certain ghastly
> blemishes. He then remembered hav-
> ing abandoned it there, one day, in or-
> der pointlessly to examine some empty
> sepultures. Seeing it so sad, so pro-
> foundly sad, and so beautiful, he took
> it by the hand very tenderly and escor-
> ted it all in tears to the House of the
> Father of the Living, whose way it
> showed him.

29. – Judas is nought but Blessed still. One would
voluntarily work for his canonization, but his thirty
deniers do not suffice the Sacred Congregation of
Rites.

From a preface by Paul Bourget to a novel
written by a lady:

> *I have always thought that the psycho-
> logical novel attained its full develop-*

ment only on condition of its being placed in a milieu of leisure, as formerly tragedy did not affect people other than queens and lords. That's not to say that over-the-top idlers are more interesting than humble folk. (But yes, my old Paul, but yes!) They are simply a human terrain more particularly adapted to certain efflorescences of the soul...

I ask pardon for that ridiculous citation.

30. – Lectures by Jacques Maritain on Bergson at the Catholic Institute. Beautiful success by my dear godson. I do not know – God alone knows – if Jacques is capable of an act of genius, but he certainly has all the gifts of a superior man. His entirely philosophical lectures are of admirable clarity, with the most brilliant finds.

May

6. – Note sent by a friend with regard to the so-called discoveries by Dr. Possi who made a fragment of a chicken's heart *live* for fourteen months.

Can one suppose human power to be scientific or diabolical, having realized that prodigy of making tissues and organs artificially live? With that then, it seems, death is vanquished and beings are becoming eternal. But what will happen on the day when God judges that the time is come to recall to himself the soul that gives all spiritual faculties? The bodies will continue their movements *without real life* and the world will be peopled with automatons. So...

12. – To a very afflicted female friend:

We all have one task in this world, that is to become saints, and one must suffer greatly for that. One knows this when one is a Christian, but one does not tell oneself often enough that there is only one way to suffer really. That consists in renouncing in advance all consolation. It is a totally superhuman sacrifice and that, nonetheless, is demanded of us. As long as it is not achieved, the hope for sainthood is merely a dream or a derision. Such is our task and I realize that it is very hard.

One would need to pray to the Holy Ghost to deliver us from the illusion of time that we are all victims of. In grief or in joy, we believe that time is something, but it is nothing, as it does not exist for God. It should not exist for us then. It is what separates us from God. If we could obtain that grace of never knowing the hour, we would already be in blessed Eternity, and suffering then would be for us like

a swift barque on an affluent in Par-
adise.

14. – Began *The Pilgrim of the Absolute*, sixth volume of this Journal.

"The upright Catholic who has written, sometimes in a vulgar language, so many splendid books." Thus a young, well-meaning priest says about me.

Opinions of a vicar of Notre-Dame-des-Champs:

> *As far as plainchant is concerned, for the good of the Church,* one must not obey, *so as not to be exposed to being obliged to draw attention to the contradictions of successive popes. It is, besides, only a question of artistic appreciation and not one of dogma. In this matter, one must put oneself on a* level with the average faithful.

> *As for children's first communion, the only usages that one must respect are those of the tradition in France. If the bishops* attempt to obey, *it is because of the Cardinal's hat. In Switzerland, where there is no cardinal, they do not obey (which is wrong). The first thing to do is to develop the intelligence of the children. Grace* can *well add something to it but one must not count solely on God to make miracles for every soul. What al-*

lows us to retain the children is the meal of first communion.

> *A few words on the clergy. You would want that we become saints. That would be* deplorable. *They do not have a practical mind. The most important thing is administration of the parish, etc., etc.*

21. – *Re-read Balzac's* les Chouans. *It is nothing but dust anymore.*

25. – Printed dedication for the new edition of *Sweating Blood*:

> *To Ricardo Viñes. Your Catalonian ancestors, who were named* Almogavars, *conquered, at the end of the thirteenth century, Asia Minor and Byzantium. At the beginning of the twentieth, dear great artist, you conquered Léon Bloy, which was perhaps more difficult.*

28. – Letter from a lady of Dijon, saying that my books do her well, that she waits for me to give commentary on the Gospel, congratulating me for no *longer* being a scatalogue!

June

3. – Words attributed to the billionaire Carnegie:

> *I am the happiest man in the world. I estimate that I make, at this moment, my paradise on earth. I ask nothing better than to continue doing what I have done up to now and I am ready to give five hundred million dollars to whomever will demonstrate to me that I could lead a happier life than what I currently do.*

That is roughly what a cow, gifted with speech, could say, in its prairie, before the last train departs.

4. – Someone reminds me of the lines that Paul Bourget wrote in *Paris Echo*, at the moment of Separation:

> *Four barriers separate us from bar-barousness:*

> *THE GERMAN GENERAL STAFF, the British House of Lords, l'Institut de France, and the Vatican.*

> *(The German General Staff!!! O Paul of the Institut de France!!!!! 1915.)*

5. – Postal dispatch of *The Woman Who Was Poor* to Raoux:

> *The saddest of books, while waiting for the magnificent bloody ones that*

will come.

8. – Alfred Pouthier brought me a copy of *les Droits de l'Homme*, a dirty rag edited by the son of the late Hyacinthe Loyson, apostolic ejaculation worthy of his procreator on all points.

His paper informs me that we live under a *clerical* republic (!), that Joan of Arc was a martyr for liberty of conscience and an *ancestor* of the Revolution, which is surprising for a virgin. The child of the incestuous and sacrilegious Carmelite, having for his ancestors all the imbecilic yellow-bellied chickens or cockroaches that promulgate the Rights of Man, owes his ascendency to not botching any democratic commonplace, and he conscientiously accomplishes his mission. But today, it is magnificent. Did anyone know that a Zola Association exists and that that association celebrated, last Sunday, the commemoration of the transfer to the Pantheon of what, by a strange euphemism, one wishes to call Emile Zola's *ashes*? Multitudinous attendance, affirms the newspaper that drops some names, among which Anatole France, whom one is always certain to find in the front row when the urgency for some foolishness or turpitude is pointed out. Pigswill and discourses, naturally. Here is what that tadpole of a barefoot Carmelite puts forward:

> *When the confused aspirations of op-*
> *pressed consciousness seek an expres-*
> *sion that liberates them, men find it in*
> *the name of a man. The Christian cries*
> *out:* Jesus! *and the Mujik cries out:*

Tsar! *We, for fifteen years now, when
a hope sighs in us, when a need of
protestation rises up in us, when a call
for social fraternity, human fraternity,
hastens from our hearts to our lips, the
cry that rises in our consciousness, the
cry that comforts and protests,* the cry
that zigzags like a lightning bolt, *the
cry... (etc., and damn), it is ever and
spontaneously:* Zola! *(impassioned* applause*)*.

At the end of that harangue, the priest's child
quickly lays bare his liturgical entrails:

*Young republicans, young laics, re-
member that you are the children of
the Dreyfus Affair; that your cradle,
like that of the prophet, was launched
on stormy waves. As Hugo was the Father of Poets, Zola was the Father of*
Citizens. *All of you, friends, are his
children. That is why I raise before
our rallying palladium, our own* mon-
strance, *laics, that medal of glory that
was awarded to Zola by all his battle
comrades!*

P.-H. Loyson removes from the table where it
was placed, in front of Anatole France and Mme.
Emile who had lent it for this occasion, the large gold
medal engraved by Charpentier with the effigy of the
author of *J'accuse!* and bearing this inscription:
"Truth is on the march."

He raises it for the attendees to see, in the direction of the table where the young militants are grouped. Everyone is standing. Intense emotion; then tremendous acclamation...

I am well aware that there is no law against ridiculousness, but here, really, they are pushing it.

10. – I understand that there exists a *modernistic mysticism* nowise invented. It's the renewed heresy of the *Quietists*:

> *What distinguishes above all the apostles of the modernistic Gospel, says* l'Univers, *is their love of shadows. They envelope dogma and law with a sort of aristocratic fog, only penetrable by their initiates' eyes. When one opens their books, one has the impression of descending into those nocturnal crypts where, in an abstruse language, mystagogical rites are celebrated. They no longer speak our language; the old vocabulary of Catholicism becomes, under their pens, a kind of Chinese dialect, each word of which makes you pause and corresponds to neither traditional ideas nor images. They plunge you into the unconscious and the subconscious with the rapidity of the cage that swallows the coal minor six hundred feet beneath the surface of the earth. Above all when they*

mix in asceticism, they are profound and tenebrous like shafts in the bowels of the earth. Read this end of a letter by a nun who frequented their small chapels; she writes to a priest:

> *"I am at the divine disposition for respiration of the Lord. His sufficiency, which suffices unto himself, wants to be for my being his sufficient... The effect of divine sufficiency in a simple act puts the being in a correspondence that is known only by the charity that made that expenditure; it unto itself knows how to effect the appreciation; the effect of that appreciation makes the being triumph in the life here-below. Etc."*

Look at us now, – in Byzantium; the Turks must not be very far off.

14. – A recomfort comes to us today, Saint Basil's feast day. The old saint consoles us, himself having the need for being consoled. All the so-called *orthodox* schismatic monks follow, I believe, the old rule of that patriarch who must groan, for more than one thousand years now, over his unfaithful children.

To Father S.:

You appeared to me too unpleasantly upset by the ferus homo[13] *that I apply*

---
[13]*ferus homo*: Latin for "wild man."

temerariously, according to you, to Our Lord Jesus Christ. But you are familiar with my Salvation Through the Jews[14] *and you know in what manner I read the Holy Book. I firmly believe that* all *biblical individuals, the bad as well as the good, are figures of the Savior, the which was, at the same time, Innocence itself and Sin itself, having inexpressibly taken on everything.* Omnia in eo constant.[15] *Such was the feeling or, to better express it, the doctrine of the ancient and holy Interpreters whom one calls the Fathers of the Church.*

It is in this way that one can say without any temerity that Abel is a symbol of Jesus and that Cain is no less an evident one as well. Same thing for Isaac and Ishmael, for Jacob and Esau, etc., etc. Have you not noticed the striking prefiguration signified in the two dreams: that of the cupbearer and that of the pantryman in the prison that keeps Joseph, who explains them to them. The first, the cupbearer, needing to be established again in his charge and to give the chalice *to the King once again, the other who gave*

---

[14]*Salvation Through the Jews*: in English translation, Sunny Lou Publishing, 2020.

[15]Omnia... constant: Latin for "Everything [is] consistent in him."

bread, needing to be put on the cross, *and both of them in the span of* three *days. I would think I might insult you, my father, on insisting on the admirable symbolism of that story wherein Our Lord is shown under his double aspect of glory and ignominy. The detail is of inexpressible beauty.*

There would be no end to it if I undertook to multiply the examples. The immense calamity is that, for more than a thousand years now, the Tradition of the Fathers is completely lost, and intelligence of the Divine Word has been replaced by an incredible and diabolical sentimental stupidity. Morality has supplanted Revelation, and nobody understands anything anymore in the Scriptures.

*We spoke of Ishmael (*id est: exauditio Dei[16]*). Does it not, that name alone, give you something to think about?* Secundum quod dictus est: ferus homo, designare potest fidelium populum qui ferus homo est contra dæmones et hæreticos... Ismaël ludens cum Isaac (Gen. 21:9), designare potest carnem blandientem spiritui. *Thus spoke Origen, Saint Jerome, Saint Augustine, and the Venerable Bede.*

---

[16]id est: exauditio Dei: Latin for "i.e., God's answer to a prayer."

"Jesus non fuit ferus homo," *you wrote to me. The name of Ishmaël was given by an angel, one would need to note.* Ecce, ait, conceptisit et paries filium, vocabisque nomen ejus Ishmaël. *Exactly Gabriel's language to Maria, which implies a mysterious connectivity. And he adds:* Eo quod audierit Dominus afflictionem tuam. *As for what is from the text:* Manus ejus contra omnes et manus omnium contra eum, et e regione universorum fratrum suorum figet tabernacula, *text that must be read* extra tempora et extra tecta, *in its mystical, prophetic, and universal sense, – do you mean to tell me, my dear Father, something that could be formulated more exactly by someone who wished to show the dreadful situation of modern society with respect to God and the necessary attitude of God with respect to that apostate society.*

If, in a moment of zeal or enthusiasm, that is to say of compassion, for the oppressed, blinded, assassinated souls, I have applied those redoubtable words to myself, it is because I am a soldier trying to align himself with his Chief and because that imitation of Jesus Christ is recommended to all Christians. His sorrow did not prevent him from flagellating the sellers and uttering terrible Vows.

Persevera in obsecrationibus pro mendico Christi.[17]

17. – From Pierre van der Meer, to whom I had confided [a copy of] the preceding letter:

> *I do not feel myself able to express what I think. Everything becomes so mysterious and above my comprehension. And yet my soul understands, it knows more than me. It comes from God, it wants to return to Him. And it avidly receives everything that brings it closer to God.*

18. – One of my dearest friends is afflicted by the poor health of his son. I would like that he be given to me to heal. What a mystery! It is proven that I have the power to assist souls sometimes, and I can do nothing for bodies which are infinitely less precious. But also what a motive of fear for me! To be beneficial to souls, it suffices that I give them what God has confided in me for them. To be beneficial to bodies, I would need to give much to God, as did the Saints, and I have nothing but vain and sorrowful tears.

---

[17]*Persevera... Christi*: Latin for "Persevere in obsecrations for the begging of Christ."

20. – Jeanne found this in her notes, which is perfectly exquisite:

> *Jesus is at one and the same time pastor and lamb. The Lamb had himself killed so as not to accuse the Pastor.*

22. – Response by Father S. to my letter of the 14th, which he did not understand:

> *My poor lines proceeded from the desire to see your idea of the Absolute traced advantageously onto the Christ who, incontestably, is the Absolute Man being the Man-God. Would it not be necessary for each one of our words to be able to be spoken by Him so that we ourselves could say we are in the Absolute and speak in the Absolute? That is the question that haunts me...* Lucem inaccessibilem.

Why the disquietude? The *divine* Absolute manifested by Jesus is in the Revelation and the Precept. My entirely *human* idea of the absolute is in Faith and Obedience, and that's all there is to it, honestly.

25. – To a friend who reproaches me for having addressed him "dear sir":

> I am all the more inexcusable for having used "dear sir" given that I myself have a horror of that protocol which I

regard as a grave insult, unable to be surpassed except by "dear mister" which summons all vengeances. My excuse, which I humbly offer, is due to this, – that my mind is solely occupied right now with imminent holidays, and the tribulations I foresee trouble me and turn me into an idiot. It is inevitable, my poor children and their mother having an absolute need for a change of scenery. We are going to Saint-Piat in l'Eure-et-Loir. We will need to remain there for three months, I do not know how, and my fright is intense.

27. – A surprising piece of filth is brought to my attention: "*Le Fraterniste:* a general periodical of psychosis, the largest French journal of spiritual conquest and metaphysical studies."

Every criminal is not responsible for being a victim of the "psychotic mechanism." That jumps out at me at once, and I have lost all courage to continue reading. I notice however that universal disarmament and amorous intertwining of all peoples are asked for by the people of that paper and I discover principally, not without some fright, a list of "Important French and foreign works and periodicals treating of Spiritism, Spiritualism, Magnetism, Theosophy, etc." I counted 71 periodicals of which 25 in France alone.

One sees clearly that the Demon is becoming the Master of the world.

29. – I am introduced to a Japanese Catholic, a very good friend of France, Léon Matsouoka, collaborator of the *Ossaka-Assahi*. This young man, who has a distinguished place in the intellectual world of his country, has decided to make me known in Japan, when he returns, by articles and conferences where his enthusiasm will shine.

A priest brings me an old copy of *Sweating Blood* for the benefit of a dedication. I write this madness:

> *I have ceased to sweat blood since Our Lord has stopped being the archbishop of Paris. Now something else leaves me.*

July

3. – We dine at Meudon, at the home of Mme. de la Laurencie, whom I had never seen before, even though we had written several times. She charms me instantly. Although very ill, she was able to rise. Ruin of a delightful woman. Her malady seems to have made her into a completely spiritual creature, no longer living except through her soul. I have the joy of finding several words for her...

(We were unable to see her again. She died several months later. Memory of an infinite sweetness and sadness... Here is something that appealed to Jeanne, two years later, November 26, 1915, second anniversary of the departure of that marvelous and unforgettable friend:

> *Dear predestined friend, I do not have the right to approach you, privileged woman of suffering, and it has nothing to do with me. It has to do with God, his impenetrable and adorable plans.*
>
> *The real maturity of the soul is not that which comes with years, it is the perfect life in God. It is in this way that you had already run your course on this earth, when it was permitted me to get acquainted with you.*
>
> *It was the evening of your life and the morning of our friendship. That is what explains how it is still filled with radiant youth. It was soaked in eternity and born on the sill of "the gate of the humble," through which you have vanished, so soon afterwards.*
>
> *I have promised to follow you. I want to know you, to speak with you in God, to tell you things that I was unable to say here below.*
>
> *Do you remember our first en-*

*counter? An irresistible force com-
pelled me. One day, I took the train
and was at your house with confidence, as if charged with a mission.
What mission? That of receiving. You
welcomed me like an old friend already. We understood each other, and
the richness of your heart, – I caught a
glimpse of it. Unforgettable moment.
Our souls melted with tenderness. We
wept over ourselves, over our misery
in this life, over our children. Our
tears mounted towards God to disappear in his Bosom.*

*We saw each other again one
week later. Do you remember the divine hour with our spouses, there in
your room, at Meudon? It was there
that the words spoken by Léon Bloy –
"Health is a gift of God, and malady
is another." – consoled you. We were
four souls of goodwill...*

*We separated, never to see
each other again on this earth. You
were already immolated, and you had
need only of God at that point.*

*But I bring here now my emo-
tional testimony of the intimate communion of two souls. It did not deceive
us. It goes beyond the tomb, and grief
mixes with joy. Today, second anniversary of your departure, I wanted*

*to find myself with you again as in that
month of July, 1913, and to make that
memory felt again in the heart of your
dear husband.*

*Would that he might pardon
the indigence of my words.)*

5. – Setting up at Mévoisins, near Saint-Piat.

7. – To inaugurate my holidays, here is *La Vigie*, a
Catholic weekly unknown to me previously. Henri
Merlier, Director. That issue is addressed to *the author of "Salvation Through the Jews."* The lead article marked in red and entitled "Historic Modernism"
concerns Péladan who has just published a little ploy:
The Secret of Joan of Arc. "That book," says Merlier
"is an elegant piece of filth." Only the adjective is
contestable. Péladan despises the Church, the Old
Testament, the New also, by consequence, and does
not believe in miracles, which does not stop him from
proclaiming himself Catholic. Joan of Arc never had
a supernatural life. "She was initiated, chosen, prepared for her mission and counseled during all that
mission," by the *Franciscan International*, "veritable
secret society" whose ancient Sar affirms its existence
in the 15th century. Joan of Arc's victories are explained (?) then by the occult power of that society!!!
The supernatural not existing, Cauchon is naturally
rehabilitated. It was his duty to condemn Joan.

"We are no better than our ancestors," the imbecile says. But "at least our religious conception has been purified, the devil has disappeared from our thoughts. We know that man is the author of evil." I most certainly will not read Péladan's book.[18] It's been too long a time since I renounced boring myself in that way, and that *ex-Son of the Angels* is really too stupid and too unsavory. But that that impious cretin should be accepted in Catholic circles, admired and glorified by the so-called religious journals such as *The Sun*, recently blessed by the archbishop of Paris, is a marvelous shame, and I have need of no other proof of the existence of the Demon.

There is another cretin at least one notch below him, if one can say that. It's Joseph Serre, verminous author of a book on Ernest Hello dictated in part by Mme. Hello who, not content with having debased her husband while he was alive, thought to demean him in this way after his death. That man Joseph Serre is the apostle of *theosophical modernism*. He too claims to be Catholic.

One is ashamed to know how to read when one encounters stupidities of this sort:

> *Nature is an immense ascending stairway all the steps of which are at the same time* natural *in themselves and* supernatural *for the steps below them. Reason is supernatural for matter in the same way that the eagle is super-*

---

[18]Péladan: J.-K. Huysmans purportedly had an affair with his girlfriend in real life, just as the character Durtal, in *Là-Bas*, had an affair with Mme. Chantelouve, who is based on her. See Bloy's *On Huysmans' Tomb*, Sunny Lou Publishing, 2021.

natural for the mole, that the Christian is supernatural for the man... I apply this theology to miracles...*! A miracle is one of the great* scientific *laws of the world... A miracle is the point of view* from *below.*

Dogmatic transubstantiation, this good Christian declares, is nothing but the religious crowning of that scientific law whose famous evolution Darwin is but the forgery of!...

Necessary conclusion:

The Imitation of Jesus Christ, *preferred reading for pious Catholics, – is it not* a work of pure Buddhism, *of superior and Christian Buddhism?*

That infect book on Ernest Hello, work of modernist and theosophical propaganda, was published in 1894.

It is the *Bonne Presse* that recently republished that excrement, justly qualified as "a religious and literary attempt" by the Abbot Barbier (*Masonic Infiltrations*). One has to ask oneself just what a *bad* press could publish.[19]

8. – Reading in *The Conquest of England* by Augustin Thierry whose Voltairianism is particularly repugnant to me. When he speaks of the Church, – and he is forced to speak of it nonstop, – he lies or he deceives himself, and that happens all the time. Saint

---

[19]bad press: *Bonne Presse* in French means *Good Press*.

Edmond, for example, so admired by Carlyle himself, is expedited in a few lines, and saintliness is accorded to no one.

9. – To Mme. de la Laurencie:

> *Madame and dear friend, I am happy to have been able to be agreeable to you by offering you this book, which is already old, but always so* present *for me.* (The Ungrateful Beggar.) *It's a tableau of sufferings to complete* The Woman Who Was Poor *in some of its pages. There are souls from whom God asks a lot, knowing them capable of giving a lot, and it is a great honor that he does for them. You do understand me.*

> *I would not exchange the horrible life that I have recounted for anything in the world, and I am deeply astonished to have been judged worthy. I have had the iniquity to complain sometimes. I beg you not to pay any attention to it, and to preserve your esteem for me notwithstanding, by considering with kindness that I am a very poor man, and by making use, in my regards, of the natural compassion that you have for an excessively weighed down old ass. I ask for nothing more.*

Very boldly I called you "dear friend." That appellation, so banal in the language of the world, has however an infinite value in the Invisible. It is written that the abyss invokes the abyss. I think that such is the prodigy of a veritable friendship, given all human souls are abysses. Here are the words of a sublime fool: "I am the son of a man and a woman, according to what I'm told. That surprises me. I thought I was more than that." *He was seeing his soul, that latter fellow, he leaned over the edge of the abyss, and he died because of it...*

As for me, I will die without having understood the monstrous blindness of men who attribute an importance of some sort to what is not their souls, and each of my books is an attempt to express the stupefaction that that inexplicable blindness procures for me. We think of you, Madame, with extreme sweetness.

To an Albert Telbisz of Buda-Pest, asking me for an autograph:

Sir, I do not know the Hungarian language. It is possible that in Buda-Pest the word "master" signifies some honorable thing. In Paris, the same word, addressed to a veritable writer, is an insult, in the sense that one ordinarily

*reserves that protocol for soilers of
paper of the lowest rung. If it pleases
you then to write to me again, spare
me that opprobrium and be content
with calling me by my name.*

11. – Devastating news of the death of our dear curate
d'Anesse (St. Expédit. See *The Pilgrim of the Absolute*, p. 187.). We were his only parishioners, two
years ago, and we cherished him. That death is overwhelming. Certain details are, moreover, horrifying.

13. – Lachrymose letter from a colleague of the deceased. He claims to have had his complete confidence, which is exactly the opposite of the truth. Hypocritical and unexpected letter that leads me to believe that that soutane is afraid of my testimony. What
I have already written appears to suffice. (*The Pilgrim of the Absolute*, pp. 180 and 187.)

20. – The clergy of Paris pitch in together to offer an
automobile to Cardinal Amette. It appears that that
was a scandal which he wanted nothing to do with.
M. Quignard, curate of Saint-Louis d'Antin and dean
of the curates of Paris, revolted by that indigence of
the first pastor, launched a circular to all the other curates, inviting them to invest 100 fr. each. The religious communities are taxed 50 fr.

As there are in Paris about 80 parishes and as

many communities; as it is, what's more, facile to predict that the titulars of the most important curates and the richest communities will want to distinguish themselves, one can hope that that direct contribution, more or less voluntary, will permit to offer to his Eminence wheels worthy of a prince of the Church.

One divines the enthusiasm with which the poor curates, and even the rich, will pour out their contributions.

As for the diocese's beggars and down-and-out, they can, as one says, *pound sand*.

22. – Sainte Marie-Madeleine. Mass at Yermenonville, neighboring village whose impiety is almost surprising. I was informed of the heroic tribulations of the curate of that hateful parish. If that unfortunate priest isn't assassinated by his rustics it will be a miracle. It won't take much. It's a Beauceron[20] Christianity.

23. – Visit by Philippe Raoux who had just completed his military training as lieutenant of artillery. He informs me that the French artillery today is extremely redoubtable and can defy all others.

26. – My dear godson Pierre brings, on a visit to me, his compatriot, Henri van Haastert, the young Hollan-

---

[20]Beauceron: a French breed of dog, one of the breeds used to produce the Doberman Pinscher.

der that I spoke of on March 1st in a letter to Termier. He immediately rushes towards me sobbing, extraordinarily moved to meet me. It is one of the beautiful moments of my life. Pierre told me he was "charming." That young man is better and much more than that. He is a marvelous Christian soul, so far as it seems to me.

30. – *The Desperate Man* by Crès was released. Received author's copies. The corvée of envois and dedications is about to begin.

August

1st. – *The 600 martyr-priests of the Isles of Charente*. The author of that curious brochure, M. Gabriel Aubray, recounts, with as many details as possible, the enormous sufferings of all those priests, deported, in 1792, from all the French provinces, to the isles situated at the mouth of the Charente, and it is a painting of infinite horror, but not without grandeur.

The object of that brochure is principally to call Christian France's attention to the incomprehensible act of forgetting those victims whose bones, deprived of graves for more than a century, fill the earth and silt of those isles. It appears that one is beginning to think about it.

The author could have abstained from the qualification of *martyrs* so easily lavished by modern sentimentality. Doubtless there must have been, among those unfortunate priests saintly souls resigned to acceptation of the worst torments: but how many others expire in the same way from strange sacerdotal infidelities! What would happen to our contemporary clergy, bishops first, if a *veritable* persecution were unleashed? A man, priest or laic, but very virtuous, is not a martyr just because he suffers or because he dies. The Martyr is something else...

2. – Mass for the burial of the wife of a good man of the countryside who was one of my war companions, in 1870. Numerous attendance by black frocks and robes that one never sees at church. It is evident that only the priest prays. I spoke sometimes to the deceased, a year ago, telling her in vain how the impiety of that village disgusted me. Did she receive the priest just before dying?

Today, almost everywhere, in contempt of ritual, one receives into the Church the impenitent deceased, even the most scandalous, and then it is recited over their bodies the terrible orison: "... *quia in te speravit et credidit, non pœnas inferni sustineat...*"

Small event. An old domestic that Jeanne employed for laundering and sewing came, this morning, all in tears, having been chased from the house of her son-in-law because she works for us who are *bourgeois* (!), that is to say, in the minds of the villagers, good for nothing folk who make idle and party. Jeanne, moved to pity, decided to keep her.

3. – To Rachilde:[21]

> *My dear friend, I wrote and pre-scribed to Crès to give you a copy of his* The Desperate Man. *If he obeyed, as I hope, I entreat you go get a move on. It is a novel, as you know, and even a famous novel, having deter-mined a persecution. That would change the ordinary outpourings of vomit. Then this would be a sacred justice, am I not right? to honor a book whose author was condemned to twenty-five years forced labor in a kind of hell. Today, he barely exits from that penal colony, at about 115 years old, to a continued state of men-acing ruin. You are familiar doubtless with the Tour de Vésone, in Périgord. It is an enormous ruin of Roman pow-er. In the epoch of the first edition of* The Desperate Man *that Tower was in the middle of the fields, and kindly beasts reposed in its shade. Today, it is the ornament of a square whose caretaker sells postcards. That is what I'm asking for from you, Rachilde, a postcard,* in color, *of* The Desperate Man.

Dedications of *The Desperate Man:*

---

[21]Rachilde: most likely Marguerite Eymery (1860-1953), whose *nom de plume* was Rachilde.

*You regret not being one of my god-
sons, my dear Henri van Haastert, and
I regret not being your godfather. But,
for want of that spiritual bond, there
must be, between us, a very distant or
very near kinship of souls, to make
them, the holy angels who brought us
together finally, weep with compassion. I felt that from the very first moment we met.*

To Christine van der Meer:

*I offer to you the new edition of this
old book dedicated to my great godsons. Old, clearly, as it was written
more than a quarter of a century ago,
but, all the same, contagious with
youth, as it is impossible to read it,
even if one were a hundred years old,
without feeling eighteen years old
again. The author himself who was already an amorous young man under
the first Capetians, begins to grow
green again... Youth is a fugitive bird
that returns towards those who suffer
in order to sing their agony.*

4. – To my dear Philippe Raoux:

*This veritable tale of ancient dolors
that God made use of to fabricate a
writer who would accept to suffer still*

so that those who had compassion for him should find paradise in their hearts.

5. – To Brou:

There is no desperate man nor despair when one has a friend, whether down-and-out or proscribed. Think on it, while re-reading this old book of do-lor.

To Madeleine B.:

If this book full of suffering had ten thousand pages *and each expressed a sentiment of fraternal love, it would imperfectly express my tenderness for the very dear sister who was sent to me, at 65 years of age, by My Lady of Compassion.*

To René Martineau:

Why are you not a negro? I was on a deserted isle, and you came to me – the first – one Friday. *Now, that was precisely the Friday of Our Lady of Seven Sorrows, feast of the Compassion of Mary, March 29, 1901. Because of that, dear friend, and whatever might be your skin* color, *you will be judged with a great misericord.*

To my sumptuous friend, Alfred Pouthier:

Exactly prefigured by Leverdier[22] who never had an existence except in the prophetic vision of the author. A unique Pouthier for a unique Léon Bloy! Here you have it, what was needed in the end, what was asked for in the Absolute.

6. – To Raïssa Maritain:

So that she herself might offer this book to the dedicatee in eremo,[23] the which has grown so much older, after some time, that he appears more like my brother to me than my godson even. We are all converts, born blind, whom the King of the Jews illumines when it pleases him, and the Solitary saints who adored him gropingly under the sun had reason to think that Paradise was situated in the middle of the desert.

To Pierre who is supposed to bring Henri van Haastert to me, absent for several days now:

Exspectantes, exspectamus quotidie, cum gemitibus liberos spirituales et amicum dilectissimum Henri, cum in eremo eremitarum, hoc est in pago dicto: VICINI NEQUAM.

---

[22]Leverdier: Marchenoir's faithful friend in *The Desperate Man*.

[23]in eremo: in the desert. A reference to Jacques Maritain.

10. – The curate tells us, in a very amusing way, the story of his installation here, several years ago, in the middle of a hostile population that he subdued by dint of good-naturedness and rustic ruse. Primary school of diplomacy for the installation of country curates.

12. – Arrival of unexpected guests. Now look at us, nine people under the same roof, not counting our guardian Angels. God will provide.

17. – Dedications of *The Desperate Man*:

To Elisabeth Joly:

So that she might not forget that the worst human torment is the thirst for Grandeur and Beauty and that there are poor poets who suffer for thirst as much as guilty angels can suffer. Ah! It is not the world's contempt that tortures them, it is exile from the paternal House and the necessity for those miserable wretches to watch over loathsome swine whose nourishment they are reduced to envying. The author of The Desperate Man *has known that excessive misfortune, and he will know it doubtless to his dying day. It is for that reason that he begs pity from hearts on the highways and in the cor-*

*ner of woods, being, besides, always
armed to the teeth.*

To Jeanne Termier-Boussac:

*Who has so generously spoken of me.
Mediocre gift by an old, very poor
bonze visited by too rare pilgrims who
make too few miracles. This book is,
moreover, sublime or insupportable,
according to the reader's temperament. Its principal interest is in proving that the author, come into the
world under Louis-Philippe, although
engendered under the first Capetians,
continued that miracle of not catching
up to his 18 years until the dawn of his
fortieth. That exceptional case is the
only explanation to offer for the* optimism *in reverse, but real and constant, of that strange* Desperate Man.

21. – Mass at Chartres, in the Chapel of Notre-Dame-
sous-terre. The famous Basilica is visited for the first
time by Henri van Haastert who will bring back to
Holland the dazzlement of that marvel that I do not
grow accustomed to.

Article by Aurélian Coulanges. *Journal artis-
tique* of Marseille, August 20:

The Desperate Man! – *It is a sign of
the times that one republishes Léon
Bloy. Has cretinism finally decided to*

leave French literature? Or rather has unanimous bad faith felt some remorse?... Georges Crès has just honored his series of Maîtres du Livre *by adding* The Desperate Man *to it, and the intense radiance of this book – of that molten gold – resplends over the books of lesser value that stand near it. Nothing is faded in this autobiographical novel that remains as fresh, as lively, as full of vibrant and grievous life... A superhuman force radiates from it... That such a book, after twenty-five years, and so many readings, should retain its power of moving me, and carrying me along, and troubling me so profoundly, of pulling me entirely into the whirlwind of its enormous genius, it is the superabundant proof of its force, of its worth, and of its perennity...*

26. – To Coulanges:

I have read your article with a bit of emotion. You do not write Criticism, *you are like a traveler from the Year 1000, come on foot, from very far away, and who simply gives his impression in the presence of a monument of a prehistoric or antediluvian age which reminds him of his childhood. How could I not be touched? I love you much, my dear Coulanges, I believe I have told you so already. Would that this testimony of a mammoth might console you for contemporary promiscuities.*

You will be reproached for loving me too much, above all in pious circles. So you must feign to believe and proclaim loudly that I am converted. *It's the only thing I lack. Lack of conversion is my failure as a Catholic writer, after the disgrace of being unable to write like a pig. Don't forget it.*

Response to a person whom I do not know and who wants to write something on La Salette and who consults with me:

I have absolutely nothing to give you. All that I have concerning La Salette will be found in She Who Weeps *and* The Life of Melanie, *books for which I have not asked for the* imprimatur, *perfectly assured that I would not obtain it from any of our bishops who are all cowards, when they are not Judas. I should have written the* Life of the Shepherdess *integrally. I was singled out for that. The necessary documents having been refused me, I no longer had anything to say or do. By publishing the two books that I just mentioned to you, I have done exactly all that I possibly can, all that God asked of me. Then silence.*

27. – Two dedications for Henri van Haastert:

> Salvation Through the Jews. – *Sou-*
> *venir of terrestrial Paradise where we*
> *met in an immensely unknown epoch.*

> The Byzantine Epic. – *What is the*
> *Byzantine Epic and what is the*
> *Napoleon Epic, would you care to tell*
> *me? When one thinks of the prodigious*
> *Poem of a poor man trying to mould*
> *himself in the likeness of Jesus Christ!*

29. – A certain gentleman sends me a booklet, arche-ological work on an ancient Roman city in Vosges, and a letter that delivers me from any need to nurture that relationship. He is one of those men who makes predictions by *dates*. "The date of the end of the pow-er given to the Beast to make war on the saints," he says, "is in December of this year." Unfortunately, he does not say where the *saints* might be found, nor how many of them.

31. To Jean de la Laurencie:

> *I cease today to have any excuse for*
> *not writing to you. I have just finished*
> *the correction of two books supposed*
> *to appear next month, and I have*

reached the beginning of an idiocy that gives much to hope for to those of my contemporaries who might dream of an academician's mechanical arm-chair for me.

All that I can say in response to your frightening letter dated July 24 is that, on account of my wife, I find myself in an impossible situation. She made you believe that I had invented the next best thing to sliced bread and that I am in a condition to respond to divers questions, luminously. You have embarked on that boat and, all of a sudden, you interrogate me on the History of France, since the invasions of the Barbarians in the 5th century to the time of Charlemagne, and even up to the Port-Royal recluses. Nothing but that. But how could you suppose me so different from everyone else in-sofar as knowing the History of France, which is certainly the most unknown and most unknowable of all histories?

My Byzantine Epic *has hypno-tized you. You have believed that after my having read the so very clear text of Schlumberger that it would be noth-ing for me to decipher the infinitely complicated and muddled Chinese of the Merovingians, of the Carolingians, and the first Capetians, where so many historians have gotten stuck in the mud. What a difference!*

The autocrats, from Anastasius to the last Constantine, that is to say for one thousand years, – the thousand years of the Middle Ages – are merely the line, often horrible, and ever diminishing, of the formidable Roman emperors. In France, or to say it better, in all of medieval Europe, it is exactly the opposite. The barbarian chaos constrained itself painfully, how painfully! towards the excessive Unity that was realized under Augustus and which took fourteen centuries to disintegrate completely.

The history of the Later Empire is a straight line from the first to the last Constantine, an uninterrupted line of atrocious heroes and splendid riffraff, a sort of Appian Way, *always contracting, from the Irish Sea to the Propontis. The history of France, on the other hand, is a poor stepladder planted in the infinite rubble of the immense, overturned empire. The first six centuries of Christian France, or so-called Christian France, from Clovis to Hugues Capet, appear absolutely impossible to sort out, inextricable to me, and what comes next is not clear. I have gotten bogged down several times in the swamps of blood of the 14th and 15th centuries. It was necessary for me to get to Louis XI, authentic father of the French monarchy, so as to find a little light finally. But I am extenuated by my experiences and perfectly incapable of satisfying people who do me the excessive honor of consulting me.*

Not only am I not a historian, but I am ignorant of history. You should see in me a sort of dreamer, a visionary, if you will, but nothing more. What could I tell you about the Jansenists whose name alone gives me convulsions? With the exception of Pascal, who was a great poet struck by mathematics, with the exception, perhaps also, of Arnauld, who left estimable translations, I see in them only heretics full of hypocrisy and dreadful prigs such as Nicole or Lancelot.

Their history was written by Sainte-Beuve in many volumes the reading of which no man is capable of surviving. Balzac tried, one day, to express the mortal boredom procured by that inhuman work, and his ink froze in horror. I would have but one word to say to the "well-thinking" bourgeois woman whom you mention. That would be a phrase by de Maistre with regards to Voltaire: "If you are attracted to that side, God does not love you."

There you have it, dear friend, all that I can write to you. You will think, no doubt, that that is not worth the ink nor the paper it is written on.

September

2. – Dedication of *The Desperate Man* to my friend, Eugène L***:

On desiring for his literary heroism a recompense better than the spider's web of the defenders of Hunnigue.

That spider's web is an impossible story to recount in a book, if not elsewhere.

3. – Extremely agreeable visit by the Abbot Cornuau accompanied by our friend Pauline B***. I'm asked to read *Born Blind*, unpublished commentary on the ninth chapter by Saint John, and many other things. I will never have a more attentive and more impressed audience.

4. – Departure by Henri van Haaster, who leaves us

with sadness, having lived with us for more than a month. His presence was sweet and beneficial to me, and I often thought that this visitor was sent to me by God. Only, will I ever see him again? The future has colors of agony and colors of death.

6. – Our holidays are over, and I have done absolutely nothing.

13. – New departure, of an even heavier sadness. The van der Meers quit us in their turn. Our house is going to seem inanimate. The weather has become pluviose and cold.

16. – Letter to one of my fans to put him on guard against the rapacity of booksellers selling very expensively certain of my books that can be found easily with the publishers and whom they say are sold out.

17. – Mailing of *The Desperate Man*:

> *To my very dear friend, the gentle and calm Pierre Termier, the last copy that remains to me, after having served the crazies and discontented several raving madmen. One does what one can, and the author of* The Desperate Man, *incapable of doing what he must, is always the very poor decedent who be-*

> *gins barely to revive after twenty-six*
> *years of being buried.*

19. – Just today, I discover with some pain, in the beautiful edition of that book, the inexplicable omission of the epigraph: *Lacrymabiliter*. It was, from the very first page, like a small sorrowful hill from which one could plunge one's gaze in advance down into the valley of tears...

20. – *Dico vobis, omnia quæcumque orantes petitis,* CREDITE QUIA ACCIPIETIS *et evenient vobis* (Mark, XI).[24]

     In fact, if one prayed while firmly believing that one will obtain what one asks for, being a believer in God's word of honor, one would obtain it in effect, but that does not happen once out of a hundred thousand times. Christians really want to admit that God is theoretically creditworthy, but in practice, they do not believe him to be reliable. So that the recommendations to pray for oneself and for others are absolutely in vain. Without confidence, no prayer, strictly speaking, and the confidence is so absent that, even for many priests, it is an unsustainable presumption to believe *literally* in the Gospel.

21. – Today was the nineteenth Sunday after Pente-

---

[24]*Dico... vobis*: Latin for "Therefore I say unto you, What things soever ye desire, when ye pray, believe that ye receive them, and ye shall have them." Mark 11:24.

cost. The Gospel story of the guest not wearing the nuptial dress. Jeanne points out to me that that guest thrown into external darknesses could be the Holy Ghost. Grandiose view.

24. – I write to Raoux about my small hope of success for the new edition of *Sweating Blood* which will come out soon, book that ought – under the present circumstances – to act powerfully even on the dolts. Unfortunately, I have an *interdiction*, as the imbecile says. (See *The Pilgrim of the Absolute*, p. 68.)

25. – Excursion to Gallardon. I had heard speak of that church like a marvel. Disappointment. It is a totally modern church, blinding white, with ancient stones in small number. Excessive washing and cleanliness. There are perhaps curious details here and there. I do not have the courage to seek them out.

26. – On the verge of sending out the last proofs of *Sweating Blood*, I am suddenly aware of a useful epigraph: "War is the national industry of Prussia." (That phrase by Mirabeau is found in a book on Prussia that nobody read. It had an enormous success. Since the beginning of the war, I have seen it cited everywhere. It's a gift I give to MM. the journalists. They use me, but, as always, making sure not to name me. 1915.)

28. – Extraordinary letter from Florian. He informs

me that last December he was arrested at home and thrown into a distant prison, where he was watched over like a ferocious beast, deprived of all religious assistance for two months. All that without judgment, without appearance before a court of law, and without having been informed, until that day, of the true motives for that monstruous arrest. And no compensation. The coldness of the prison gave him a painful malady in the foot which kept him in bed all spring and half the summer.

"In your last letter," he wrote to me, while finishing up, "you spoke of a 'very hard cross that would be the occasion of great suffering,' and over time the *logic* of your phase has bit me, very loyal in its mission as a mad dog."

He pointed out to me that his emperor (of Austria-Hungary) is *king of Jerusalem and apostolic*.

That persecution of a poor man who has never bothered about politics is explainable only through the good pleasure of all-powerful bishops under a senile and apostolic sovereign, punishing in that way the miserable wretch of a writer for his translation of *She Who Weeps*. He could have expected it, having received certain warnings. I have no idea of the imprudences he could have made, but I know that he has suffered and that he suffers persecution because of me.

His letter is accompanied by a translation of my *Byzantine Epic*, a small typographical marvel.

29. – Another sad letter by Jean de la Laurencie asking for prayers for his wife, who is in danger.

> Envoi of *The Desperate Man*:

> *To my friend Valentine Dupont asking her to offer this paper to her husband to encourage him in the profitable commerce of literature. It is in this way that I made my fortune which excites the admiration and envy of so many toads. I was barely 40 years old when I wrote that book of such surprising precocity. I will do better at 80, when I will be mature.*

October

4. – Return to Bourg-la-Reine.

6. – I learn that the edition of *The Desperate Man* by Crès is already completely sold out. It is true that the number of copies printed was subscribed to in advance by maniacs of luxury books who read absolutely nothing.

9. – New letter by Florian, curious and touching. He thinks like me that he has been persecuted *episcopally* and he is not alone. All those who have helped him have gotten something. The sister Veronique, who

furnished money, and one of his companions, have done six months in prison. He returns to the subject of his "apostolic" emperor, king of Jerusalem. Letters that I received from the Holy Land are, in fact, stamped with the portrait of that old imbecile. About two years ago, he declared in a discourse, in Bosnia, that he wanted the Christian and Moslem populations of that country to live in peace and that it was his intention to work for the blossoming of Mohamet. At least the newspapers said as much without impunity. It appears that that malodorous *cacogenaire* is much loved by the bourgeoisie, who see in him *the friend of peace*. (!!! 1915.)

11. – We took into our service, very imprudently, a German female domestic who appeared to us to be well-raised, pious, modest, attentive, and even very agreeable to look at. The first days, her service was nearly satisfying. Only we had noticed, with a little surprise, her frequent visits to the post office where she carried out her correspondence. Suddenly, everything was spoilt. Without reason as without pretext, she undertakes, today, to demonstrate to me the superiority of Germany over all other countries in the world and reveals herself suddenly to be so vicious and such a bitch that we immediately had to sack her, which I executed like a virtuoso and with such din that she must have run for some time.

I think she carries out in that way, like thousands of others, a very dirty profession of spying, sojourning for short periods of time in places where there is nothing to observe and making off with at the

same time wages she did not earn. Germany is decidedly most ignoble.

15. – To Benoît Joly:

You wanted to share your joy with me.
We can offer you only our prayers for
the new arrival which will clearly be a
Christian, tomorrow. I would that
mine might be very powerful, but one
never knows from what mountain or
what valley help may come. Christians
know or ought to know that prayer is
the most certain of all forces, but the
effects of it are unknown. When we
pray we put into God's hand a naked,
magnificent, and redoubtable sword,
that he does with what he will, and we
know nothing more about it. Prayer
for the little child is doubtless most
mysterious in terms of its effects. We
ourselves then are like children at the
edge of the sea or like beggars who
would look at the Milky Way. Above
and below are treasures or unimagin-
able frights.

I don't feel strong, my dear
Benoît, that is to say I don't feel capa-
ble of acting on God (prævalens Deo),
save when I feel my misery and when
that makes me weep. I speak, of
course, of the misery of my soul and

my mind which is much more real than one thinks. Believe it, when I tell you, that all I can write that is good, beautiful, and, if you will, profitable to some souls, it was given to me because I wept over myself, at the same time as over many others, over all creation disfigured by the fall – and those happy tears, they also, were a gift admirably gratuitous, in that I am, in all honesty, a very poor man, the poorest among the poor, God knows!

And that there is all that I can give most amorously to your child, to you Benoît, to your Hélène, to my sister Madeleine, to Elisabeth, to all those whom I love and who were merciful to me. When your time comes to suffer, remember that there is an old beggar all in tears, mindful of you all, at the feet of Our Lady of Compassion, and that thought will console you.

17. – Visit by a young man with the name of Laquerrière, come to propose to me the publication of such and such unpublished material that I might have. I offer him some old articles on Huysmans refused, in 1909, by Stock, when he published *Gladiators and Swineherds*. The affair is almost immediately concluded. I learn from that man that Demay, the first publisher of *Salvation Through the Jews*, died mad.

20. – Small introduction for the small volume by Laquerrière, *On Huysmans' Tomb*:[25]

Where is it then, that poor tomb?

*Here it is six years after his
death, the poor devil, and one might
believe he had been buried for over a
century now.*

*Those who wished to admire
him, when he appeared among the living, are surprised today no longer to
find an atom of his dust, and the sad
books that he left behind no longer
have their old power of boring even,
they have become so indecipherable!*

*Having been his apostle, alas!
having worked and suffered for so
long a time to make him a Christian,
the excessive mediocrity of his nature
required that I should be paid immediately with the most glaring ingratitude, and that I should contemplate in
him the most extraordinary abortion
of Grace.*

*My disciple was acclaimed by
our Catholics, and that says everything.*

---

[25]*On Huysmans' Tomb*: in English translation, Sunny Lou
Publishing, 2021.

His bibelot and bric-a-brac religion appeared to them the result of a divine intimacy, and they accepted that the hopelessly thick Naturalist of À vau-l'eau should compare himself to the greatest Christian writers.

The pages that one is about to read mark two periods.

The first were written before Huysmans' conversion, then when, full of hope and not foreseeing the atrocious disappointments he had in store for me, I caressed him with a great zeal. The others express the bitter disenchantment that followed.

People will not fail to accuse me of contradiction or inconstancy, which is entirely all the same to me. Some have come in vain to ask me for these chapters, which have not been printed in book form until now, having been refused by the publisher Stock in his edition of Belluaires et Porchers,[26] *and which might have some importance from the point of view of our literary history. Why would I not consent?*

I will also be reproached perhaps for failing to show respect for the deceased. "Death," said Jules Vallès

---

[26]*Belluaires et Porchers: Gladiators and Swineherds.*

in the past, "is not an excuse."

– October 1913. Apparition of Saint
Micheal on Mont TOMBE

22. – Dedication of a luxurious copy of *The Desperate Man* for van Bever who persuaded Crès:

> *I owe you now not only for the magnif-
> icent republication of a book I thought
> deeply buried. I owe you also for the
> happy consequences that one can hope
> to derive from it. You will have been in
> this way the first demolisher of that fa-
> mous conspiration of silence that I
> have suffered for 25 years now. It is
> something, dear friend, that I could
> never forget.*

26. – Pleasant recitation of the interview between one
of my friends and a loathsome bibliopole who stole a
great deal from me, which authorizes him naturally to
claim to be my victim. All of the sudden, the recrimi-
nations began, then the slanging matches. A little
more into it and they would have gone to fisticuffs,
extreme result that would not have been to the advantage of that usurer and second-hand dealer; my friend
being very sturdy, but not having come for that.

27. – A relative sends me a small portrait I did of myself for my parents, in 1865. It is not without emotion

that I see it again, after so many years, that curious image, drawn with a finesse that is really extraordinary.

29. – My dear Abbot Cornuau had dreamt of a collaboration for me at *l'Univers*, where I had debuted in 1874, under Louis Veuillot. It appears that that paper has changed its ways. Quite a pointless endeavor no doubt. Those people have been able to modify their orientation, but how would they be accommodated to my absolutism and my literary style? Cornuau, having written to the director, who is a priest, did not even receive a response.

31. – Visit by my godson Pierre. We talk, as always, about the frightful mediocrity of the Catholic world. Wherever we find ourselves and whatever the object of our thoughts, an irresistible slope leads us there, and the occasion, this time, was given to us by a young Dutch priest who is a friend of my books, harshly oppressed over there for that reason.

November

1st. – *Saint Augustine*, by Louis Bertrand. Plausible restitution of the African Christian in the horrible days of the Donatists[27] and Vandals. Honorable medi-

---

[27]Donatists: a North African Christian sect that broke away from the Catholic church in the 4th century A.D.

ocrity and intense success.

2. – To Jacques Maritain:

It is time, isn't it? that I respond to the reception of your book on Bergson, and my embarrassment is huge. I was unable to begin reading it until yesterday evening and I confess that by the twentieth page I was completely wiped out. It is so distant from me, all that, and the atrocious barbarisms of philosophical language are so contrary to my temperament as a Latin writer. I will continue, however, persuaded to find your soul and receive a little light from you. But beginnings are hard.

Intuition, duration!? O what talk! I know quite well what you want, my dear godson, but I do not know what Bergson wants, and I will never know doubtless, as he himself did not know. 466 pages on that imbecile, it's enormous! Three or four words, one only *maybe would have sufficed.*

Enough, I will succeed in finding the courage. Even though I am submerged in proofs, for four months now, and forced, at the same time, to work on the Pilgrim of the Absolute, *I do not abandon the project of an arti-*

cle. I said it to Pierre, it would be unheard of if my constancy were not recompensed by some enormous Bergsonian joke, which I would know how to take part in, which would earn for me, I really hope so, being deprived of all credit among lofty thinkers.

(I acknowledge never having been able to realize that project [of an article].)

3. – From Termier sending me a booklet:

To Léon Bloy, the greatest, doubtless, of geologists, the only, in any case, who posed the question of the true shape of the Earth, the question of knowing why it is called the Footstool of the Lord.

4. – Response:

You award me the title of geological grandee. It's inebriating and monstrous. From there to hurl yourself "into the frozen crater of a volcano," as you said in Toronto, it's only a step. One has claimed that I was that volcano myself, which is possible, God being admirable in his works. But my crater does not grow cold, as you know. One will need to take care.

7. – Apparition of *Exegesis* (new series).

9. – Great bustle in Bourg-la-Reine. Today is the inauguration of a ridiculous statue of André Theuriet, who was the mayor of the city and a glorious academician, ceremony presided over by Poincaré, Faguet needing to expectorate I do not know where. All that under the rain and in the mud. The entire city is afoot and the crowd is compact with the passing appearance by that miserable Président, condemned by his office to all farces of this genre. I would prefer the hard labor of breaking flint.

10. – Theuriet again. Discourses *in extenso* in the *Paris-Journal*. There are four of them of an almost improbable stupidity. The large piece is by Emile Faguet. I read things like this:

> *The so kindly, little French bourgeoisie, all things considered, has nothing more proper to depict...*

> *Theuriet's novels are not written marvelously. He wrote reasonably, judiciously, finely, in the least fatiguing style in the world...*

> *It seems that he always heard Fénelon saying: "So many bright lights blind me, I want a gentle light that comforts my feeble eyes."*

> *Speaking of an illustrious novel that I don't wish to mention, Lamartine said this: "It is a book that smells bad." Theuriet's books smell very good... Theuriet culled his books in the woods, like strawberries or bilberries...*

Poincaré gobbled all that up.

10.[28] – Printed dedication in the booklet *On Huysmans' Tomb* to Marguerite Termier:

> *I offer these pages to you, my dear child, because you are gentle and good in my eyes. When I wrote them, you hadn't yet entered into the world and I myself had no other experience than that of poverty and many other torments. If you should ever happen to suffer, one day, remember, as a Christian, the old writer who will have passed before you like a grievous shadow.*

Several dedications written by hand for *Exegesis of Commonplaces* (new series).

To Christine van der Meer:

> *If you take the trouble to read "between the lines," you will be surprised by the tenderness that I have for you.*

To Raïssa Maritain:

---

[28] 10: sic

*Me too, I made the "choice of a ca-
reer." I am your godfather for now
and for eternity.*

To Madeleine B***:

*So that she might have compassion for
the poor adopted brother whom this
book will separate a little bit more
from other men.*

To Pierre van der Meer:

*You were closer to me than anyone
else, and I took more than sixty years
to find you, the spectacle of imbeciles
having, alas! "plucked the eyes out of
my head."*

To Philippe Raoux who dreams to be
married:

*The reading of this book, is it a good
preparation for the Sacrament of Marriage? Who can say? But the author
has certainly foreseen the coming
union of the sentimental impieties of
modern Christians with the complete
cretinism desired by Satan. You are
already the witness of it.*

To René Martineau:

*You had the first series, and that was
so successful for you that you have
wanted to have the second also. But I
am an equitable prince, and I want all*

*my people to be happy. If Elisabeth is
not content, I will offer her your head.*

To Elisabeth Joly:

*This morning, at church, I thought
much about our dear Elisabeth, and I
saw her, as in a dream, aged 70 years
old. It was a totally small, old Elisabeth, who was remembering still the
dedication of this book and who went
to pray over my tomb in an unknown
cemetery. Supernatural refreshment
for my poor soul.*

To Eugène Borrel:

*It is not enough to disembowel the
Bourgeois, one must even make blood
pudding of them for the delight of the
poor. I abandon to my disciples and
successors that disgusting cuisine.*

To Termier:

*It is because My Lady of Compassion
put you on my path that I was able to
write my last books and that I will
write others still, if God gives me life
still. I will say this to you until my dying breath, and then I will say it in
eternity.*

To Mme. P***:

In homage of profound affection, this book which superficial folk might believe full of malice and which is in reality the cry of a suffering heart.

To Jeanne Termier-Boussac:

This book which may appear to you without savor, having heard me read it too much. I am horribly deprived of virginity.

To Léon Bellé:

So that he might know that "I do not speak by chance," that "I was not born yesterday," and that I am "a heart of gold."

To Emile Baumann:

Lapides clamabunt. *The* hearts *of the bourgeois who will read this book.*

To Ricardo Viñes:

In order to "clarify his religion."

To André Dupont:

From a "disreputable" writer, who has little to "line his pockets" with, who is ordinarily stepping "on hot coals."

To the Abbot Jules P***:

A mask of irony on a visage streaming with tears.

To Jean de la Laurencie:

This book, amusing for the superficial and terrible for the profound.

To Marguerite Levesque:

Behind that irony, you will run into God at every instant and, right next to Him, my Mother in tears.

To Marguerite Termier:

An edifying life *is certainly mine. To think that for two months I have written only naturally admirable dedications. It is almost "the choice of a career." But I am at the end of my strength, and I can say nothing to you, other than that I love you.*

13. – Someone sends to me, under wraps, a long band of paper that has been distributed up and down the boulevards. On one side it reads: "The perfect woman, Annette Kellermann, who just terminated her triumphal engagement at the Alhambra in London..." On the other side, the measurements of different parts of that person's body... less... It's too much or not enough.

17. – Anecdote given by Félix Raugel. One of Beethoven's brothers, Jean, a cretin, domiciled in the neighborhood of his colossal brother Louis, only not

visiting him, limiting himself to sending him a card, at the end of the year: "Jean van Beethoven, proprietor." To which the author of *Messe en Ré* responded once, by sending back to him the tip of the card with this written on the reverse side of it: "Louis van Beethoven, *Hirnbesitzer*" (proprietor of a brain).

19. – Léon Bellé, announcing his near visit, wrote to me that Bourg-la-Reine is not a *common place*, given one can meet me there.

20. – Brou sends me his epitaph:

> *Jean-Frédéric Brou*
> *(in his lifetime, statuary)*
> *Lies at the bottom of this hole*
> *Solitary.*
> *Provisioned by good means,*
> *Able to do anything,*
> *Through*
> *Reverses of fortune*
> *Did a bit of everything, nothing good*
> *And died in misery.*

Barthèlemy tells me that after *The Soul of Napoleon*, I should write *The Terror*. Why not?

23. – Read in the weekly *Semaine Religieuse* a Brief by Pius X to François Veuillot, Louis' nephew, on the occasion of the centenary of that twice-dead journalist, about whom a great deal is said, at this moment,

by men of M. de Mun's intellectual stamp.

> *With the flame of his zeal of an apostle, he entered into the lists, ornamented by precious gifts that make the* writer, *the* artist, *and the* thinker *of GENIUS (!), by which he* equaled *and* surpassed *the most illustrious masters (*sic*), for in the holy battles of the defense of sacred principles, his quill was at one and the same time a sharp sword and a luminous torch.*

Such are the stupidities that that unfortunate Pope has been made speak!

25. – Introduction to the *Histoires désobligeantes* that Crès wants to republish:

> *THE VOLUNTARILY ENRAGED*
> *or*
> *THE CONSPIRATION OF SILENCE*

> *We have been taught since our infancy, Apemantus[29] said to me, that there are ten subjects of discourse. The profound grammar of the future will say that silence is the eleventh and most fearsome, being called on to devour all the others, like Aaron's serpent devoured the other serpents.*

> *The commonplace of "eloquent si-*

---

[29]Apemantus: from Shakespere's play *Timon of Athens*.

lence," for example, is not sottish, and the "silence of passions" has more to be feared than the worst loquacity. The "conspiration of silence," another commonplace, has nothing chevaleresque about it, clearly, but it is indisputably efficacious for the killing of a superior man whom it is impossible to dishonor. It is the desert of the immense steppe around the conqueror forced to die of inanition. It is the infinite solitude of God himself whom nobody speaks of and does not want to hear speak of...

Does anyone still remember the marvelous extermination of Saint-Pierre Martinique, when thirty thousand human beings were annihilated, in thirty seconds, by the silent *blast of a neighboring volcano?*

You told me, Marchenoir, that at that very instant your daughter was taking her first communion and that there had been no need for a victim apart from that innocent in order for the prodigious act that she accomplished to be ineffaceably and very singularly marked out for her by the colossal gesture of Death. For that is in fact your way of explaining the events of this world, O frightening concentrator! and I believe that you are a thousand times right, and there is something to dream about while leaning over that gulf.

When the little girl who came before her received the Body of Christ, an entire people was still alive;... when the turn came for the one who followed her, all was over for that people. Custodiat animam tuam... *That phrase had sufficed. No more banks, no more boutiques, no more tribunals, no more business bureaus nor love bureaus, no more churches even. At fifteen hundred leagues, we were the dead, a dead city, we had become Silence, suddenly.*

Someone said to you, however, that there was a spared man, one only, and that that man was precisely A MAN CONDEMNED TO DEATH? *One rejoiced, I suppose, to be present at his execution, one spoke about it in honorable families, one was doubtless impatient for that punishment, and he was the unique witness of the execution of that multitude!... You think, perhaps that I am telling you an apologue. Eh! well, no. That man, condemned to death, he is you. They wanted to execute you by silence and they did not succeed except by turning you into the solitary inhabitant of a silent necropolis.*

My dear Apemantus, I replied, I really want to believe that you are not speaking in apologues to me, but you appear to me to be touched by a bizarre monomania. You want, by all means, that I should be a persecuted man, and you do not see that I am, on the contrary, a persecutor. Ask my contemporaries. Everyone will tell you that I am a monster and that there is no way to escape my ferocious bite. For all that, I have been caressed, covered with flowers, told the most amorous things, offered money and delicacies, – nothing works. Saint Martha herself would renounce taming so ferocious a tarasque.

I confess, there is nothing in my power to keep me tranquil. When I do not massacre, I must disoblige. *It is my destiny. I have the fantasy of ingratitude. Not being blind, I see clearly that everyone is good, that, from the lily of purity to the most notable ruffians, it is up to whomever might love me more tenderly and prove it to me by the most meritorious of sacrifices. I will never finish if I recount to you the little concerns, the delicate attentions, the enflamed declarations that I am the object of, not to mention anything about the many heroic immolations indignantly and abominably paid for by my blackest ploys. What do you want from me? I am a man voluntarily enraged.*

You will object perhaps that one has tried to make me die of hunger for thirty years now, that one has caused two of my children to die by that means. Not having the heart, I accepted my part with an admirable nonchalance. But being, all the same, a just man, I can put myself in the shoes of the good souls to whom I owe all that. Their intentions were so right and so pure!

One has thought stupidly, to be quite honest, that silence would kill me. That was like wishing to empoison a crocodile with the bouillon of toads. I have only become stronger and more toothed. Without wishing to, my enemies have been my benefactors. Silence, misery, horrible disappointments, that's all one needs to become the invincible monster.

Your last words prove that you have understood that. Why then speak to me of inanition and desert? I have never been so visited nor so flourishing. Silence is a prairie favorable to the ruminants of eternity, and very sympathetic animals are attracted to me, almost daily, by the luxuriance of

*pasture. The day when there is no
more silence around my person will
certainly be a terrible day. I will see
myself standing on a dungheap of silver where the lovely daisies or pascal
anemones of Sorrow no longer grow,
and my discouraged companions will
go away grazing on the laburnum of
unicorns in the mountain.*

*Be quiet then, Apemantus, keep
calm. The* conspirators *of silence, the
silentaires, as they were called in
Byzantium, are nothing but poor bai-
liffs who kid themselves, believing to
see in me a loud perturber. You were
my host multiple times and you know
that I have a silent jaw. My laugh
even, when I devour my contemporaries, would not arouse a spinning
spider, and my paces make less noise
still, when I walk among tombstones.
If they were clever, they would clarion
night and day to denounce my presence and deprive me thus of the incog-
nito that favors my expeditions of a
vampire.*

*Do not speak to me about those
imbeciles.*

27. – I learn that Mme. de la Laurencie died yesterday. That shocking catastrophe had been felt by

Jeanne the night before, in a grievous dream. We will have just gotten to know that admirable person then only to lose her immediately afterwards.

28. – To Jean de la Laurencie:

Dear friend, we are with you, with all our heart. We weep with you and we pray. Would that God and his Mother of Compassion be with you, assisting you. There is no other consolation for Christians, and he who writes to you has often had a broken heart. Having seen, once only, alas! her who has disappeared for a short time, *I know what you must be suffering. God tests you remarkably, like a beloved. "All that happens as a result of his holy will is adorable," I said one day when I was agonizing under the knife, and that certitude consoled me.*

Have pity on yourself, you poor soul! She who has left you has not left you. She is actually with you and with your children, closer doubtless than before, no longer having the obstacle of any illusion. She has become the companion of Jesus, who is closer to us than all other creatures. She has an infinite compassion for you, and she will be helpful to you. This morning I prayed for her and, be-

*cause I too was in pain, I prayed to
her for myself, knowing that the deceased have the power to protect the
living. Instantly I felt a little recomfort. How much more for you, the
greatest friend she had in this world?
Throw yourself at this idea and weep
with confidence at the Master's feet.*

Jules Lemaître and his lectures on Fénelon.
That Jules congratulated Mgr. de Cambrai for having,
during the course of his mission among Protestants,
suppressed the Angelic Salutation, which, he said,
greatly facilitated *conversions*!!!

29.   – The *Matin* is supposed to publish one of the
stories from *Sweating Blood*. I had chosen a particularly impressive one. It would have been an enormous
bit of publicity and really patriotic at the very moment of the ignoble German provocation at Saverne.
But I hadn't counted on the great eunuch of that publishing house: Georges Lecomte, who does not see it
that way, and who, unable to worm his way out of it
completely, makes me wait. It is important not to
print horrible things such as might discredit the good
Germans, and it is also important that the piece not be
too lengthy. Etc., etc.

December

1ˢᵗ. – Appearance of *Sweating Blood*.

"You are the apostle of Certitude," someone wrote to me.

3. – The eunuch of the *Matin* continues. It goes without saying that the amusing person protests his goodwill and his admiration for the "magnificent writer" that I am.

Funeral service for Mme. de la Laurencie in Meudon. The unfortunate survivor, very distraught, told me, on exit, several words of the departed who prayed, not to be healed, but to be gay and smiling to the end, among her own, and I recall the exceptionally touching phrase by Bossuet in the Funeral Oration of Madame: "Just as she had been sweet towards everyone, she was sweet towards death."

Rather villainous letter from a lady who received the *Exegesis* and *Sweating Blood* and who repays me by begging me no longer to send her anything, her husband, a Normand notary, having read and *criticized* (!) those two books.

5. – The eunuch has finally decided. He will publish one of my stories, the least *scandalous*. It is a matter, above all, of not offending Germany. Still I must strike a certain number of lines. I resign myself to it, so as not to afflict the publisher who is counting on

that probably pointless publicity at this point.

Several dedications written by hand for *Sweating Blood*.

To Cornuau:

This book by a very wounded old soldier, but still living, and how!

To Mme. Termier:

These stories will cause her fright, maybe, by filling her with pity for France menaced today by the same horrors.

To Edmond Barthèlemy:

This is perhaps the truest account *of 1870. It is a story of the French Soul at that time.*

To Florian:

This book of sorrow, while waiting for the last punishment forecast for all Europe by She who weeps, sixty-seven years ago. Arescentibus hominibus præ timore et exspectatione quæ supervenient universo orbi.

To Louis Q***:

Suppose, if you will, that I am in the last wardroom and that I call myself Cambronne. It is my personal vision of a new German war.

To Friar D***:

Examination of conscience prelimi-
nary to the coming events.

To Léon Bellé:

While advising him to prepare his
boots for the next one.

To Jeanne Termier-Boussac:

"Clairvoyant for suffering," you said
of me. On reading this cruel book that
reappears today, ask yourself serious-
ly what could be my very clear vision
of the near future.

To Henri van Haastert:

Gallia moritura te salutat.

To Léo Funtek:

While waiting for the next massacres.

To Blanche L***:

With the counsel not to read this book
if she has the sentimental *illusion of*
war.

To Termier:

One awaits the ham-actor emperor's
announcements to know whether these
things will begin anew. With great
peace at heart, I await God's move, an
imperceptible nutation of the Father of

*the poor who will instantaneously mo-
bilize France's Guardian Angels.*

To Doctor Joseph Termier:

*In 1870, I was so gravely wounded
that it was necessary to operate on me
on the battlefield, while proceeding to
the ablation of the brain, the heart,
and another organ that I do not otherwise mention. It is in this way, say
some quite uninformed men, that I was
able to become a writer.*

To Abbot J. M***:

*While waiting for the fulfillment of the
Secret of La Salette, the very near fulfillment perhaps, of which this was
merely the prelude to.*

To Pierre van der Meer:

*Before your baptism, you did not know
that a Léon Bloy was even possible.
Since you've become a Christian, it
seems to me that I possess some supernatural parentage with the Prince of
Apostles – being, otherwise, the fisher
of many other luminous fish – and I no
longer know myself whether I have not
actually become impossible because of
spiritual paternity. Hence I hardly
ever find myself anymore in that ancient nightmare of horrors, to the degree that I see myself caught up in an-*

other magnificent dream.

To Ricardo Viñes, to whom the book is dedicated:

> *Was I worthy of dedicating this book to you, or were you worthy of this dedication? Obscure question put before divine competence. Whatever the case might be, you are horribly compromised, my poor Ricardo, and it is quite over for you. That will teach you to discern good literature and not to risk the honor of the Catalog in dangerous promiscuities.*

To René Martineau:

> *You are, dear friend, a witness to my dolorous life for more than ten years now. Will you finally be a witness to my glorious life? God and his Angels know. Whatever happens, I will remember that you were the first-born of divine Compassion, born in order to succor and console me. I embrace you while weeping over the ruins of poor France.*

To Henri Barbot:

> *One of the rare seers who prophesied with me the probable renewal of these abominations.*

To Jacques Maritain:

It appears that your old godfather sells.
One thinks even that he will become a
thing, *which would evidently be the*
summit of glory. Why would that need
to disgust me so terribly? Yesterday I
received a visit by a very rich lady
who admires me, but who does not get
involved in the banality of an effectual
assistance. It seems to me that we
were speaking at an infinite distance
from one another, above the abyss,
and I felt it more profoundly this
morning on reading the day's epistle.
What have I come to do in this world,
my poor godson?

To Marguerite Termier:

While waiting for the Grave *that I pro-*
mised you.

To Aurélian Coulanges:

This book which ought to be in all the
military libraries, if the red pants
weren't scared stiff at the same time
as the black pants. Crappy opportunity
to continue with the conspiration of si-
lence.

14. – At the very gracious request of Jeanne
Termier-Boussac, I accept with joy to becom-
ing the godfather of the child she expects in
February.

16. – A publisher friend of Crès', Eugène Figuières, asks me, in the form of a dedication, for a thought (!) to be written on a page removed from *Sweating Blood* which he sends to me, having, he said, the intention of propagating this book in Algeria. I do as he asks:

> *In order to show evil with precision, with a rigorous exactitude, it is indispensable to* exaggerate. *I believe that I wrote that somewhere. It is precisely what I tried to do in* Sweating Blood. *But the evil of 1870 could not be exaggerated.*

A rich and probably greedy individual declared to me that the book of mine he likes best is *Blood of the Poor!* A tiger's preference.

17. – I am told of a Catholic bourgeois person not believing in the immortality of the soul. Paradise, for her, is being rich, Purgatory is being in financial difficulties, and Hell is being poor. What idiocy and banality.

18. – The day before yesterday, X*** tells me about one of his colleagues, an engineer who passionately loves my books, to the point of being unable to read others. He adds that that admirer possesses a revenue of more than one million francs. – So, I exclaimed to him, will he do nothing for me? which made him smile...

I imagine that man then, whose exorbitant riches are already *satanic*, reading my books, my dolorous books, full of my suffering, as he witnesses a séance of torture, and enjoying sadistically the expression of that suffering that has lasted already more than thirty years – a thousand leagues away from thinking that a totally small gesture that would cost him so little would instantly deliver me; and even further, if that is possible, not realizing that the author who is, in his eyes, only an instrument of pleasure, has perhaps a *mission*; that it is the duty of the rich to assist him, and that he himself is evidently designated for that; finally and above all that that would be a means to distance himself from the horrible threats contained in the Gospel. But it appears that those are comical ideas, sentimental and religiose sillinesses.

Who knows? A dirty Belgian journalist wrote, last year, a surprising article on me, wherein he said that it would be an act of *vandalism* to attenuate and, even more so, to suppress my poverty. "He lets out such beautiful cries when he suffers!" Would this not be the obscure and deep thought of that same multimillionaire?

Dedication to Ricardo Viñes:

The Revealer of the Globe, *1884. – You had just been born then. Perhaps even you were still to be born, for I am not certain of your age. In any case, you were not yet the revealer of yourself and you did not think to conquer Léon Bloy any more than Byzantium. Now that this is a done deal, be a gen-*

*erous vanquisher and let me reign a
little over the Catalog.*

*The Desperate Man. — The Im-
beciles are in the Church like bugs in
old houses. They frighten visitors and
make renters pack up and leave. I
hope that you do not find bugs in this
old book.*

*Gladiators and Swineherds. —
The basis of modern literature is in
this blasphemy: It is the spirit that
kills and the letter that gives life.* Quod
erat demonstrandum.

26. – As a kind of Christmas bonus, Father S***, ad-
dressee of my letter of June 14, and who hardly lets a
week pass without expressing his affectionate feelings
to me, drops this on me finally:

*Here it is 4 or 5 months since your
books have fallen into my hands. It
was on reading the accusation of simony that you made against the Holy
Congregation of Rites. How can you
judge in that way an organ that keeps
so close to the head of the Church and
that functions under the Pope's very
eyes?... How you make your friends
suffer!...*

30. – I said to Termier that, by now, the certain insuccess of *Sweating Blood* is a new proof of the existence of God who has decreed without a doubt that I
would never find success. Decree that I suppose con-
temporaneous with the Fall of the Angels and by consequence much anterior to the creation of the hills and
fountains.

31. – To Cornuau, with regards to all the playacting
on New Year's Day:

> *I recall that admirable place in Cath-*
> *erine Emmerich's revelations where*
> *the Saint recounts that for several*
> *years before the Deluge, when Noah*
> *was building his mysterious Ark, –*
> *enormous work that earned him the*
> *reputation of a madman – the sky was*
> *almost continually dark and fraught*
> *with frightening lightning. I wonder*
> *what the men of that time said to them-*
> *selves each time one of those menac-*
> *ing years began. It seems to me that*
> *today it is the same thing, with this dif-*
> *ference that God's horrible discon-*
> *tentment does not manifest itself in a*
> *perceptible manner. One enters into*
> *the most horrible abysses with a great*
> *sense of serenity and the* Good Press *is*
> *there to tell us that all is going very*
> *well and that. the faith is making*
> *progress.*

Here now are some lines from the last letter by Father S***... How to respond to that? I cannot doubt the charity of that religious. But he is one among a herd of Catholics (the best!) who believe that everything that comes out of Rome is admirable and who confuse so easily the head *for the* belly *of the Church! The greatest saints, among whom one could cite Saint Bernard, had a surer optic. The word simony terrifies Father S***, but everyone in the universe knows that the Congregation of Rites does not "function" except when stimulated by gigantesque allocations and nowise "under the Pope's very eyes," who does not see but what others want to show him. The pope knows quite well that he is surrounded by crooks and scoundrels, and he dies because of it, that's all there is to it. I will not respond then, considering that life is short.*

1914

January

6. – The curate of Saint-Piat comes to lunch at Bourg-la-Reine. Always affable and joyous, but how changed! He is no longer at all the same curate of two years ago. He appears completely one with my views and my feelings. Miracle operated by my books.

7. – Here is one of the best men ever found. But he is Protestant, lock, stock and barrel. He should be immensely proud of his son, become a Catholic however. Nothing doing. The Jews' *velamen* is also on the Protestants, and perhaps more blinding, for they have placed themselves outside of divine law entirely.

Short letter, really ridiculous, from M. A., "literary critic and journalist!" in Beaumont-sur-Vesle (Marne). That individual asks me for four of my books, with *dedications*! Four only. He is moderate.

17.[30] – To Termier:

> *"One more step towards death," you said to me with regards to the* end date *that you send me. I have just taken an-*

---

[30]17: sic

other [step]. The Pilgrim of the Absolute *is almost finished. It will be the
same thing, I think, with this new book
of mine as with the others that give life
to some, I'm told, without procuring
anything for their author but the hope
of Mercy to assist him in dying well.*

*Death is the constant object or
subject of my thoughts, and I imagine
it so much more amorously than I predict it to be cruel. I have my reasons
for that. I do not believe it very close
however, certain of having not yet fulfilled my mission, of having not accomplished a certain work that I am
obliged to accomplish. In the event
that I am mistaken on this point, I
have my sack over my shoulder, I am
ready to depart, and this world has really too little caressed me that I should
leave it with any grief. In any case, my
dear friend who calls himself too
humbly my "little brother," know that
God sees your works and that I will
not allow him to forget them.*

14. – *Paris Odors*, old book re-published by Crès. I
cannot re-read it, in spite of the fifty-year-old mold,
doubtless because it reminds me of my youth. But
what are Louis Veuillot's famous violent expressions
today compared to mine, and what to say of his style
à la Sévigné or à la Bruyère? I quickly renounce it,

the author being so base, so totally devoid of art!

15. – Unusual letter from Florian trying to explain to me the defection of his friend, the priest Deml, so faithful prior to now, become the "Czech inhabitant of Olympus or Parnassus," among the "national gods of Free Thinking." He shacks up with a married woman. That letter, which I do not have the permission to publish, is full of very curious satirical phrases.

Another letter from my excellent friend the Friar D. to whom I sent a reliquary. The heart of that religious is a harp.

20. – Printed dedication for *The Pilgrim of the Absolute*, to Philippe Raoux:

> *Remember, my friend, that happy day last year when you came to visit me at Mévoisins before returning to your very sad Poland. You could not stay for more than a couple hours and we had too many things to say to one another.*
>
> *So our two souls looked at each other in silence, our two poor souls that we did not know, and which do not know themselves. We knew only that Our Lord Jesus Christ was with us and rejoiced to see us together.*
>
> *I offer you now this book in*

which foreigners *perhaps will not dis-
cern the malice that is in their hearts,
but I know that you will find mine,
which is all yours, my dear Philippe.*

23. – Letter come from Dusseldorf. The doctor Her-
man Platz, professor, writes to me after having read
Barbey d'Aurevilly's Letters to me. That professor,
who appears to me a fearsome pedant, would like to
know "what position I hold in contemporary tradi-
tionalism from the point of view of ideas!?" If life
was longer, I could respond to him that I know no
other tradition than that of the Roman Catholic
Church. Has that Germanic prig read me at least? Impossible to unravel. But I have never had a stupider
question put to me before.

24. – Our doctor sent me a note with his honorariums.
My name is written *Blois*. Response:

> *My dear Doctor, my having, as every-
> one knows, "a heart of gold" and the
> ancient habitude of paying for every-
> one, I do not hesitate for one minute to
> settle your honorariums on the ac-
> count of* M. Blois, *who is absolutely a
> stranger to me.*

> *A simple glance at the book
> that I had the pleasure of giving to you
> would inform you that my name is but
> four letters, being a sort of very myste-*

rious tetragram.

25. – An illustrious photographer, having taken the portrait of Pope Pius X, solicited him to write several words above that image. The Holy Father wrote this: *Diligentibus Deum omnia cooperantur in bonum.*[31] Saint Paul's expression inscribed on my work table for many years now, and which I re-read constantly. Unexpected encounter, a bit surprising.

29. – I was speaking about the impossibility of a reason to conceive what has no limits, infinity. My little Madeleine then said, with a surprising profundity, this:

> *"Is it then less impossible to conceive finity? Isn't any sort of limit disconcerting?"*

February

2. – I am famous in Holland. I learn that a lecture by Henri van Haastert, in Amsterdam, had much success. He spoke well of me, contradicted only in a very weak fashion by an ecclesiastic closed to all comprehension of art.

8. – Found this in a journal:

---

[31] *Diligentibus... bonum*: Romans 8:28.

The Death of a Millionaire. New York.
– The precious tube containing
500,000 francs worth of radium,
which had been inserted into his
shoulder, was unable to save the life of
the American millionaire, M. G. Bren-
ner. It was in order to treat his cancer
or at least to retard its fatal issue that
the doctors had decided to attempt the
supreme method: placing a tube
containing half a million francs' worth
of the precious metal into small
incisions made under the patient's
skin. After four weeks of suffering, the
patient died with his treasure under
his skin.

12. – *The Baptism of Pauline Ardel* by my dear friend
Emile Baumann. The quite incontestable originality
of that new novel by the author of *The Immolated* lies
in its being highly Christian in a language entirely superior to that of our Catholics; but the ending discon-
certed me. A marriage of devotion after a marriage of
love prevented by the beloved's death! It's enough to
bring him back to life.

13. – To Baron Lumbroso, director of the *Revue
Napoléonienne*, in Rome:

    ... Your request for all *my books, many*
    of which cannot be found, and your

dispatch of 50 francs for that puts me in a predicament. I am a very poor man, almost septuagenarian and incapable of multiple errands. Being neither the possessor nor the seller of my books, I find myself ordinarily forced to redirect those who ask for them of me to my publishers. I entrust what I have at hand to the post for you, excusing myself for their small number. Eight volumes in all, which I ask you to kindly acknowledge receipt of. After that, I am entirely tapped out.

In the spring, I will be able to send you a copy of The Desperate Man, *republished finally after twenty-five years, the book that made me famous and poverty-stricken, being the origin of the conspiration of silence which I die of for a quarter of a century now. You will receive also a republication of* Histoires désobligeantes *and* The Pilgrim of the Absolute, *sixth tome of my journal. If you really wish to get to know me, you must read all six volumes and above all* The Woman Who Was Poor, *which unfortunately I cannot give you a copy of.*

It costs me nothing to tell you that your 50 francs have been received with pleasure. I am a beggar, and I will die a beggar, having never wished to prostitute my thought. One accords me to be a great writer, some even go so far as to suppose me a genius. But the newspapers do not mention my books because that would make them sell, and because the equilibrium of louts demands that I should perish in misery. The Soul of Napoleon *or* Blood of the Poor *signed by another person's name would have enjoyed twenty editions by this time. The first is still not sold out. Same comment for* Sweating Blood, *which appeared at the moment of the provocations of Saverne, a book which should be in every French person's hands. One will discover me little by little, with difficulty. Many good people who would love me are unable to know even that I exist.*

After so much trouble and work, with the responsibility of a family and feeling myself growing old, I am reduced to dreaming of an encounter with an admirer *capable of repairing the injustice of contemporaries by giving me the means to achieve my work without too much suffering. But that does not exist.*

15. – Baptism of Christophe Boussac, born the day before yesterday. When that little Christian will have

reached twenty years old, where will I be? Assuredly not in the Panthéon, no more than at the Academy, even less, perhaps, among the Glory of God's elect. I do not see the benefit of the poor child having so poor a godfather.

16. – Trip to Argœuves (Somme) by Pierre van der Meer in the company of Barbot and an imbecile. The curate of Argœuves, the Abbot Rigaux who knew Mélanie very well, is, it appears, the most interesting man around. He is full of memories of the Shepherdess whose thousands of confidential letters he possesses which he cannot communicate, keeping them to serve for her future canonization which he believes completely certain. The entire life of that saint has been the same since her childhood, full of prodigies. Stigmata, prophetic gifts, marvelous visions, continual encounters with Jesus and Mary. She saw, above all, with anguishing precision, the *near* fulfillment of the most terrible threats by La Salette. What I would have given to know her!

17. – Enormous sadness. My situation as a *kept* writer of genius and always uncertain of tomorrow weighs down on me. Often I have seen assistance arrive after such crises. Perhaps it will come. But that does not console me, given it is precisely the perpetual necessity of that assistance that breaks my heart.

19. – A lady mentioned *Sweating Blood* in a review. "Nobody admires Léon Bloy more than that lady. But she deplores that the splendor of his style should be in the service of that so very un-Christian sentiment, hatred." When you get right down to it, I have been too hard on the Prussians.

As for the recent batch of academicians of whom Bergson is part, Raoux is surprised that it takes so many zeroes to add up to the number forty.

26. – In a paper:

> The election of the Jew Bergson. – *Israel then will be superiorily represented in the illustrious campaign, and it is good that one of our own, who has succeeded in vanquishing a position taken up by religious biases and social prejudices and which detonates over the liberalism that reigns in other classes at the Institute, should be a mind of rare caliber before the profoundness and ingenuity that the more established Catholics incline to, like the d'Haussonvilles, the Denys Cochins, and the de Ségurs. – PRAGUE, director of the* Israelite Archives.

As for myself, I don't incline at all. It being true, however, that I am not an *established* Catholic.

27. – Letter from Lumbroso sending me another 50 francs for an article to be written for his *Revue Napoléonienne*. He has procured fifteen of my books and sent me the half-titles for dedications.

I am not exactly overwhelmed. One article and fifteen dedications for 50 francs! But the sender of it knows quite well that the poor ought to swallow everything.

28. – With fatigue, disgust, and sadness, confectioned the article and dedications. Work that certain collectors would pay very dearly for. The swine will have his money's worth.

> The Ungrateful Beggar. – *To Albert Lumbroso, who declares himself an admirer of* almost *all I have written. That "almost," which gives me sea sickness, does it include the* Beggar *or the* Ungrateful? *It is agonizing. The "small Léon Bloy museum" that he announces, will it only be* almost *a museum? What discomfort for the poor tramp of the Absolute!*

> My Journal. – *The author, in 1904, did not know if he would continue. The title of that volume was going to be "Seventeen Months in Denmark." Notice to the bookbinder.*

> Four Years of Captivity in Cochons-sur-Marne. – *Sixty-seven years of pe-*

nal colony at Cochons-everywhere. Better title for the collection of my works.

The Unsellable. – *"The Unreadable" would be perhaps more exact. Who today then is capable of reading a book in which God is constantly spoken of?*

Chosen Pages. – *The hardest forced labor that has ever been imposed on me. Stupid choices. The next page is always better.*

Gladiators and Swineherds. – *There aren't even any more swineherds, the Republican Circe having worked so well, and the gladiators have totally disappeared.*

Le Pal. – *These four brochures which will never be reprinted, the author judges them puerile and often absurd.*

The Chevalier of Death. – *This little book too much in imitation of Carlyle is my first work and I do not recommend it. It was written in 1877. I was then, or I must have been, 15 to 18 years old, being born in 1846.*

The Desperate Man. – *The conspiration of silence was determined by this book, twenty-eight years ago. It continues still. The author also, by a miracle. This edition (Stock) is, moreover, execrable.*

The Woman Who Was Poor. – *The second part of this book, one of the saddest that has been written, is the author's exact story* – the second part only. *But it is disgusting to think about the total incomprehension of the reader.*

The Son of Louis XVI. – *The dirty race of Bourbons was supposed to finish like this, by a poor tortured imbecile.*

Christopher Columbus Before the Bulls. – *Those bulls have turned out to be very old cows, and it is what one calls today the Roman Curia.*

Léon Bloy Before the Swine. – *It's changed, I am behind now.*

The Last Columns of the Church. – *Today, as ten years ago, there is nothing but those shitty columns. It is what Pius X thinks.*

The Resurrection of Villiers de l'Isle-Adam. – *Poor Villiers did not believe in death. He was right doubtless. It is why I persuaded the sculptor to write on the back of the coffin these liturgical words:* Vita mutatur, non tollitur.[32]

---

[32] *Vita... tollitur.* Latin for "Life changes, is not taken away."

March

2. – Barbot is immensely preoccupied with the curate of Argœuves and the revelations of Mélanie touching on the burning of Paris. If that happens, one will never have seen anything so frightening.

3. – *Journal of a Convert.* Title of a very fine book by my godson Pierre wherein his conversion to Catholicism is recounted. I had advised him to translate it from Dutch to French, last year, in Rotterdam, and I have been rather happy to settle on Crès as the publisher of it. In my quality as a godfather, I ought to write an introduction, of which this:

> *"Vobis datum est nosse mysteria regni cœlorum.*[33] *The mysteries of the kingdom of heaven have been made known to you." Thus says, in the Gospel, Our Lord Jesus Christ.*

> *The modern multitude, which does not believe in that Kingdom, naturally seeks the mysteries of the* other *kingdom. For there is no means for getting around the Mystery, when one is "in the image and in the resemblance of God." One can live without bread, without wine, without a roof over one's head, without love, without*

---

[33] *Vobis... cœlorum*: Latin for "The mysteries of the kingdom of heaven have been made known to you."

happiness; one cannot live without Mystery. Human nature demands it.

Ah! Well do I know that there are many animals, so-called reasonable, who seem to live to sixty or eighty years old, and whom one will carry, one day, to the cemetery, without their having ever been able to leave emptiness. Many even have been famous in their translation "from the uterus to the sepulture." Only the contingent from the Sorbonne, from the Academy, or from Parliament is considerable. That distinguished crowd is ignorant of the Mystery's torment. The apparent realities suffice and all the rest is non-existent.

But true men, those truly living, those who have not "received their souls in vain," suffer and weep like abandoned souls, as long as they have not found the Church which keeps the key to all the mysteries. Such was the history of my beloved godson Pierre-Matthais van der Meer of Walcheren, whose very fine book I present to all those who have hearts capable of beating.

* * *

It is true that this latter man is a poet and one of those poets even whose na-

tion can be proud of, that is to say a vase of suffering, one of those beings who does not fall but from on high and who are, for their continual anguish, captives of the mud of this world. Without a doubt they will return to dust like all other human beings, but their dust will add something to the Milky Way.

* * *

Pierre van der Meer was born in Holland, behind that insuperable dike built by Calvin, four centuries ago, in order to separate forever from the Church one "marshy people" already prepared by nature to croak in obscurity.

How could he, at thirty years of age, scale the obstacle? Is this the effect of his aristocratic ascendancy, forcing him to reintegrate the spiritual House of his most distant ancestors? Is this all simply the horror of an artistic soul evading, with the cries of joy, the infinite hideousness of Calvinism; or rather, as he himself supposes, could one say that it was in him, – by the universal Communion of saints, – the mysterious germination, finally obtained, of one of those humble prayers of an unknown man carried by God's Breath, like those grains flying on the

*wind that come one does not know
whence and that fall where they must,
exactly?*

*All that is infinitely hidden,
and it will be up to Paradise to know,
one day, to which brothers, according
to the Spirit, we owe this divine Gift!*

* * *

*But, what tortures exist for such souls
while waiting for the miracle! There
were few things so poignant and penetrating as the clamor of that poet incapable of being satisfied by what is not
the Infinite and crying out in his despair for not having found issue from
his jail of contingencies.*

*He knows that the Truth is un-
known to him, he believes it is inaccessible, he feels caught in an immense
net of mysteries that he cannot break a
single link of, and he lacks all hope of
being assisted. For Protestantism does
not forgive. A Jew, a Muslim, a Schismatic, an idolater, a negro, can seek
God without despair. Sometimes even
his soul can break out magnificently in
a work of art expressing his nostalgia.
That is not possible for a Protestant
always forced, by his principle, to rely
uniquely, exclusively, on himself!*

The frigid and pale demon of Mediocrity, which inspired Heresy, has taken it upon itself, after four centuries, to denature the Face of God at the same time that it extenuates his Word, realizing thus the insuperable ugliness of all sects given birth to by the so-called Reformation. Really atrocious ugliness that ought naturally to produce an instinctive – and now archisecular – repulsion against the splendors of Catholicism.

* * *

When a poor soul, cooped up since childhood in horrible obscurity, is cherished enough by God to conceive the desire to get to know him, it will seek everywhere with anguishments and infinite deceptions, except there where it finds itself, in the indefectible Church of Christ. That same church does not exist and cannot exist for it. One has told him as much! It alone is impossible, given it is supernatural, by consequence infecund, inept to live and inept to give life.

There is a sadness, a nameless pity, to see miserable beings listening at the bottom of their souls – as if to a distant and supplicating church bell – to the call of God, and weeping here and there outside the Church, without thinking to enter! No one has known that dolorous burden better than Pierre van der Meer, that excessive pain exhaled with so much vigor in two thirds of his book, until the moment of his miraculous conversion.

"I don't believe in anything," he told himself, having received with horror the confidences of a wicked man. "I cannot then condemn this man and his acts. In the name of whom or what could I? Why would he need to act otherwise, given it pleased him to act in that way? All is permitted, I know. Haven't I myself thought more abominable things maybe, and am I not complicit by those thoughts? Each one of us is free to act as he desires, if only he has the courage. That man did not let himself be imprisoned by opinions and strict proprieties. To whom or to what must he reckon with for his acts? Evidently no one, for there is nothing above him. He is right, I am wrong. Everything is permitted. He has no limits, he has no law. Neither good nor evil exist. All is permitted... But why, my soul, do you sob?...

"Why can I not be content with what stands before me, palpable, limited, real? Why does my spirit invoke Infinity and Eternity? I cannot think of

the End *and Infinity is like a gulf in which a stone falls that will never hit, never ever, the bottom. The one and the other of these things are inconceivable to my reasoning...*

"The spectacle of that starry night over our earth bowls me over. How many men have cried like me in their anguish, on innumerable evenings for thousands of years, since suns have been illuminated in the night from the beginning of time! And nobody has heard liberating words. And the most frightening or most risible thing is this that, very probably, there are no mysteries and that we torture ourselves in vain...

"But what is terrible is that we think. *The solitude of man, the only being that thinks, in the midst of worlds, is it not frightening?*

"According to a very acceptable hypothesis, the earth, that old planet, will become, after several thousands or millions of years, inhabitable, then perish. And that will be as if humanity had never existed. All will be precipitated forever into emptiness and absolute oblivion. Nothing will carry any longer in itself the memory of what those strange creatures, who one day lived on earth and whom one

*called men, accomplished and suf-
fered. The symphonies of Beethoven,
the Bible, wars, the most sublime
thoughts of saints, Napoleon, Dante,
despair, love, the succession of empires, the Christ, – all that was perfectly, absolutely vain, and the gigantesque drama that had lasted so many
centuries and to which not one witness
remained any longer, – could have
also not taken place. Is it not a terrifying derision, is it not enough to make
one hurl with anguish or find escape
in death?...*

*"For a moment as brief as a
flash of lightning, we are here, on
earth, living, with eyes wide open,
with the wild tempest of our passions,
tortured by every desire and every
dream, wishing to embrace the impossible and to hold it fast to our heart.
We interrogate the past, we read what
men have thought; we cannot understand. We interrogate the earth, the
sky, the stars, the abysses in space,
and the abysses in our soul; we sob
with ecstasy and with nostalgia at the
sight of a beautiful thing, we make
great passionate efforts and then, all
of a sudden, we lie flat out, immobile
and there is nothing, nothing, nothing... The stars, at which we looked
with such immense desire, will no*

longer remember us...! Anne-Marie!...

"Beauty," he said much later, "is always tragic, for it is the song of a privation.*"*

Where will you find, even in Pascal, as dolorous and as profound a foreshortening of the human Lament as that last expression? How many are there, and where are they today, who can feel like that?

* * *

I spoke of Mystery at the beginning because it is the first thing to be seen, as soon as one opens this book, this very simple and very beautiful recitation of the peregrinations of a soul in search of God.

The soul knows nothing about Him, does not recognize His Face, but knows that there must be One and that, unable to be an orphan of Nothingness, it is necessary for Him for the soul be conceived and given birth to.

His tears, his sighs, the beatings of his heart have taught him that it is somewhere, very far away or very close by, and that by searching for it he would find Him.

But that is difficult and more

dolorous than one can say, because of the darkness, the layers of darkness over the paths. Darknesses of things, darknesses of men, known and unknown darknesses. All lamps are spent, from the time of the first step taken, and it is indispensable to continue, return being already impossible.

* * *

I was born somewhere however, says the poor soul who weeps, and I would like to return to the House of my Father. Since having dissipated my substance, I herd swine while dying of famine, how many times and with what terrible regrets have I recalled that house full of light where one had warmth, where the poor satisfied their hunger, where the Master came himself to wipe away the tears of the unfortunate!

But I no longer know where it is, that House that should be my inheritance, and the Sphinxes encountered everywhere and consulted at every instant, they mock me, while waiting to devour me.

The one says to me, "I am the mystery of Life"; the other says, "I am the mystery of Death"; a third one says, "I am the mystery of your thought"; a fourth one, and the most troubling of all, says finally, "I am the mystery of your heart." And if I do not guess right, they threaten to tear me apart. O my unfindable, invisible Father, have pity on me!

* * *

Such is, as much as can be translated into words, the frightening dereliction of a superior man to whom God was not introduced, but whom mediocrity disgusts, and who no longer expects anything from philosophies nor even artists, if not deception and derision – until the marvelous hour when Our Lord Jesus Christ, suddenly manifested, divests him of his old heart!

* * *

And as for me, I tell you, one more time again, that it is anguishing and magnificent to find these things in the Journal *of Pierre van der Meer. Even though I occupy a large place in his book which well-informed critics will not fail to judge as too honorable, I believed myself unable to forego – in my quality as a godfather – presenting this superior writer, translated for the first time into French, at the risk of seeing him enveloped in the famous conspiration of Silence that some peo-*

> *ple try to assassinate me by, for thirty*
> *years now, and which I have succes-*
> *sively buried the instigators of.*

6. – Stroke of inspiration found in I do not know what
paper: *The Baptism by Air!* with regards to an aviator.

12. – To Lumbroso:

> *I inform you of this that, on March 2,*
> *ten days ago, I sent to you, by*
> registered *mail, a letter containing the*
> *article you had asked for and a packet*
> *of fifteen half-title dedications. Those*
> *two objects, capable perhaps of excit-*
> *ing the covetousness of a collector, –*
> *did you receive them?*

Two volumes by Selma Lagerlöf: *Jerusalem in Dal-*
carna, and *In the Holy Land*. I do not know why
someone recommended them so highly to me. They
are not exactly boring, but their meaning escapes me.
What do they mean, those Swedish and Lutheran
peasants whom God (?) commands to go to Jerusalem
to chant their psalms or their imbecilic canticles,
without thinking, for a single instant, to visit the Holy
Sepulture, and who return to their country disgusted,
not having done anything intelligible? In love as well
as in religion, they absolutely do not know what they
want, and I shut these sad books as I would seal off a
cave inside which I found, instead of treasures, nothing but darkness and the mold of an abandoned sepul-

ture.

15. – *When the Spirit Blows...* by Adolphe Retté. The first chapter concerns Huysmans. Extreme poverty. Admiration almost without limits. He trots out the things written by Huysmans without adding a personal view to them and in the style of a consecrator. Sometimes he uses me without naming me.

As I was cutting the pages of the book,[34] I saw however my name in another chapter. "*The Soul of Napoleon*," he says, "very beautiful book by an exciter of high thoughts, unfortunately ruined by unhealthy pride and too human rancors."

And there we have it! My greatest misfortune, in such a pair of eyes, it is not being a *converted*.

17. – Enormous news. Mme. Caillaux, wife of the too famous minister of finance, killed, yesterday evening, the Director of the *Figaro*, who was threatening the married couple with publishing I do not know what fearsome document. The victim deserved better than the assassins? Excellent occasion for copy by the newspapers. But what a deluge of filth when one opens the floodgates of that trial!

It is the year for the republication of my books. After Crès, the *Mercure de France* has expressed interest in reprinting, it also, *The Desperate*

---

[34]cutting the pages: at that time, as even today can be found, esp. in France (and probably elsewhere in Europe), books were published with the folios folded and the pages needing to be cut.

Man, but with a curious image. Three years ago, when I was in Périgord, Doctor Ampelosse, mentioned in *The Pilgrim of the Absolute*, had the idea of photographing me before a group of pigs. That photograph has become the fitting frontispiece of *The Desperate Man*.

Occasion for new dedications. Of which, here are some for admirers.

To Louis Q.:

The image represents Marchenoir twenty-five years later. He is awfully beautiful still, no? What would you have said in '86, when he was in the presence of real swine whom those here give too flattering an idea of?

To Cornuau:

Melancholic attitude of an old author before adolescent swine.

To Viñes:

Incontestable superiority. Do similar exist in Catalonia?

To Léon Bellé:

Marchenoir's swine have, in sign of mourning clearly, a black crown on the derriere, which differentiates them from other swine. One is invited to study that admirable symbolism.

To René Martineau:

Look at that image. Before making your acquaintance, my good friend, I hardly saw contemporary humanity otherwise, and I really had my back against the wall. God bless you for having distanced me from that drove.

To Georges Rouault:

With a little image of piety to remind one of the Last Judgment, when our contemporaries will have been restituted to their veritable form.

To Vincent d'Indy:

Lacrymabiliter, Miseranter, Speranter. The title is an antiphrasis. Fundamentally, this book is the expression of unchained *optimism.*

To Félix Raugel:

Imagine that to music, with the grating sound of the saw into the prophet's vertebrae, and the bonging sound of the poor old church bell tolling for the dead.

23. – Pierre tells me about a great commotion going on in Holland, on the subject of my books, the Catholics down there being stupider than those here, judging me to be a great *pernicious* author. I ask him to have van Haaster let me know exactly everything that I am reproached with so that I might respond.

24. – Read *Cromwell* by Carlyle, 3rd volume, translation by Edmond Barthèlemy. The author absolutely
wants his hero to be the most immense of men. He affirms it with all the force of his extraordinary talent,
without succeeding in rendering sympathetic to me
that blasphemer inimical to all beauty, that insupportable and unintelligible preacher who understands
nothing about the Texts that he fills his Letters and
his interminable Discourses with.

Carlyle, idolator of Cromwell, and who has
contracted his Puritanical scabies, wants by all means
to defend him from the accusation of hypocrisy that
weighs down on him for generations, without understanding that that wicked man was a dyed-in-the-wool
hypocrite, that is to say compared to himself, and that
such was his appalling innocence.

25. – *The Schismatic Russian Church* by Father
Theiner. This old book shows quite clearly the horrible state of that domesticated church, more deformed
and more debased than the so-called Protestant
churches. Abyss of darkness.

26. – Response by a lady who received *The Desperate Man* and who does not know that she is a dolt.
She writes to me that one needs, in order to understand my books, a "certain moral superiority," and
she considers herself happy to note, by my parcel to
her, that I have accorded her that superiority!!!

29. – Henri van Haaster confirms to me what Pierre had told me, the great battle going on in Holland around my name and the menaces or insults by Catholics, recompense for my defenders.

April

2. – Finished reading *The Schismatic Church*. Terrible indictment against that miserable church that dishonors Russia. One understands Catherine Emmerich who saw so somber a cloud over that empire.

3. – To a friend:

> Quare tristis es?... Spera in Deo.[35]
> *What could I possibly say to you that might equal those words that you read daily before mass? I know the pain that your son gives you. It is doubtless great and for me unexpected. I had at first thought that it had something to do with those foolish carnal acts that young people are exposed to. Then I would have recommended commiseration and gentleness, while guarding yourself against bitter blame that withers the heart and destroys confidence. "If you do not have the strength*

---

[35]*Quare... Deo*: Latin for "Why are you sad?... Trust in God." Psalms 42 (Vulgate).

> *to control yourself, my poor child,"*
> you would have said, *"I will do*
> penance for you.*" And that language*
> *could have penetrated deep into his*
> *soul. I learn that the situation is much*
> *graver, as his very character would be*
> *in question. Then, my afflicted friend,*
> *there is nothing left for you but prayer,*
> *prayer through the sacrament. Some*
> *years ago, you did me the honor of*
> *consulting with me. I responded to you*
> *that I myself had no other resource*
> *than quotidian communion which,*
> *moreover, is not a counsel but a for-*
> *mal precept, and that there is nothing*
> *else, in all honesty, for obtaining the*
> *Faith that can move mountains.*

5. – Palm Sunday. Advertisement in the *Matin* whose edifying piety is known by everyone. One would think he was reading the *Croix*:

> *Everyone should go to the cinema,*
> *during the religious holidays of Holy*
> *Week and Easter, to see the film that*
> *reconstitutes faithfully and respectful-*
> *ly, in conformity with the texts of the*
> *holy books, all the phases in the Life*
> *of Our Lord Jesus Christ. Never has a*
> *similar effort been produced in cine-*
> *matography to give, with as much* truth
> *and intensity, the splendid, unique,*
> *and definitive* Living Illustration *of the*

Holy Gospels (!!!). The last word of perfection. Ininflammable *film.*

Resolution to write a book on Joan of Arc, irrevocably influenced by my friend Brou who spoke to me of the Heroine with extraordinary strength of penetration and love.

To Rachilde who communicated to me the proofs of a very good article on *The Desperate Man*:

> *I send you your proofs that I read with attention. I have corrected some errors! I have even dared to change an inexact word and I audaciously suppressed two others that bothered me. I hope that you will forgive me for that. I love you much, my poor Rachilde, enough, believe me, to accept new suffering, if it should need to come to that, so that you might believe, like me, in God and in his bounty. Tears, my tears, you have seen quite clearly that they were, that they still are, more sorrowful than bitter. Be persuaded, however, that they are not without a sweetness and that they often help to support life in this appalling world. I wish you such tears, dear friend. That would be the surest collyrium for your eyes damaged by too many vain or abominable readings.*

8. – A maniac of antisemitism, whom I have spoken of already in *The Pilgrim of the Absolute*, has felt the need to write to me that his feelings for the Jews have not changed and that "this week he curses them more than ever." The Church prays for them, and that man believes he's a Catholic.

9 . – *France Before the Swine*. (Published in the *Works* by Gustave Téry, the 16th.)

"All France," someone said to me, "consists however of nothing but idiots and scoundrels." So be it, but the triage is problematic, the identification enigmatic, and the disproportion appears fabulous. Would the boldest optimism dare to hope today for the ten just men asked for in the pardon of Sodom?[36] As for thinking individuals, – who would undertake to isolate them? Let one search for them in the clergy, in the army and in the navy, in the literary world or the world of science, in the swarming of the magistrature or finance, at the Sorbonne, at the Academy, and above all in Parliament, one will be frightened.

More than sixty years ago, when M. Ernest-Judas Lavisse was not yet operating for the integral demolition of the ruins of the French spirit, a great philosopher, already frightened by the universitarian cesspool, groaned with a prophet's eloquence over the *Weakening of Reason* consecutive to the inanition of souls. What would he say today on seeing the

[36]ten just men... Sodom: for an entertaining retelling of the story from Genesis, see chapter XXX of Bloy's *Salvation Through the Jews*, published by Sunny Lou Publishing, 2020.

Durkheims, the Aulards, the Lansons, or the Seigno-
bos, and what would he not say about the spectacle of
mud-splattered and probably definitive cretinism invoked by universal suffrage.

One buries, each day, venerable old men who
have believed, to their dying hour, in Democracy, and
I confess that that idiocy confounds me. Since the ripe
old age of 18, I recall very clearly that I had trouble
conceiving there should be beings so beneath negroes
as to believe that children had the power and even the
duty to engender their fathers. The old fable of Menenius[37] is particularly discredited. One has to believe
that, five hundred years before the Christian era, the
people of Rome were less stupid than we are, given
that illustrious and dusty triumphant general could
make them accept him. Today, one would declare him
doddering and send him to La Coupole.

All the same, it is mind-boggling to think on
the inexplicable self-survival of the Republican
regime. For forty-four years now, if not longer, one
would believe that all experiences had been had and
that that regime of disgust had become impossible.
Universal atrophy of intelligences, unprecedented
limpness of characters, endemic execration of Beauty
and Grandeur, national obsequies for all human or divine authority, furious bulimia of sensual pleasures,
destruction of the family and vivisection of the fatherland, mores of enraged swine, systematic empoison-
ing of youth, election and selection of scalawags or

[37]fable of Menenius: presumably in reference to Agrippa
Menenius Lanatus, who obtained the consulship in 503 BC, and
who in 493, during an uprising of the plebs, claimed to have
originated from among them.

goitrous fellows in the caverns of politics or on the sidewalk of candidatures, etc. such are the fruits of the tree of Liberty.

No matter, it is understood that all goes very well like that and that one must guard against weakening it. It is the tree of life planted by giants, and it would be a sacrilege to touch it.

Let's us admit something, though. It is true that not everyone is an idiot or a scoundrel, but what an appalling destiny for the few exceptions, that is to say the very rare people who still represent the generous France of bygone days! Perfect ignominy, the silence one dies of, the misery that kills, that is their share; while waiting for the corporal punishments that, one day, will be the largess for those Witnesses of Divine Life.

A review sends me a questionnaire. Every writer having two-sous-worth of notoriety is exposed to it. It is the epoch of surveys, with or without commission. If the responses flow in, that makes up the copy *free* for the picking, and the writers consulted are really before the swine, like eligible candidates.

It's a matter, this time, of repolishing the shoes of the French Academy just a bit. – In your opinion, it asks,

> *1) The French Academy, is it or is it not in decline?*

> *2) Do you think today that it would accept a Flaubert or a Baudelaire?*

3) Does its current influence on letters seem to you good or bad?

My response could be nothing else than this:

1) [38]

2) Not only would it not accept a Flaubert or a Baudelaire, but it would plot to prevent them from being able to pay their debts, reducing them to the bleakest of famines, and it would overwhelm with its oldest favors the most fetid Rosand or Hanotaux that it could unearth.

3) Its present influence on Letters is absolutely nil, it being understood that Letters no longer exist.

They can interrogate me on whatever topic they wish, on the Caillaux-Calmette affair, for example. My response will contain the same grace and will shed the same light, exactly.

10. – Holy Friday. Jeanne and the children are unable to penetrate Notre-Dame, or any other church for that matter. At Saint-Eustache one would have to pay 4 fr. for certain seats, 1 fr. for others. Our poor people cannot attend the offices. Our cardinal archbishop is certainly not ignorant of this traffic.

---

[38]Editor's note: the response to question number one was apparently struck by the original censors.

To Father D*** who sent me 20 francs on the occasion of the feast day of Saint Léon the Great, which is tomorrow. Every year, no matter what I might say, he makes it a point to make me the same gift, at the same time of year. I am ignorant of the privations represented by this gift by a very poor monk:

> *My dear friar, guessing what your gift to me, arrived this morning, must certainly have cost you, I am pleased to tell you that these 20 francs have arrived at a moment when one was quite nearly at one's wits end. For it is always like that. No matter how many publications I might put out, the enemies of my books multiply their efforts to stifle them and my situation remains the same. God wants me poor, and even indigent.*

# # #

Re-read *The Ungrateful Beggar*, p. 240, last paragraph, and above all p. 371, first paragraph. In exchange for the voluntary and spontaneous sacrifice of all earthly prosperity, I have received the power to act on certain souls to the degree of leading them to supernatural life and making them the souls of apostles. I can suffer then without too much bitterness, sometimes even with the feeling of a profound joy.

By distinguished privilege, I have understood in time that it is necessary to pay for those who cannot pay for themselves, that it is the entire mystery of the Redemption, and that one cannot gain souls except by suffering for them. Today, nevertheless, I grow old, not in spirit, but in body, and my force diminishes greatly. It is a great struggle, for I am far from having accomplished my task. I have the head and the heart completely full of new works that I must realize and, if my fate is not softened, I fear that I will be unable to make it to the end. I believe that it is in this sense that it is appropriate for people to pray for me.

12. – To Raïssa Maritain:

> *My beloved goddaughter, I would like, on this day of the Resurrection, to take you into my paws of an old* lion, *you, Vera, and Jacques and devour you amorously. But why send me money? You do not know then that I have a banker, always the same. Besides, you invert the roles. It's not for the godchildren to give, but for the godparents. So many things you have yet to learn, my little Raïssa!*

> *You are right, however, to see some symbolism in my life. There is more to it than you think, more to it than I know myself, and that is the story of each of the creatures made in the resemblance of God who cannot be conceived of save through symbols.*

*But I have been singularly privileged,
that is for sure.*

*The end of Lent this year has
seemed very rough. Today, my soul is
exceptionally at peace. Easter Sunday
has often been very painful for me, being one of those who are sad and who
weep still, on Monday, with the disciples of Emmaus. The transition seems
too brusque, from immense grief to
full joy. One has need of habituating
himself to that prodigious transition
and twenty centuries have not sufficed.
Jesus himself could not manifest himself in his glory except after having
descended into hell. That text of our
Symbol is overpowering.*

13. – To Jean de la Laurencie:

*How happy I am, my dear friend, to
have been able to give you a little recomfort! God knows that I would like
to possess a greater power. But I am
merely a poor man. All that I can do is
to show, to those who suffer, my
wounds, which have been deep and
which I do not stop suffering from.*

*You said correctly that "com-
plete faith" is a divine grace, but you
were wrong to add that it is not ac-*

corded except to those who merit it, as if it could be merited. Alas! what do we deserve, any of us? And what would become of us if we were treated according to our merits? That's enough to instill fear.

Believe me, my friend, that is not it. God gives faith, not to those who might be thought to merit it, but to those who desired it, and he gives it gratuitously when he pleases and to whom he pleases, even to those who do not desire it. Think on the Good Thief, who had begun – as the other – by insulting him on his Cross, as Saint Matthew tells it expressly, and on Saint Longinus who pierced his heart. What surprising choices! Those men hardly desired it, one might suppose. So...

Try to persuade yourself that I have a little experience in the matter and tell yourself forcefully that you have only but to desire, to desire veritably. What you lack will be given to you, and you will be able to speak as a master to the mountain of your grief. Without a doubt, you will suffer still as we are all members of a Chief crowned with thorns, but you will suffer without bitterness, and with a profound peace of heart.

> The Woman Who Was Poor,
> *loved by the dearly departed whom I*
> *name every day at the* Memento[39], *fin-*
> *ishes with this: "All that happens is*
> *adorable... There is only one sadness,*
> *and that is not to have been made*
> *saints." Ah! if you knew from what*
> *abyss of pain came those words which*
> *have consoled many souls!...*

15. – Reading in the *History of Charles VII,* by Vallet de Viriville, for my book on Joan of Arc. Horrible chaos at that beginning of the fifteenth century.

18. – Henri van Haastert asks me for a preface to a book on me that he is going to publish in Holland, and he gives me a series of fifteen imbecilic objections by my Dutch critics.

19. – All is pointless, except suffering.

29. – Preface for van Haastert:

> *I thought, for a long time, that one*
> *cannot be stupider than the Catholics*
> *of France. Today, I am forced to rec-*

---

[39]Memento: Memento (or Remembrance) of the Living; it is a prayer at mass beginning with that word, in the Roman Catholic Church.

*ognize with ill-humor that the Cath-
olics of Holland are, in that regard,
very superior to us. It is difficult,
doubtless, but not impossible, to encounter in France a Catholic gifted
with intelligence, capable of understanding something. That has been
seen, I could site some examples. It
appears that in Holland that is completely impossible. That deeply hum-
bles me. I am struck, grievously
wounded in my patriotic feelings.* Et
egressus est a Gallia omnis decor
ejus.[40] *It was perhaps the last superiority that remained with us, the superiority of stupidity in matters of religion, and there you go – it has been
taken from us!*

*Why must it be, alas! that my
poor books, so little worthy of the attention of men, have been the occasion
of that extraordinary unleashing of
Dutch Catholicism's imbecility? According to your journals, my dear
Henri, not one of my lines is not without reproach and there would be no
end to it if I undertook to respond to
all the accusations, but above all and
before everything one does not forgive
me for being a "man of the Absolute,"*

---

[40]*Et egressus... ejus:* Latin for "And all its majesty has left Gaul."
A modification to the original, from the Lamentations of Jeremiah,
"*Et egressus est a filia Sion omnis decor ejus.*"

that is to say, to affirm absolutely *that God exists, that he was made man, and that there is no truth outside the Church. In the eyes of Dutch Catholics, that is the irremissible grief, the supreme heresy. All the world knows, behind the dikes, that the Truth has nothing of the absolute about it, that it is undulating and multiform, that the "yes" and the "no" are equally plausible, that a friend of God must "conform to his century" and make all concessions to the devil that are demanded by whichever way the stock market or the opportunity for political transactions goes. Judas, who was very calumniated, even by Saint John, who accuses him of having been a robber, Judas was simply a victim of the Absolute, and that is why he so sottishly went to give the silver back to the Prince of Priests, instead of investing it in an annuity as an honest Catholic bourgeois person from Amsterdam or Rotterdam would have done.*

After that capital accusation, it seems that one could stop there, my other sins being nothing more than an easy-to-foresee consequence of that original prevarication. French imbeciles would have understood that that amply sufficed. But the Netherlander imbeciles are not so easily contented,

at the foot of the altar.

> *I lack common sense and prac-*
> *tical sense, they say. They are right, I*
> *am forced to admit it. Common sense,*
> *such as they intend it to mean, consists*
> *in not getting all worked up about*
> *martyrdom, nor even for a sacrifice*
> *whatsoever, even if it were the sponta-*
> *neous giving of several pennies to an*
> *indigent. As for practical sense, the*
> *small children of the catechism, as*
> *well as the most charitable ecclesias-*
> *tics, know that that precious sense is*
> *superabundantly demonstrated by the*
> *invincible resolution to fill up on tripe*
> *and make a good cake out of the blood*
> *of the poor. Yes, it is true, I have al-*
> *ways lacked those two senses.*

> *The same imbeciles, encour-*
> *aged by that avowal, say then that I*
> *demand from Christians more than the*
> *Gospel does even, because I believe*
> *poverty necessary for whomever wish-*
> *es to follow Jesus. This also is true.*
> Vende quæ habes, et veni, sequere me.
> – Qui non renuntiat omnibus quæ pos-
> sidet non POTEST meus esse discipu-
> lus.[41] *Instead of condemning me, O*
> *Catholics from behind the dike and*

---

[41] *Vende... discipulus*: Latin for, "Sell what you have, and come
follow me. – Whoever does not renounce all that he possesses
cannot be my disciple."

from behind the faggots, instruct me, for I do not know how to read the Gospel. It's gotten to the point that I denature the texts by translating them, for example, Væ divitibus[42] *into "Woe unto the rich." The French editions of the Vulgate are defective. It appears that the Dutch editions, much more faithful, contain* Gloria divitibus in excelsis.[43] *And that completely floors me.*

It goes without saying that I am accused of exaggeration, which is grave. In my Exegesis of Commonplaces, *however, I have tried to explain that exaggeration is to firmly say Yes or No,* Est, est. Non, non *as my defective Gospel claims. But the* Exegesis of Commonplaces *is an obscene book that is not permitted to be read from the pulpit in Dutch churches.*

As for the obscenity, one voluntarily notices that I have a Rabelaisque and even Zolaesque *predilection for disgusting words and impure things that "defy Latin even." This last reproach strongly vexes me, because of my pretensions to pure Latinity. From now on, I will write all my pigswill in Latin and I will dedicate*

---

[42] *Væ divitibus*: Latin for "Woe unto the rich."

[43] *Gloria... divitibus*: Latin for "Gloria to the rich in excelsis."

them to the Dutch clergy.

It appears also that there are in my books atrocious blasphemies that one would search for in vain in the works targeted by the Congregation of the Index,[44] the which does not do its job properly, by leaving me perfectly alone. It is quite simple. I have corrupted it by dint of money. The incorruptible imbeciles no longer practice their profession of imbeciles, given they omit that discussion.

I ridicule the delicatesse of pure people, I praise immoral books such as The Flowers of Evil; *I lack the Catholic spirit, and the proof is that I speak of the "swine of prayer," which however cannot outrage Catholic Holland, being much closer to Boetia than to Chicago. I mention also the "livestock of the sacristy," inexact citation, it seems to me. I believe I wrote "the mares of the altar," a more epic expression.*

It goes without saying that I lack charity and that my pride has no bounds, reproaches that were served up to me very often by Parisian jour-

---

[44]Congregation of the Index: the Sacred Congregation of the Index, or *Index Librorum Prohibitorum*: a list of books held heretical to the teaching of the Catholic Church, and forbidden to be read.

nalists of inferior imbecility.

Finally, a reading of the Catholic papers from Holland reveals to me my own history. I learn with surprise that I have been a Communard. I had thought until now that in 1871 I had taken up service to combat the Commune. A matter of nuance probably. I learn also that I have done four years in prison at Cochons-sur-Marne. Behind the dikes one knows that a famous fortress is located there where blasphemers of bourgeois villainy and pious cretinism are rigorously locked up. What else will I learn?

That's all, dear friend, all that I can respond to your consignment of papers. They have made my head spin a little, I dare say, which will not surprise your imbeciles, the which have inexplicably forgotten my well-known intemperance however. But I do not hide from you that I would prefer to get drunk on something else.

21. – Gaëtan Bernoville, the young publisher of the *Library of French Letters*, full of enthusiasm for me, has decided to republish *Je M'Accuse*...

27. – Barbot speaks to me about a short novel on the burning of Paris that he is in the process of finishing, wherein the predictions by La Salette would be verified.

28. – Dispatch from Lumbroso announcing to me his visit tomorrow.

> To Lumbroso:
>
> *March 2, nearly two months ago, I had the honor of sending to you, on your request, by registered mail, a packet that many collectors would have regarded as rather precious: a letter-article for your review and numerous dedications. I continue to wait for your acknowledgement of receipt. Ten days later, on March 12, a reminder letter goes without response. Having no reason to think you are a* Republican, *which would be an extremely insulting explanation, I supposed I do not know what insurmountable obstacles [prevented you from responding]. I will expect you tomorrow then, Wednesday, while postponing, not without some risk, a profitable endeavor.*

Jeanne judges that note too stern, I am rather stupid not to have sent it.

29. – Punishment does not keep people waiting. New dispatch by Lumbroso. Visit put off to tomorrow.

Perfect vexation. I must renounce a plan that was particularly pleasing to me. Is not that dispatch an *Italian* scheme to be followed up by several more? I know from experience that there are humans made for deceit – always. Horrible bitterness. Who would one dare to treat like this among the triumphant?

Charles VII. That history is extremely painful to me. Around Joan who is so marked for suffering, I search for a sympathetic person. One would think that there were only cowards and blackguards.

30. – Lumbroso, my having waited the entire day, *does not show up*. Admirable transalpine churlishness!

May

1st. – *PARIS IN FLAMES. Novel of National Expiation,* by Henri Barbot. Extremely odd work whose manuscript was confided to me. That small, encompassing and deeply moving book is helpful to me in the state of grievous depression that I find myself in, procured by Lumbroso's ignoble behavior. One could wish for a more artistic use of language, but Barbot was forced to write with extreme rapidity. That goes perhaps better for the diffusion of a book whose unique object is to propagate the Secret of La Salette, by exciting to the highest pitch of curiosity.

2. – I was about to exit when Lumbroso finally arrives, accompanied by his daughter, a small, rather insignificant person and two women or exotic girls, one of whom interrogates me immediately on theosophy! "Madame," I responded, "the theosophers are imbeciles devoted to the devil." Those people came simply out of curiosity. I am photographed, the young woman having brought an instrument. The father, who resembles a fat insurance broker and who does not pardon himself for anything, overwhelms me with questions on those of my books that one finds difficult. Finally, the album, that same young woman having also brought that object. I write:

> *Mademoiselle, one absolutely wishes me to be a monster, an abominable pamphleteer. Now, I am a tender person, a lover, and I have always been* knocked about *by everyone – Mademoiselle!*

When it is visible that my patience is on the verge of evaporating, which scarcely ever tarries, those grotesques depart in a cushy automobile, leaving me a little more somber than before.

To Lumbroso:

> *You like autographs. Here are two. The first dated, Tuesday, April 28, as you can see, responded to your first telegram. I was wrong not to send it to*

*you. I do not resist the desire to send
this also to you.*

*It is evident that you came to
visit me only* out of curiosity, *as one
might visit the Jardin des Plantes or
go to the cinema. I expected as much,
moreover. Such appears to be the only
effect made on you by my letter of the
13th of February. I would reproach
myself if I did not tell you that the result of your visit has succeeded in
leaving me sadder and more bitter.
You did not come alone, having perhaps foreseen it all. It was impossible
then for me to speak with you as I
would have wanted. The offhand manner of your dispatches, immobilizing
me at home for 48 hours, because they
gave me to suppose that you would not
be a "pointless visitor," has deeply
hurt me, I want you to know, and that
persists.*

*I am really quite aware that
with my being a great writer, who is
poor and without prestige, you needn't
be too overly concerned about me. I
have seen it all too often. But I do not
succeed in playing my part, any more
than being visited like some curious
beast. I have spent several excessively
bitter hours because of you, Sir, when
I bit my nails while waiting for you, all*

the more bitter as I was precisely tor-
tured in another way and that I had
stupidly hoped for some improvement
to my situation from you, imagining
you to have been sent.

I think that you have nothing to
reproach me with. Your promise of an
important article in the Revue Napoléonienne *(Italian promise that was*
never kept) had disposed me such that
I did for you what I do not do for
strangers. A multitude of dedications
and an article that didn't really cost
you all that much. But can you under-
stand the language of those who suf-
fer? You are a man of the world, and
all is owed to you.

4. – Remarkable article by Termier in the *Revue Heb-*
domadaire. Response to an inquiry on the "Witnesses
of Experience." It is very nobly written, and I am cited in the most honorable manner. Termier presuppos-
es a meeting in Canada, whence he returns, with a
young man who would have read much of me, and he
says to him this to finish by: "If you know such books
by heart, in truth, my dear friend, I have nothing more
to inform you."

5. – Response by Lumbroso. He defends himself
against the charge of having come by out of curiosity
and asks why I call him a "man of the world." – "One
cannot have rents and busy himself with history and

literature?" He does not deserve any reproach, etc. Finally, he offers me another 50 fr. to have translated, into Italian, my pages on the Grand Chartreuse. Decidedly, his price is always 50 francs.

To Lumbroso:

You say you didn't come by out of curiosity. So, I ask myself why you did come. You also do not wish to be confused with my enemies, which my letter nowise implied. I am, perhaps, disposed, on the contrary, to consider you well-meaning, although obstructed. And you have annuities, I did not make you say it. Annuities! In other words, the most efficacious thing for petrifying the heart and obnubilating the intelligence. A rich man – how many times have I observed it – will never be capable of a chevaleresque act. Ah! of course not, and never will he understand what justice demands of him. It is a poverty inherent in his status. Væ vobis divitibus! said the Lord. Assuredly a person of independent means can occupy himself with history and literature, but profundity is interdicted him. That is the privilege of the poor. They alone can comprehend and even divine, because they know suffering. They alone know how generously to devote themselves, to share the little that they have with their brothers.

*What did you understand from my let-
ter of February 13, which I kept a
copy of, that I just re-read. Absolutely
nothing.*

*Today, you offer me 50 francs
(it appears to be your figure) for the
right to translate pages from* The Desperate Man. *It's like offering me nothing at all. Only my publisher Vallette,
the director of the* Mercure de France,
*can give you that authorization and it
is to him, not to me, that you ought to
address yourself.*

*Now, to elucidate the auto-
graph of April 28 and given you have
no repugnance for numbers, take this.
I received from you, two times, February 12 and 27, the sum total of one
hundred francs for one article and
twenty-three dedications, including
eight volumes expedited to start with,
taken from my armoire for you, and
which I will need to replace. Now, an
article by me has never paid less than
one hundred francs, sometimes much
more, even if it were a few lines. As
for my dedicated books which only my
friends obtain for free, they are not
sold for less than ten or twenty francs,
being most sought after by admirers of
autographs, as you are free to verify
with the book merchants.*

> *I do not insist, because that disgusts me, knowing moreover how useless it is, given you said you do not "deserve any reproach." But do not ask for my admiration. – The Ungrateful Beggar.*

Culled from *l'Action française:*

> *Yesterday in the ninth chamber [of justice]. Introduced into the box of the accused was a poor wretch who holds his possessions in a ball wrapped tightly in a green coat. The president Huet sets out his case before that delinquent, that he was found at Les Halles in a reprehensible state of vagabondage. His short discourse terminated, the president invites François Dramb, that's the name of the man, to provide the judges with some explanations. And one hears him say these strange words: "My president, with respect to society, I say to you: M****!"[45] The president Huet is stopped short in the same way as the soldiers of Wellington must have been stopped short by the same syllables... And Dramb was condemned to two months for his vagabondage and two years for his plea.*

---

[45]M****! One has to assume that the word was "Merde!" which literally means "shit" and in context would probably be, idiomatically, something else: "Bloody hell!" or "F***!"

He is exactly the man that is needed to respond to Lumbroso.

7. – To Termier:

I already knew that you were a writer. After your response to the inquiry by the Revue Hebdomadaire, *I know it a little more now. In the same number, M. Charles Richet says that "the future and salvation reside only in science." Soon you speak of the soul, exclusively, and that immediately puts things prodigiously on another level. You do not merely cite me here and there, you espouse all my thoughts, and you love them to the point of losing sight of the geology which has the air of being an old neglected mistress of yours. Do you not risk afflicting some of your disciples like that, by exposing yourself to the vengeance of the abandoned woman?*

My thoughts will not lead you far. They are ruinous and unrelenting. They do not let go of their victims, and they take pleasure in putting them out of sorts. Think on it closely. *There you are now, infinitely far from the commonplaces of science; you will find yourself in the desert, in eremo, in the company of my unfortunate godchil-*

dren, and it is not sure that you will be visited there by the nourishing crow of Saint Paul, the first hermit. So be it, I abandon you to your destiny.

Ah! you take the soul seriously! You believe that it alone exists really and that everything else is appearance. Look at where I have led you then, by handing over my progeniture to you. You will go as far as to say to those who know my books by heart that you have nothing more to inform them. What a strange and dolorous scholar you are going to become! You will finish by confessing, in tears and covered in ashes, that it is I who told you the last word on science and that I won in that way the battle of Waterloo against the coalition formerly gathered under the Terrible Tree in the Garden of Voluptuousness by all Death's powers. Then, doubtless, you will be visited under the Olive Trees of divine Peace, by the comforting Angel of the other Garden.

Lumbroso's response. It deserves to be conserved:

Sir, you are right to sign off as "The Ungrateful Beggar." I proposed to you 50 fr. for the right to translate a page that I can translate without paying anything, given the works pub-

> *lished over ten years ago can be trans-*
> *lated without any formality. You re-*
> *spond to a proposition made to you to*
> *show some thoughtful consideration –*
> *with an unfriendly letter, little merited,*
> *and not at all agreeable to receive.*
> *But all that, I confess, does not sur-*
> *prise me in the least. It is precisely*
> *your bad character that pleases me.*

It is I who am the exploiter, and it is he who is conned. I hope that everything is over with that Italian swine. The rastaquouère wants to be mistaken for a dandy. It's "my bad character that pleases him." The case of this peninsular reminds me of the expression by Murat about Talleyrand: "He would receive a kick in the seat of his pants with the same smile."

8. – To Gustave Téry:

> *I didn't quite understand your dis-*
> *patch to Mamers. The insuccess was*
> *so certain!*

> *Caillaux will be president of*
> *the Republic, and maybe even emperor*
> *and king, Jo I, [passage suppressed],*
> *acquitted by an infallible jury, will*
> *sleep at the Elysée, and together we*
> *will go to the guillotine. A stranger to*
> *all politics and a contemner vomiting*
> *on about universal suffrage, the enor-*
> *mous ridiculousness about the polling*

booth is not going to convert me to that institution of imbeciles and scoundrels. I will vote however on the day my voice will have the weight of twenty thousand voices, something that will not happen overnight probably. Omnia evomenda et cacanda.

10. – One of the people who accompanied Lumbroso on his visit to me, the one who spoke to me about theosophy, wrote me a grotesque letter, saying that she had come to see in me a man "in whose soul God *was born*" and that she was hoping I would "make her participate in that high joy...!? I am persuaded of my ignorance; unfortunately, I cannot strip myself of my *critical sense*." What can I do for such souls?

Letter from Lumbroso's daughter, rather nice under the circumstances. She sends the photo to me, otherwise execrable, that I let her take. Response:

... You seemed to me, all things considered, a good little person, and I want to believe that you didn't stop by out of pure curiosity, but I am firmly and unshakably persuaded that your father had no other intention than that. He belongs to the race of collectors, unjust and cruel race that I know too well. He knew that I was very poor and, having already copiously conned *me, he enjoyed seeing me suffer at home. That's all there is to it. That not*

sufficing him clearly, he gratified me in addition by a base insult in his last letter. It would have been easy for him to gain my friendship, but he preferred to make himself contemned... I have nothing to say to the ridiculous letter by Mme. Z. that I just received at the same time as yours. Life is too short, and Christians have better things to do than to engage in discussion with students of demons.

20. – Gabriel Gargam, person cured by miracle at Lourdes. Where does this printed matter come from?

Garbiel Gargam, Post Office employee, was the victim of a railroad calamity, on December 17, 1899. Broken to pieces so to speak, he was de-clared incurable *by all the physicians and remained struck by paralysis and muscular atrophy. The civil tribunal of Angoulême "given the Company of Orleans had reduced him to the most pitiable of conditions and had made him into a veritable* human wreck, *sentenced it to give him a pension of 6,000 francs and an indemnification of 60,000." Gargam was soon cured in Lourdes, in 1901.*

Apostil by the anonymous sender: "I demand that the Civil Tribunal be appealed to rule on this new case. If the cure is complete, they should suppress the pension. What does the railroad company think about having been sentenced to pay? But will the Tribunal recognize the *legal* existence of the miracle! What will the person cured by miracle say? Will he prefer to remain a *wreck* and collect his pension?"

28. – I don't remember having been more deeply miserable. *Diligentibus Deum omnia cooperantur in... angustiam*[46].

30. – New catastrophe in the Saint Lawrence Bay. Breach in the hull of a Canadian ocean liner, *Empress of Ireland*. More than one thousand dead. A large number of Salvationists perished, sixty, it is said. It is remarkable that God wanted to destroy *at that very moment*, on the eve of cataclysms, those poor caricatures of Apostles of the Last Days.

June

1st. – Ridiculous visit. After lunch, I went to lie down for my habitual nap, and I was beginning to fall asleep when my door opened wide and I saw an unknown person enter, a young man who asked to be excused and told me that, on returning from America, where I do not know what he did, he took advantage

---

[46]*Diligentibus... angustiam:* Latin for "God participates diligently in every... anguish."

of a journey to Bourg-la-Reine to come and see the great writer that I am. Extremely badly disposed, in such circumstances, for this unexpected bore, I asked him amicably to tell me what he wanted. He did not want anything, except to see me, and I let him go, without having been able to wake up completely. I do not even know his name, which he told me perhaps, but I forgot it almost immediately.

3. – Some dedications for *Histoires désobligeantes,* which is going to be published.

> To Jean Boussac:
>
> *That these stories might not disoblige. Far from maltreating Geology, I favor it in a deep sense, as I am constantly inviting boors to restitute their dust to it.*
>
> To Jean de la Laurencie:
>
> *The underside of the bourgeois aristocracy.*
>
> To Vincent d'Indy:
>
> *There are two sorts of men, those who seek Beauty and those who seek money. The first, of which I'm one, ought naturally to perish in ignominy.*
>
> To Elisabeth Joly:
>
> *I struck hard. No grave opened up. In the cemeteries of intelligence, there*

*are more than concessions in perpetu-
ity.*

To Philippe Raoux:

*Contemporary society, from the pinna-
cle of the Absolute.*

To Josette Bernoville:

*This book written by a virtuous author
for seventy-five-year-old virgins.*

To Georges Crès:

*You wanted to be the publisher and
friend of Léon Bloy. Unfortunate man!
To say nothing of the proverbial ingratitude that that author will inflict
on you, have you thought about the
dreadful rigor of your sentence on the
last day?*

To Termier:

Uncle Louis finds my Histoires *horrible. It is true that they are not for very
young girls, but does he not understand what must be the vision of modern society for a contemplative, and
how does he not divine the infinite at-
tenuations that the writer has had to
impose on himself?*

To André Dupont:

*Have you thought sometimes of the
horrible cataclysms that one would*

see unleashed on the day I became obliging? My continual disobligement, would it not be the secret to the equilibrium of the world?

To Abbot P***:

A verbo aspero, quis nos liberabit? clamabant putrescentes.

To Jacques Maritain:

Sepulchral literature of an old godfather who thinks a lot on death.

To René Martineau:

The voluntarily enraged man is an antiphrasis, do I need to tell you that? It suffices to read this book to be convinced of the considerateness of my feelings and the chaste love that my contemporaries inspire in me. Unfortunately, they do not feel good, and I see strange birds in the blue sky which I am told are aeroplanes, but which I believe to be horrible vultures.

15. – For several days now, the *Matin* has opened an inquest into the *Ideal Future of the Republic*. Those words are already of an unordinary comicalness. The responses naturally flow in. Here is, today, one from Marc Sangnier:

"Love one another."

In my opinion three things are essential for the greatness of the Republic: first, sovereign democracy establishing the perfect concordance among citizens; second, hatred banished from the here-below; third, love among men... (sic)!???

That Marc really exaggerates cretinism. But what to say about a similar inquest into the light of democratic Thabor, when the Turks are at the gates of Byzantium!

16. – Paris crumbles. Yesterday, during a storm, a hole opened up in the vicinity of Saint-Augustin and the passersby were buried alive. Warning.

17. – Letter from a stranger sending me a circular, an "Appeal to the Clergy," for the renaissance of Catholic Art. A reading of the pages from *The Desperate Man* where I shout down Sulpician imagery gave him hope that I would do something for what he calls the "Renovation of great Art in the Church" – as if I had not already done all that I could, at the same time that I proclaimed the evident inutility of such efforts.

18. – Gathered from a paper:

For the last few days, in Versailles, the following card was distributed: Mr. and Mrs... have the honor of ask-

> *ing M*** to kindly attend an evening*
> *of music and dance, which will be held*
> *on Saturday... starting at 5 o'clock, on*
> *the occasion of the baptism of their*
> *Scotch collie "Thanus."*

> *Fifty people showed up.*

Good formula for attracting lightning. (Of those fifty people, how many are still alive today? August 1915.)

19. – Jeanne to René Martineau on the occasion of his book, extremely honorable for me, *One Living and Two Dead*, which has just been republished:

> *I have just gone through your little*
> *book, little in format, but big as a drop*
> *of truth cannot fail to be. I thank you*
> *for the several lines that concern me,*
> *for their discretion, and the affection*
> *that you have for me. It turns out that*
> *God had need of me (if one can blas-*
> *pheme thusly) to weave together in his*
> *fashion the dolorous existence of the*
> *greatest of Writers, of the most humble*
> *of Christians, of the contemned Beg-*
> *gar whom you know. You would weep,*
> *my dear René, if you only knew how*
> *the task is so far above me, and you*
> *would pray for me. But it is not about*
> *me that I wanted to speak. Your article*
> *on* The Soul of Napoleon *seemed to*
> *me something out of the ordinary. You*

know how Napoleon counted on his little corporals, he, the first of that phalange; eh! well, it seems to me that I see you, relative to Léon Bloy, in that same category. What you have received from him you have given back to him with interest, and you invent great and beautiful thoughts on the occasion of his. It is always beautiful to see a soul come out, and you show yours in a beneficial and peaceful clarity, the ambiance created by your loyalty, your probity as a man and as a critic. To that you add your heart, and, with the discernment that is proper to you, you find the happy phrase to express your thought which is never banal.

There you have it, my dear René, the feelings with which I read your pages. You evolve from on high... and the envious are forced to look up into the air while waiting to sprout wings.

24. – Véronique being rather seriously ill, I go to the curate to whom I express the desire of our child to receive communion. He consents to give it to her on Friday, at 7:30, but declares that he will only be able to do it once a week, citing a law (?) that opposes a more frequent administration of the sacrament in the domicile of a sick person. I leave him horribly scan-

dalized.

26. – Not having received a package implored for several days now with urgency, I dispatch to my publisher Crès, otherwise a very lovely man, the following precious autograph:

> *My dear publisher, if I was rich enough and different enough from myself to buy stamped paper, I would send to you one sheet begging you to write this on it:*

> *"I am committed never to send copies of* Histoires désobligeantes *to Léon Bloy at his domicile in Bourg-la-Reine. I will have them arrive after his decease, in the paradise of poor writers, so that he can offer them to some of the blessed."*

> *You have no reason to be in a hurry then. I will live for another few years, maybe.*

30. – I learn that Jacques Maritain is named chair of the history of modern philosophy at the Catholic Institute.

Several dedications for *Je M'Accuse...*, which was just published with a rather nice portrait. (*Bibliothèque des Lettres françaises*.) The first edition, having become unlocatable, is from 1900.

To Friar D***:

The stones that Saint Etienne was lapidated with were not appropriate here. Something else was needed.

To René Martineau:

Such is Emile's glory. In twenty years, this book alone will prevent him from being forgotten.

To Elisabeth Joly:

There is nobody else but me still to eat Zola. Even the swine don't want him anymore.

To Emile Baumann:

In what other manner, in what other tongue, could an artist fearing God speak about that miserable man?

To Philippe Raoux:

The Gospel tells us that no less than two thousand swine were needed to lodge comfortably the demons that inhabit a single man. That figure is much inferior to the number of Emile Zola's admirers!

To Georges Crès:

What is a scatalogue? It is an author who does not sell himself. A novelist who takes in one hundred thousand is never a scatalogue.

To Benoît Joly:

Impossible to offer this book to a vir-gin, impossible to offer it to an honest woman, impossible even to offer it to a gendarme. I offer it to a lawyer.

To Pierre van der Meer:

On inviting him, when he is at the foot of the altar, to measure, if he is able, the feelings of a godfather who travels a million leagues each day to see him, after having contemplated Zola.

To Jeanne Termier-Boussac:

Who has the gift of seeing profoundly. This book wherein the hatred and dis-dain of objects are sometimes exalted to lyricism, will it not, one day, be considered like my work of art? Ques-tion.

July

1ˢᵗ. – *No more cretins!* said the Doctor Serge Voro-noff. It suffices to graft the thyroid gland of an ape onto a backward child. "Equip a cretin or an imbecile," said our Slavic, "with a good thyroid gland, and you will see a lively intelligence manifest itself to the point of genius... but it is to apes that one must address oneself for that."

No more cretins! That would be the end of the Rights of Man and the ruin of our literature.

5. – In the *Intransigant*:

AN EXTRAORDINARY BOOK

PARIS IN FLAMES! by Henry Barbot. Novel of national expiation. Paris and Hertzian waves against German airships. (Bibliothèque des Lettres français, 62, rue de Seine.)

Do you have a case of the nerves? Hang them where you like, behind the door, in the cave, or in the garret, not to take them down again until after you read Paris in Flames. *Then only will you have any chance of surviving this tremebund book.*

Who then is Henry Barbot? Whence comes that frightening man who appears to know the nearest future and who recounts it with the precision of a damned man come back from hell? One does not invent such stuff. People don't just imagine the clamor of agony of three million men, and it is not in the power of any apocalyptic novelist to conceive of so supernatural a conflict of all known and unknown Forces. One must have seen it, and Henri Barbot appears to be the veritable visionary of those unheard-of horrors, unrevealable until now.

If his book is read by the multitude, – as it is easy to predict, – a historian no less extraordinary will be needed to recount the enormous bourgeois panic, preliminary to the catastrophes glimpsed, which will necessarily follow. Everyone will want to flee at the same time, and gunners will be requested for the police contingent at the boarding of trains. Such is the future of tomorrow, Barbot not being the man to get bogged down in contingencies. That will happen, or it will not happen immediately, I grant, strictly speaking; but no other conjecture is admissible, and I think that that prophet is very probably right.

That magnificently dreadful book is not, moreover, completely without consolation. France, Paris principally, must expiate. The exorbitance of its infamy demands it, that is incontestable. But everyone is not exactly and indistinctly wicked or idiots. There are all the same a lot of good people, a very small lot, it is true. One can find two of them here, two extraordinary individuals, two total athletes of heroism and faith. They are, by good fortune, situated in an inaccessible place where they are given to combatting marvelously. One must read this to know what the imagination or thought of a writer born of despair can come up with, in the presence of menaces by German riffraff and immense French viciousness!

Here, for example, is a poor individual, like you and me, totally devoid of miracles, but armed however, and how! He cannot save Paris, because Paris cannot be saved, but he avenges so terribly, at this very moment, that one would think it was God himself who was fighting.

Invent or conjecture all that you can, you will not succeed. I am telling you, once and for all, that this is not something that can be invented; and something that can be invented even less, above all today, is French heroism pushed to the extreme limit of the Supernatural, to the point of crossing that limit even, to the point of terrifying, striking right at the heart of the filthiest nation in the world, Prussia, in 1814, 1815, and 1870!

– LÉON BLOY

Saw, for the first time, a young Belgian,

Léopold Levaux, professor of French at Samara in Russia, where he wrote to me several letters that gave me the desire to get to know him. He presents his wife to us. Very favorable impression. They are going to leave for Liége and – God permitting – regain Russia finally.

9. – Preparations for my annual execution. I am in the middle of crates. We leave tomorrow for Mévoisins. Visit *in extremis* by Félix Raugel, who helps the commissioner bring down the heaviest parcels. (I can still see, with extreme melancholy, that noble artist assisting me in that fatigue, and I do not know if I will ever see him again. After ten months of continual risk of life, he was hit finally in Alsace and languishes at the present hour in the hospital at Montpellier. July 1915.)

10. – Difficult arrival at our hermitage in an excessive heat. All the work of setting up shop here, tomorrow and the day after tomorrow, is to celebrate my 68th birthday here.

14. – Began the Introduction to my book on Joan of Arc. Enormous difficulty.

18. – I am horribly troubled in my work by an ignoble and already comminatory demand by my proprietor at Bourg-la-Reine. I am three days behind in the July rent, which the funny old man does not accept. I ad-

mire how that genre of vermin has always had the power of making me suffer so much. (The devotion of my dear adopted sister Madeleine B*** allowed me to force-feed that animal soon thereafter, integrally and for the *last* time. He has needed, since then, to put up with other delays.)

19. – *Prelude*. Anonymous booklet. An attached card gives me the name of the author: Jeanne Peyrabon, with her address. There are some remarkable phrases contained in it. Do I have to respond?

20. – We had found in the village a little maid who appeared to be a good fit. The curate informs us that her parents were furious to see their daughter with people who go to mass every day, threaten to take her away. Such are the villagers of this place. They would prefer to prostitute their daughters or see them die rather than have them exposed to religious practices.

Lumbroso again. He sends me this note: "Dear sir, do you want some work? Can I ask for an article from you? Yours truly." Decidedly, Murat was right. Kicks in the seat of the pants have no effect.

Return of the card with this:

Léon Bloy, having given Lumbroso fifty *times more, more or less, than he received from him, has been treated by that Italian as a "mendicant." Now, mendicants do not work, people ought to know that, and above all* ungrateful beggars. *Léon Bloy has never worked in his life, it's well known. He restricts himself only to* giving *autographs to other mendicant-collectors.*

To Jeanne Peyrabon:

Madame or Mademoiselle, I rarely respond to small books that are sent to me. Life is short. This time however I would reproach myself for remaining silent. I have found in your Prelude *some remarkable expressions that I have the duty to thank you for, as you appeared to have written them for me:*

"How beautiful are the words that touch my thought! – To be born is a terrible engagement that Death is powerless to take away from us. – He who suffers is alone against the universe. – God, when I speak of him, is my pseudonym. (After this phrase, one has almost the right to send Pascal to bed, as you have done.) – Leave our sins behind us, their fate belongs to Jesus Christ! – Capital sins are, in potency, the most beautiful virtues. – Absolute Emptiness cannot make me not exist. – Death takes only what one gives it. – Hope follows Eternity like a

*shadow. – O men whom you believe
are all the same and all mediocre... O
blind by persuasion!"*

*And there are others still. But
who will notice them, my dear sister?
In fact, I know nothing about you. Are
you an 18-year-old virgin or an 80-
year-old ancestor? The two hypothe-
ses are equally plausible. Or are you a
man of a certain age, employed by the
administration or a captain of artillery? Which is also plausible. Are
you poor or rich? In the latter case, I
would no longer understand, being
used to considering the rich as intolerable idiots. It is true that I have never
understood much.*

*Despite the impression your
pages have made on me, I would not
perhaps have written to you, my being,
moreover, extremely occupied with a
book on Joan of Arc. I was persuaded
by your dedication wherein you offered to me your "deep affection, if I
want to accept it." Of course, – if it is*
deep. *Yes, but the protocol and my experience! If the man of the Absolute
and the miserable soul that I am asked
you for an* immediate *and palpable
proof of that deep affection, you would
burst out laughing, and how! No matter, I am one with my conscience, hav-*

ing told you, Mademoiselle, Madame, or Monsieur, what I think of your small book and that, you must believe me, is not at all a protocol.

22. – To my new godson, Christopher Boussac, in his cradle:

You do not know perhaps, your education being up to now extremely incomplete, that in three days from now, on July 25, it will be the feast day of your patron, the great Auxiliator Martyr Christopher, miraculous precursor of Christopher Columbus, and companion forever of Saint James the Greater. In three days time then, I will ask on your behalf, through his intercession, that you should have a certain part in all that I have been able to do for others, by accepting suffering all my life. I hope that Saint Christopher, so long honored by me now, will accord to you by my prayer the gift of Strength, privilege of martyrs, and a marvelous facility to pass, like him, through the most furious torrents, and carrying on your shoulders the baby Jesus who weighs as much as all the worlds combined. In your language of an innocent tell your father and your mother that your old godparent loves them deeply and that he does not know

> *how to express to them his joy of hav-*
> *ing been chosen. I had much need of*
> *you, my dear little man, to complete*
> *my old guard, my last handful of god-*
> *children for my supreme battles. While*
> *waiting for you to be able to pray ex-*
> *ternally one day, someone will teach*
> *you how to make the sign of the cross*
> *for your godfather. That, I ask, per-*
> *suaded that such an act will be, in that*
> *very precise intention, an* interior
> *prayer of your innocence which will*
> *keep the demons at bay from me. I em-*
> *brace you while weeping with love.*

The curate comes to lunch. We speak of his lamentable flock. He tells us, among other things, that his parishioners are in such a deadened state of mind that they die like beasts, *without agony*, having destroyed in themselves anything that could be the occasion of a litigation of soul, at their last hour.

23. – Raugel sends to me, by way of curiosity, a grotesque cantata for railroad employees, work of poetry and music approved naturally by the Archbishop of Paris who has it played in Notre-Dame; His Eminence estimating correctly that ridiculousness is the surest method to exterminate religious sentiment.

23.[47] – For the people of this village, we are *those who go to mass*. It is as if one said: those who have

---

[47]23: sic

gone bankrupt or who have been in the penal colony.

25. – Response by Jeanne Peyrabon:

> *Sir, the words that you address to me are those that rouse courage until death. I find in them the wherewithal to despise future work and cherish past sorrows. It would be enough for my little book to have been written only to please you. What is more natural? The person who seeks God is sure to find you along the way. I am a young woman, but it would not surprise me to be an officer of artillery. My father was, in my place, and it's he who raised me. As for the affection that it pleased you to acknowledge, I dare say, Sir, that the human heart has too few objects worthy of love to let such an opportunity as Léon Bloy get away. Very respectfully.*

26. – Finished the Introduction to my book on Joan of Arc.

27. – Financial situation all the more anguishing as Madeleine is on the verge of leaving with a group of young girls for a holiday in Normandy, which would be very beneficial for her.

29. – Universal disquietude caused by the menacing attitude of Austria toward Serbia takes shape all of a sudden. That war being able to have a European conflagration for effect, all available combatants having been called or will be. Are the announced cataclysms close finally?

30. – I received copies of *The Pilgrim of the Absolute*, put on sale under the worst conditions. Some envois:

> To Termier:
>
> *This sixth volume of my Journal will not be the last if God lets the author live some time still before probable extinction of all people and bookstores.*
>
> To Jeanne Termier-Boussac:
>
> *This book wherein she will find her name sometimes which will surprise her, knowing that I am in the ancient habit of pouring my heart out at my escritoire.*
>
> To René Martineau:
>
> *To make him believe that I am still "a living person" and even a very good living person, something that he certainly will not swallow.*
>
> To Christine van der Meer:

So many things between us, dear friend, and so many kilometers separating us! How large this little world appears to those who love and who suffer!

To Pierre van der Meer:

Poor pilgrim that I am! It seems to me that I reach the end of my voyage, as having already met Jacques, Raïssa, and Véra, I have finally come to you, to Christine, and to your son. I hope, my beloved friends, to see you one day all together, fainting for love, a little above me, before the altar of Notre-Dame of the Absolute.

To Alfred Pouthier:

One was put on this earth in order to amuse oneself, isn't that right? This sixth volume of the Journal of my life confirms one more time, in the least refutable manner, that chevaleresque belief.

To Marguillier:

The absolute *insuccess, what a dream!*

30. – Jeanne and Madeleine leave for Paris, Madeleine needing to join her little companions who will spend some weeks together on a beach in Normandy. (Extreme imprudence, if only we had known.)

Pierre knowing me to be alone with Véronique for two or three days and probably devoured by sadness has come to succor me with his presence. (The enormous tribulation had not yet begun. But one felt it approaching, one heard it rapping at the door... What a memory!)

31. – The order for general mobilization has been given. The drums are beating in the villages, informing the cultivators that they have to prepare for the requisition of their horses and their vehicles. What's more, there is the issue, as in '71, of 5- and 20-franc bills, the government wishing to make off with all the specie. Certain panic.

Austria has just begun its war with Serbia which will infallibly unleash everything. What to think of that miserable François-Joseph, so often and so severely warned, over the course of his turpitudes, and who ought, at eighty-eight years of age, to be preparing for death not rushing to pour the most dreadful misfortunes all over Europe!

August

1st. – Assassination of Jaurès,[48] yesterday evening. Will anyone be found weeping for that criminal.

---

[48]Jaurès: Jean Jaurès (1859-1914) was a French Socialist, head of the French Socialist party in 1902; he was an antimilitarist and against the imminent war with Germany. He was shot by Raoul Villain.

First disquieting disorder. Impossible to find any specie. I offer everyone a 50-fr. bill, our last resource, and nobody wants it. We converse sadly, Pierre and I, about the current situation. Only, can he remain in France? And how will we survive, we and the others?

We must separate. I see my beloved godson depart, with a terrible tightening of my heart. (I didn't see him again until eight months later, after what anguish and what torments!) Jeanne returned that same evening, most fortunately, but without Madeleine, alas.

Conclusion of an article from the *National Zeitung* of Berlin, come out today (three days *before* the declaration of war):

> *Whatever Providence might have reserved for Germany, it is on France that it must recur for indemnification, but in a different way than 44 years ago. It will no longer be five million that France needs to pay, but thirty million.*

> *The Holy Mother of God of Lourdes will have much on her hands if She, the Miraculous, must heal all those poor people's bones that our soldiers will break on the other side of the Vosges.*

> *Poor France! There is still time for her to change her mind, but,*

in several hours, it will be too late.
Then France will feel the blows re-
ceived for several generations. But
you wanted it, Georges Dandin!

The defiance is in this way presented to the
Immaculate Mary, Queen of France, in the heavy and
villainous style that suits the German spirit.

The Expiation

(Before continuing in this journal, and at a distance of
thirteen months, it seems to me beneficial to clarify
the situation of the French Soul from August 1, 1914
until the present hour, August 25, 1915.

It has not changed.

Death, mutilation, or the most horrible captivi-
ty of two million Frenchmen seems to have been, in
that respect, absolutely ineffective. The warnings of
every kind, their fulfillment even, so terribly begun
already, the most authentic predictions – seem to have
had absolutely no effect. France continues no longer
to want God. Theoretical atheism among disbelievers,
practical atheism among believers. Unanimous refusal
to believe in the Supernatural and, by consequence, in
Punishment.

Must everything become appalling then?
From the Vosges to the extremity of Western Flanders, the front line is a cemetery. All Belgium and all
our departments of the North are sacked, sullied, tortured, destroyed by the dirtiest barbarians. It appears
that that is not sufficient. Reason deprived of faith is
in such agony that it cannot see the causes anymore.

One was speaking to me yesterday about a monstruous and abominable flying insect – a dragon-fly from the marshes of hell – seen in Paris and killed, with difficulty, by one of my friends who saved himself from the horror of it. That horrible being seemed sent by the dead. Will that be necessary again, and must an unknown terror come?

God cannot be replaced except by monsters from the Abyss, and the Germans are not frightening enough. They will disappear, moreover, however many there are of them, their not being but the dust kicked up from the Executioner's steps.

So this will be the veritable Expiation, in inex-pressible fright, expiation for France at first, because of its pre-eminence, then for the rest of the world guilty of the same prevarication, and any human or angelic voice will be unable to say just how far the earth's desolation will go.

But France, always necessary to God, will be the first to rise up again from among the agonizing nations in order to fulfill its complete destiny. With-out a doubt, it will have lost its flower, its noblest sons having given their life for its ransom. But that enormous sacrifice will be taken into consideration by Him who weighs the spheres and atoms, and it could very well be that, in the end, a mysterious and im-marcescible virginity becomes its portion.

Today, whatever the events of this unprece-dented war might be, which will leave all peoples wounded, I wait for an incredibly unknown Man, next to whom the greatest strangers will appear like first cousins, a bum, I suppose, a barefoot person, I really hope so, but sent and given a mission to fulfill everything. He is close by, perhaps, waiting for the right moment...)

2. – Ninth Sunday after Pentecost. Gospel passage of the day: "Here they come against you, days when your enemies will surround you with *trenches*."

(Liturgical prophesy whose surprising precision was not known until six weeks later. Those trenches, which continue still, have cost the most beautiful blood of France. August, 1915.)

3. – The situation becomes very sinister. No news of Madeleine. The small merchants of this place threaten to close their shops and here we are without a sou. Never, even in Denmark, had we known such distress. The mail collector acknowledges the complete interruption of service. The curate tells us that the Germans have crossed France's frontier, without declaration of war, which would correspond with their practices of brigandage. We know nothing, except that Germany declares war on Russia and that this evening it will come to declare it on France by the intermediary of its ambassador M. de Schoen, who appears to be a really ignoble puppet.

6. – We learn that Germany has declared war on England also. Wilhelm's impertinence is extraordinary.

There he is at war with half of Europe. What an appalling conflict! That could add up to ten million soldiers in arms. Nothing like it has been seen before.

Extraordinary event. I am going to be forced to admire Belgium. A German army has just suffered a serious check before Liége. Surprising resistance for the brigands, who thought they wouldn't find any.

7. – Jules Lemaître has just died in bed. End of a mediocre life. Poor bit of news amidst the immense tumult.

8. – The Belgians continue their resistance which cannot, alas! but be desperate, but which disconcerts the German plan and retards a little the invasion. Austria, it is said, has declared war on Russia. Ample maledictions on François-Joseph and on Wilhelm.

9. – After a sad day, good news arrives finally, possibly certain, of a first victory at Altkirch in Alsace, followed by the taking of Mulhouse. All the border posts are said to have been removed. Beginning of the retaking of our lost provinces.

Countless trains filled with soldiers and war materiel. Coming from Chartres, they pass very close by our house. Jeanne and Véronique gather flowers and go to throw them to the soldiers. Is it possible to hope for what I had thought I saw in 1870: a strange and profound change in the aspect of men and things?

11. – Inexplicable dream, the night before. A name was hounding me, the name of Aeneus Silvius Piccolomini. All that I know of that historic individual is that he was elected pope under the name of Pius II, after having been secretary to the German emperor and at the Council of Basil, and that he tried rather vainly to reanimate the spirit of the Crusades. That night, that name had really obsessed me. I woke up and fell back to sleep to hear it again. It was a matter, I believe, of a prophesy concerning us...

Received several letters. Everyone believes in the success of this horrible war, in the annihilation of the German empire. The Germans, moreover, conduct themselves with an atrocious barbarity. Pillage, arson, rape, massacre of women and children, killing of the wounded. *Their* war has a diabolical aspect to it. In the end, they will stop taking prisoners. Never has a people shown itself to be so hateful and to have excited so much universal execration.

In my book, *Sweating Blood*, I showed the Germans such as I had seen them in 1870, which was however a much less abominable war. That testimony, which could have warned, was suspected, only yesterday even, of exaggeration and fanaticism.

12. – Letter from Madeleine. The dear child is happy with her little companions. They know nothing, but they cannot budge. They need passports, and that disquiets Madeleine. "If I had known," she said, "I

would not have left."

Barbot admits to having been mistaken, believing that a horrible revolution would precede the
war. In fact, he was very deeply mistaken. The reality
is plainly visible, which is that France is united *at this
moment*, and that one can hope for the destruction of
the barbarians. Actually, it is the single thought, the
one desire. The predictions by La Salette remain, and
my certitude that God wants to act soon by showing
Himself in an unprecedented manner that no one can
predict. That war then is not and cannot be the End.
So long as there is *evident* Supernaturalness, nothing
will be done. To suppose, as is reasonable, the ruin of
the abominable German empire, is to presume that
that triumph would infinitely augment the pride and
impiety of France which would not have had its punishment and which *ought* not to escape it. God has
confided his designs in nobody, but, considering the
actual events, it seems certain that the German war
being able to become European even, will be merely
an *episode* or a prelude. When the German monster is
beaten down finally, France will still have to settle its
own accounts, and that will be God's moment. So,
doubtless, it will suscitate *Someone*. It is not possible
that what I saw and heard, thirty-five years ago, will
not be realized in one manner or another.

Christine writes to us, sharing this quote from
a peasant conducting his son to the train: "God is a
miserable wretch to take our son." These people who
do not believe in God except when it is a question of
outraging him would understand nothing of the
Phrase: *Sic Deus dilexit mundam ut Filium suum Uni-*

genitum daret,[49] and it would be quite pointless to bring it up to them.

13. – Letter by a priest, dated the 6th. It is worth being conserved:

> *... There you have it then, the Great Days have arrived. Everyone has a stupid look on his face, the bishops clearly even more than others. They are incapable of seeing anything. And they let their priests depart to go kill the blind and imbeciles! They have lounged about at Lourdes however, they have paraded, chitchatted, pala-vered, – they don't know how to do anything but that, and "dominate with pride." Heaven will respond to them, from one Sunday to the next, by the or-der of general mobilization. Is God's reply bloody enough? Is it probative enough when it does not accept those demonstrations done in* a state of dis-obedience? *And the Gospel on Sun-day! What lights! What divine concor-dance! Madmen who do not wish to see! When will they see then?*

14. – Poor news, too incertain. Divers combats where

---

[49] *Sic... daret*: Latin for "God so loved the world that he gave his only son."

the Belgians and the French would have had the advantage. Disembarkment of the English army. Progress of the Russian army moving on Berlin!!? State of war with Austria which, without any declaration, silently lends its forces to Germany, etc.

15. – Japan declares war on Germany. Discontentment with Austria by Italy which may be pulled into the war in turn. Sympathy for Germany by Turkey against which the Balkan states will perhaps coalesce. Universal mess, war everywhere.

Continuation of German atrocities. One assassinates and one tortures the wounded and prisoners. A furious peasant said this morning that it would be necessary to cut the throat of all German prisoners. I think that, without going to such an extreme, it would be appropriate to massacre all the officers that one could lay one's hands on, making them responsible for the horrors committed by their men.

16. – A letter informs us that in Denmark the panic is extreme. Annexation by a supposed victorious Germany is feared. Effect of the false news that it spreads everywhere, following the unwavering system of its politics.

One is always waiting for a great battle that would decide the fate of Metz and Strasbourg, the extreme left of our army being, – it is said – in Liége and the extreme right in Alsace. A map of the theater of war that I have under my eyes makes no mention of Vaucouleurs or Domremy, between Bar-le-Duc and Nancy. It would have been apropos, and how very patriotic! to mark those two localities.

17. – Our curate fears being forced to depart, he also. So we will be completely without a priest then in this Godless village.

Letter from Pierre, without illusions. He has seen a multitude of people at the Sacré Cœur whom fear or excessive distress precipitate to church, to the sacraments, and that they are said to be *converted!* The war seems to be doing something right for us, but he thinks that if Alsace-Lorraine becomes French again, the Republican government will have nothing more pressing than to laicize those two provinces.

He saw Brou enormously occupied, in the Montmartre Townhall, with the distribution of assistance to the families of combatants. The sight of that misery is appalling.

To Pierre:

Thank you for your long letter, which is a real blessing. We are so sad, and each day weighs so heavily on us! Our Madeleine's absence is an immense aggravation. Here we are two weeks since we last heard from that child, and it is a rude test of my courage. I think quite often of you, my friends de Bures, and not without tears. When will we see each other again? And how? And in what condition? Jacques, at least, is in a secure place, on the Isle of Wight, at his Benedictines with Raïssa and Véra...

At no other epoch in History has so extraordinary a situation been seen by France, by Europe, by the entire world. Fifteen or twenty million soldiers in arms, the hateful German empire menaced with ruin after appalling massacres, and then what?... While stifling a burst of grievous laughter, I really want to give the impression of believing in fraternity, in the disinterestedness *of England and Russia, but the rebuilding of Europe will still be needed. Then, what a scramble it will be! What an unleashing of covetousness! What a vision of the Apocalypse!*

The German empire must be destroyed. That seems certain. Prussian arrogance and brutality have really surpassed all measure. God and men have had entirely enough. France is needed for that. So France will be victorious. At what price? Its extreme right, so far as we are told, is in Alsace and its extreme left in Liége. It's a vise of 200 kilometers before narrowing in on Metz and Strasbourg, fortresses stolen from France, become

*almost impregnable over the last 44
years and which are defended with the
most horrible despair. Each day, one
expects a gigantic battle that will decide perhaps their fate. It is probable
that the victory will be for France aid-
ed by Belgium and England, but, I repeat, at what price? Therefore, we
suppose the stolen provinces reconquered, the German army horribly
mutilated, pushed back across the
Rhine, forced to run before the Russians, for its extermination. In that hypothesis, all goes very well, no? And
the abominable empire no longer exists. So be it, but La Salette will remain. Will the predictions of the Secret be fulfilled? No. Will France do
penance? Not the least in the world.
Conversions caused by nervous fright
fill me with very little confidence. This
war is not and cannot be the End...*

The first German flag has been removed from Alsace.

19. – Raïssa Maritain and Jeanne Boussac, who have
written to me at the same time, are of the same opinion on this, and almost at the same time, that my book
is the only one that can be read at the present hour.

20. – To Emile Baumann:

You are right to say, without bitter-

ness, moreover, that I do not often write to you, and I'm right also to write very little, in appearance. In reality, I write a lot. For twenty days, I do nothing but that. My situation is strange. Many of my readers suppose me to have an extraordinary strength and want to rely on my support. I have to respond to frantic letters. Yet I am nothing more than a poor, very miserable man.

I had come here with my wife and my two daughters who had need of the countryside, provisioned with derisory resources. I had to kill several mandarins in order to subsist to this day. But those poorly gutted mandarins are now at the frontier. There are no others, and I do not know how that will finish for the exiles that we are here. For a great many years we are habituated to eating out of the Hand of God. More than ever, today, we count on Him, on Him alone. Among excessive difficulties, I had begun a book on Joan of Arc, seen very differently by me than historians and religiose folk have seen her. Will I be allowed to finish this book ad maximam Dei gloriam? *I have no idea.*

The present situation is not at all surprising to me. For so long a

*time I have been waiting for catastro-
phes! Those who have read me know
it. But I do not yet see the* divine *signs.
Germany is visibly designated, marked
for an excessive humiliation. Its barbarous arrogance and its ferocious
hypocrisy have gone too far. It will be
crushed then – and that will be banal.
Rivers of blood will flow – and that
will be banal. The monster beaten
down, all of Europe will hideously
scramble for the spoils – and that will
be banal. And afterwards? Yes, afterwards? there will be La Salette, that is
to say accounts to settle for France,
victorious it is true, but puffed up by
its victory, nowise penitent, and more
contemptuous than ever of the warnings provided by its Sorrowful Sovereign. There will be its hatred of all supernatural life and the Renunciation
already obtained by its Episcopacy.
Then, doubtless, God will need to
show himself, I do not know how, and
sending I do not know whom – and
that will be no longer banal at all. I
have already written about it multiple
times: As long as the Supernatural is
not* evident*, nothing at all will happen.*

Heard about the death of Pius X. Would this
be a first sign? One is familiar with the prophesy of
Saint Malachy: *Ignis ardens*, for Pius X; *Religio depopulata*, for his successor.

21. – To Jean de la Laurencie:

> *What terrible days! How many tor-*
> *ments all over the world! One asks*
> *oneself with fright what can really be*
> *the soul of those who, with deliberate*
> *intent,* scientes et prudentes, *take it*
> *upon themselves to unleash like*
> *calamities! Those rotten Hohenzollern*
> *and that deliquescent Habsburg who,*
> *with one foot in the grave, decide to*
> *send to their death before them (?) so*
> *many hundreds of thousands of men!*
> *Those criminals speak of God being*
> *with them only, they affirm, as they set*
> *villages on fire and kill people, and it*
> *is we, so they say, who are the sav-*
> *ages! The doddering François-Joseph*
> *is Apostolic, we should not forget it.*
> *One would need to know what God*
> *thinks of all that.*

> *Pius X just died. What did that*
> *holy Pope see, and what could he say*
> *in his last hours? We will find out per-*
> *haps. I have been assured that he was*
> *particularly devoted to La Salette and*
> *that he regarded Mélanie like a saint.*
> *If he did nothing for her, it is because*
> *he was afraid of some certain, in-*
> *evitable schism. For him, Mélanie's*
> *Secret was the very Word of the Holy*
> *Virgin. Who is going to replace him?*

There is not a more anguishing question for the Catholic world. You know the prophesy: Religio depopulata. *Is that to say that the Church will need to be devastated by the future pope himself and that in that way the preliminary Renunciation would be realized at the sound of the Gallic* Cock *which the world will perhaps hear? Such are my thoughts, crazy if you will, but so greatly procured by the visible disarray of the Church and the entire world!*

Would that God might be of assistance to each one of us, my very dear friend! One thinks, reasonably I believe, that the hateful German empire is condemned. 1870 does not start all over again, and the Germans start to feel it presently. But there will be a cost for destroying that vermin which will be replaced perhaps by another. Maledictio Matris eradicat fundamenta,[50] *says the Holy Book. The disdained tears can be turned into maledictions. To think that Cardinal Amette can become Pope. It's enough to instill fear in the constellations!*

No news of Madeleine. That child's silence becomes an insupportable torment.

---

[50]*Maledicto... fundamenta*: Latin for, "The Mother's malediction will eradicate the foundations."

22. – The great battle does not appear to have finished. While waiting, the Germans occupy Brussels, struck with a contribution of 200 million. The avidity of those pirates is prodigious. It is said that Wilhelm wants to annex Belgium and Holland – after extermination of the Britannic fleet.

Envoi of *The Pilgrim of the Absolute* for my dear friend the Abbot Léonce P***, who was deployed:

> *Warning him to be careful at junctions and the innumerable crossroads that he will meet along the narrow path of the Absolute, fortunately recognizable by certain signs: that it is full of stones, protected by fearsome Sphinxes, and frequented by very few travelers.*

The *Croix* publishes two long columns on Pius X. I cull this small perfidious phrase: "It has been said again and again that the deceased had already *deigned*, in his life, to give witness to his sanctity through miracles, and we can easily believe it (Eh! eh!), but *more remarkable* still is assuredly the sanctity of his actions."

It is Véronique who pointed those lines out to me, that one would think were dictated by Amette.

23. – A letter from Madeleine, long and extremely

touching, succeeds in lightening our torment a little. But the poor child does not know when she can come back.

There is always talk of a great, pitched battle, on the immense front. But one acknowledges certain, imprecise setbacks. Above all, I have the impression and agony of not knowing anything.

24. – I recall the old prophesy "of Mayence," read formerly in 1870, prophesy announcing for the epoch that we are at, approximately, the destruction, the complete annihilation of the German power, after a colossal battle of many days, in the plains of "Bouleau" near Paderborn (?).

The Russian top brass, victorious on the Vistule, would have decided to march on Berlin. God be willing. The Cossacks would know how to avenge us for the horrible Prussian brutality.

25. – Letter from Pierre. The war fills him with anguish, but without altering his internal calm. He admires the astonishing madness of Wilhelm planning to annex Belgium and Holland. He prays a great deal and waits like us for a divine manifestation. "Is it possible that the *Advent* has not already begun?" he writes to me.

All is so menacing that Jeanne sends a dispatch to Madeleine for her to come back immediately, if she can profit by an occasion.

27. – To Pierre:

I wrote to you yesterday, but I am so sad that I want to write to you again. Troubled in our waking moments and troubled in our sleep, we are waiting for a dispatch from Madeleine announcing her return to Paris where Jeanne would go immediately to find her. The absence of that child has been terrible for us, that much I can tell you. Each day then we wait for the postman and the poor paper, the Petit Parisien, *which informs us of the small bit that the minister of war consents to communicate to us...*

France's situation is clearly horrible, but what about that of Germany? Even while accepting as true the serious setbacks in Belgium and in Alsace, how not to count on the cooperation of the English, in whose so evident interest *it is to violently oppose the German expansion? The Russians and their slapped Tsar, shouted down ignobly in Berlin, in the person of his ambassador, inundate oriental Prussia and march perhaps, at this very moment, on Wilhelm's capital. However formidable his scoundrels' army might be in Belgium, it will be quite constrained, that filthy army, to make an about-face, releasing its hold, and*

*running back to face the Russians,
having five hundred thousand French,
English, and Belgians at its back, pur-
suing it, with rage in their hearts, having atrocities to punish it for, for it is
necessary that everything be paid for.
It is no question here of an ordinary
war, but of a war of* extermination.
*God has not revealed anything to me,
but I feel profoundly that Germany is
condemned and that Prussia – the military heart of Germany – must be destroyed. That* above all.

*No one can tell me what I
don't already know, that France has
merited the worst chastisements. It is
enduring them already by the carnage
of a multitude of its children and by
other horrible evils, without prejudice
of the accounts it must give – afterwards. But Germany first.*

*I live as if in a grievous dream.
This morning, in our poor church, I
was thinking of all yesterday's and today's dead, of all those dying, of all
the mourning, of all the menaces; and,
at the same time, I saw my entire cruel
life pass before my eyes! With an anguishing precision, ancient things seen
and heard thirty-five years ago came
back to haunt me, then when I was living like a contemplative and when I*

was told that there was a place —
where I do know know — reserved for
me in the immense catastrophes to
come. And I wept in the darkness of
fear and in the obscurity of hope...

What do we learn from the newspaper? This.
That in the middle of war, the government resigns and
M. Viviani, the snuffer of stars, immediately forms
another one "of national defense and union." We are
done for!

To a young friend:

Your letter surprises us and afflicts us.
"If the Belgians," you say, "had not
opposed such a resistance at Liége,
the Germans would be in Paris now."
How could you write that, knowing
that I would read it? Of course, I
won't dispute my admiration for the
Belgian army, which I was far, I have
to admit it, from expecting so great an
effort from. But, not to mention its per-
fect dishonor if it had not acted simi-
larly after the enormous German slap
in the face, nothing authorizes you to
believe that the bandits would not
have met any resistance from among
us. I add that it is temerarious to sub-
stitute by conjecture a possible event
for an actual one. It is as if one were
saying that prescience or divine provi-
dence is conditional and depends on
our adventures. I wish you would be

more supernatural, *my dear child. All
that happens in life is perfectly adorable, because nothing happens that is
outside the divine plan.*

*"You were struck," you say
also, "to see that Italy had to remain
neutral in order for the Conclave to be
able to choose a new Pope." That is a
completely human point of view. In
three days, perhaps, Italy will have
ceased to be neutral, and the new
Pope will be elected, God knows when
and how, and we will have no say in
the matter. God has no need of the
neutrality nor the heroism of anyone,
such is the supernatural point of view.
You speak of universal infidelity as the
reason for so much evil. Here, you are
almost right, and I will confide in you
something serious. It is my personal
indignity that has caused the divine
anger and I am, in reality, the only
person to blame. Mgr. Amette and
many blessed people in his entourage
know it very well. Do not accuse others. I hope that I will be held account-
able for that confession which is not
without heroism, although French and
Perigordin.*

29. – Jeanne, deprived of news and overwhelmed
with anguish, has decided to go, God assisting, to

look for Madeleine, come what may. What miseries
and what torments must we endure still?

30. – Oh! spent the night tonight at the Saint-Piat
trainstop, waiting for the trains, all the trains. They
were innumerable, but without travelers, and each one
brought me a deception. It was as if a knife, come
from afar, pierced my heart without stopping for one
second. I will not forget the fantastic and quasi supernatural impression that one of those furious convoys
of war materiel left me with. It was loaded only with
boats requisitioned here and there from the rivers, and
it was extraordinary to see them pass by at full speed
in the dark night! In the intervals between rockets, the
enormous silence of the sleeping countryside, troubled only by the quasi human calls of horned owls
and screech owls that seemed to deride the immense
distress in my heart.

31. – Blessed return of Jeanne and Madeleine, who
were able, with great difficulty and by a sort of miracle, to escape the crush of people trying to escape
Paris and find a place on a train.

(Those days and those hours spent waiting for
our child is one of the most intolerable memories I
have. Imagining two criminals who had such power
to cause such suffering, – how many times have I not
asked myself, as with so many other things, what
punishment would be suitable for them? Impossible
response. God alone knows. Their payment is, at the
end of the day, all ready, all counted, all resounding
and staggering, and something to make lions shudder,

looking at it from that point of view only.)

September

1st. – There is the story of the famous inventor Turpin who, when he was just starting out, had proposed a sort of asphyxiating machine that was capable, by its effects, of making all war impossible; he is said to have been expelled because of the apparent unfairness of such processes of extermination, as if all means of defense are not legitimate against brigands.

Tranquilized by Madeleine's return, an even more serious anxiety comes to haunt us. The Germans are said to be at a short distance from Paris. However probable might be their final extermination, the nearness of those bandits would not be without danger. Wandering bands of Uhlans are something to be feared in these parts. Resolution to leave for Rennes, where we would find Termier, having become lieutenant-colonel of artillery, in the manufactory of engines of war.

2. - At 2 am, we go down to the stop where our parcels had preceded us. We need to wait for the train, which was late by more than two hours. But that is only the beginning of our troubles. Arrived in Chartres after six hours, the train stopping for half an hour every instant, going at a speed of two or three kilometers per hour. At Chartres, immense hustle,

bustle, and disorder. It's the panic of those fleeing Paris and the North, then the necessity to let the wounded pass before everyone else, etc.

Then again the trip from Chartres to Mans, in an enormous heat, in the cram-full wagon, with new human beings piling in at each station, a terrible few hours during which time I see my girls half-asphyxiated and me and Jeanne as well in danger of it. At Mans, same confusion and jostling as at Chartres. However, from there to Rennes it is much easier. The night has come, the weather has cooled, and there are less people. At Rennes, another tribulation. We must give up trying to find a place in whatever hotel and content ourselves, while waiting during the day, with the hospitality of the benches and tables that the Red Cross prepared at the train station for emigrants and travelers without accommodations.

3. – Finally, look at us, installed in a passably sinister house in old Rennes, several steps away from the cathedral. The fearsome exodus is over. All we have to do now is live here as best we can.

Hubbub for the election of a new Pope who would be called Benedict XV.

4. – A number of masses at the cathedral, monument of the seventeenth century, whose ugliness astonishes me in a city as venerable as the capital city of Brittany ought to be.

The journals confirm the election of cardinal Della Chiesa, who has declared that he wants to take the name Benedict XV. The French government has been heroically transported to Bordeaux. The Russians, conquerors of a part of eastern Prussia, rename Saint Petersburg *Petrograd* going forward, marvelous sign – and ridiculous – of a merciless hatred. I cannot see myself reading *Les Soirées de Pétrograd* by Joseph de Maistre.

Vienna and Berlin appear menaced at the same time. There is talk of 150 thousand Austrians killed or held prisoner at Lemberg, in Galicia. Prodigious battle with millions of men. But in France, one had to do battle at Compiègne.

Found this in the *Nouvelliste de Bretagne:*

An allocution given by the Kaiser. – According to the Dortmund newspapers, the German emperor has passed troops under review at headquarters and pronounced an allocution from which here are, for curiosity's sake, the principal passages:

Comrades, I have gathered you together to rejoice with you about the victory won by our comrades. (Charleroi, doubtless.) Let us give thanks to our Old God. He will not abandon us, because we defend a just and sacred cause (!). We have more than one bloody battle to deliver. We will not lose our unshakeable confidence in

*our Good Old God in Heaven. We
want to win, we ought to win.*

Discourse by a barbarous chief invoking his idols.

Dinner on bread and cheese in a small establishment where one drinks cider. Occasion to see the soul of the people of Rennes very different from the ignoble Beauceron population. The woman of this establishment is positively enraged against the Germans. She informs us that it is very difficult to save the prisoners who pass through the city. She herself goes to wait for them at the train station with many others armed with scissors and knives in the hope of massacring some of them.

We listen to that with keen joy.

5. – The van der Meer are in route for Holland.

6. – Wilhelm is in Brussels. Innumerable cannons protect that imbecile. A formidable artillery is arranged in battery before the most beautiful monuments of the city, one of the most beautiful of Europe, to destroy it on first alert.

The German newspapers declare that that war is despicable. The Belgians and French are covered in infamy. They ought not to defend themselves. They are responsible for the atrocities. Cities and villages set on fire, women raped, children and old men assassinated, wounded, finished off, tortured, all that is their work. The Germans are perfectly gentle and magnanimous.

With regards to the election of Benedict XV, the *Matin* rejoices over a political pope, in the style of Leo XIII. "The Church has suffered too much," it says, "from the *divorce* practiced by Pius X between sanctity and politics"!!! I offer a million to whomever will explain that phrase to me.

Saw Termier. Delicious sensation no longer to think we are *strangers* in this great city.

7. – The Germans, by a maneuver I am ignorant of, would have departed from the entrenched camp of Paris and taken off in a south-easterly direction toward Dijon. Meaux is on that line and I think of my friend Léon Bellé, who had been made responsible for protecting the Meaux mills. What will happen?

(I found out, later, that that so-called maneuver, quite similar to a rout, was the famous victory of the Marne that saved France, perhaps Europe, but that the exhaustion of our troops and above all our munitions, prevented it from being decisive. Twenty squadrons of fresh cavalry, sabering that host, would have ended the war perhaps. It is true that half the German army was drunk on the wine of Champagne. However, if von Kluck had been, I do not say a great captain – something every Prussian is severely prevented from being, – but if it had simply been Blücher and if he had said: "I will lose two hundred thousand men, if that's what it takes, but I will pass," Paris would have been in great danger... However, it is unreasonable to conjecture about history, and the victory of the Marne, the sudden diversion, unhoped-for, of that torrent of two million barbarians, appears to be a miracle... in times gone by, one would have remembered, to explain it, that tomorrow is the feast of the Nativity of Mary, Queen of France, *Quos vult perdere* VIRGO *dementat.*)

10. – To Jeanne Boussac:

> *Dear friend, to begin with, I embrace you from a bit of a distance, but with all my heart. You know already, from your father, that I am in Rennes, with my wife and daughters. We came here, more than anywhere else, because of him. We had to get out of Mévoisins, which really felt threatened. Only, I would have probably remained, per-suaded that I am equal to exactly six-ty-eight men, having been born in 1846. You know how I feel about trips and my senile passion for holidays. I have had an exceptionally large serv-ing, you must admit.*

> *I would like to be able to laugh a little, my poor Jeanne, if for no other reason than to amuse you for one in-stant. I admit that my courage fails me. There are too many souls who suf-fer. But you love greatness, you are strong, and you can, more than any-*

*one else, hold on to your courage. You
have read me, you know my thoughts,
always the same, and I know that they
don't frighten you.*

*France has much to expiate,
having disdained the Tears of her Sovereign so much. She expiates without a
doubt, at this very moment, but she expiates* without repenting. *I have not
yet heard a single bishop stand up and
say: "We are chastised for not having
listened to the Mother of God who
spoke to us weeping." This is grave.
Blessed are those who think on it, but
the others?...*

*Nonetheless, the hour has not
come. I do not see the* signs. *God does
not show himself in a perceptible, in-
disputable manner. And it is that that I
am waiting for for a great number of
years now. In 1870, it was said in the
sacristies, without any more profundity or repentance than today, but without thinking the least in the world of
La Salette: "Behold the chastisement!" And one considered oneself
quit. In 1914, the same pointless saying can be heard in the same places,
as if divine Justice was in the grocer's
balance.*

*And me, I wait for the Signs
and up until now I do not see them. As*

long as the Supernatural will not manifestly appear, incontestably, horribly,
deliciously, nothing will be done.

God cannot be banal. Now,
what is happening, this European war,
as has never been seen before, with its
fifteen or twenty million furious combatants, with its apocalyptic appearance, with the enormous calamities
that follow and that will follow, all
that is perfectly banal.

All that is a prestige of the Demon, as horrible as one wants, but
nothing but a prestige, tending to
make men, particularly the Catholics
of France and Belgium, believe that
they are finally chastised for good and
that they have paid their debt.

One has ridiculously compared
Wilhelm to Attila, the scourge of God.
Do you not hear the sniggering of the
Devil and do you not feel how idiotic it
is to attribute such a role to that poor
puppet with mustaches! Same observa-
tions for the old doddering fool of Vienna. Those two scoundrels, whose
power of mud and darkness is on the
verge of ending in shame and filth, absolutely know not what they do, and
that is all one can say about it.

Two rivers of blood, infinite

*miseries, the crumbling of two em-
pires, the consecutive baying of all
peoples scrambling for the spoils; the
historic banality of all the centuries;
and then... nothing but a poor man 68
to 70 years old, a writer by necessity
or by helplessness, who waits, on his
knees, for God's Move!*

*I tell you, Jeanne, once again,
what is happening now is nothing
more than an atrocious grimace of the
Demon, an* aping of the Future, *more
abominable than others. That's it. It's
up to us not to be afraid, and to tell
ourselves that things are* not at all
what they appear to be, *that the Holy
Ghost represented by our perfectly unknown, incomprehensible, indivinable,
Lady of La Salette will not punish like
that, but in a manner worthy of Herself, perfectly incontestable, incomprehensible, indivinable. Meditate on
that, dear friend, and think lovingly,
your soul filled with hope, of your husband, my little godson Christopher
who carries Jesus on his little shoulders, your parents, all those whom you
love, me even finally who writes to you
now to lift up your heart.* Magnificat!

11. – I still understand nothing of the military opera-
tions that the Top Brass do not disclose. All that one

is able to see is the "Trenches" announced August 2 having begun, and that on that immense front from Ostende to Verdun and into Alsace, for it is no longer a question of Liége, there is on the French-English side a firm resolution to hold the most fearsome defensive and to wear down in that way that enormous army of 1,500,000 or two million men that Germany has thrown at us, while waiting for the progress of the Russians, with Austria beaten everywhere, being supposedly already out of commission, or almost.

England and Russia, no less than France, want the destruction, from now on probable, of the German empire. England wants it so badly that it brings its troops from all points of its immense colonial empire.

12. – To Alfred Pouthier:

Your letter of the 3rd, so sad and so anguished, I have received it with the expected delays. You will not be surprised to hear that we are in Rennes as of several days now. We might as well be at another point on the planisphere. This is the time for improvised holidays and you know whether that suits my type of beauty. However, I would have preferred to stay in Mévoisins and to continue working on my Joan of Arc. But we have two girls and an anguish hovers over us. Several sous having come in by a miracle, we left for Rennes where we knew we would find our friend Termier. I will recount for you our voyage through the universal panic...

You speak of Providence, which has shined favorably on you, a man of modest faith and little prayer as you seem to be. Such has been our case. Perforce, we should have been forced to remain in Mévoisins. The means to escape was given to us without my having sought it out. Today, distant spectators of the combats, we eat our poor money in a house deprived of splendor, not knowing how this will finish. Deprived of my books, for we needed to depart with very small packages, I am unable to busy myself with Joan of Arc and I vegetate on my journal, preparing thus an exceptionally strange sequel to The Pilgrim of the Absolute. *But that cannot fill my days. So I take advantage of a reading room where my name is admirably unknown.*

Would you believe it, O Pouthier, that it took setting Europe on fire and mobilizing twenty million soldiers for me to read le Bossu *finally, by my old friend Féval! Today, I read* Boubouroche, *not without delight, I dare say.*

The taciturn Top Brass inform

On the Threshold of the Apocalypse

us poorly or not at all on the facts of the war. We know only that one fights with fury and that the excessive German riffraff wears itself down each day in France and Belgium. We know also, or we think we know, that many millions of Russians march in the direction of Berlin accompanied by an appreciable multitude of Cossacks with their necks of swans. The day is perhaps no longer very far off when our affable visitors will be forced to depart or repass over the Rhine escorted courteously by five or six hundred thousand bayonets.

That day then we will return to Mévoisins, then to Bourg-la-Reine by the means and with the resources that God only knows – God only for all eternity.

13. – Must we believe that all goes very well? The newspapers, this morning, were filled with clarions. The strategy employed by Generalissimo Joffre, who appears to be an admirable *cunctator*, that strategy consisting in maintaining an inexpugnable defensive on a 300-kilometer-long front seems to be a complete success. (The insufficiency of official communiqués was such that, at that time, it took me several days to learn that we had been victorious on the Marne – which, moreover, I am still unable to comprehend. September 1915.)

15. – Continuation of good news. We are thinking of our return and Jeanne speaks about it to our hostess who manifests keen discontentment, that worthy woman claiming to have not wanted to rent to us for one month only. I am forced to intervene with firmness.

16. – The immense battle continues. The confidence and enthusiasm also continue. I want to think that something considerable will happen in three days, for the 68th anniversary of the Apparition of Mary of La Salette (The Holy Virgin, in effect, was holding a surprise for us, that day then.)

Millions of dead or wounded, immense ordeals, incalculable mourning, and, in the end, the unanimous crushing testimony of all God's or the Demon's children, – *voilà* what is shouldered by the two wicked men of the houses of Habsburg and Hohenzollern. Merely thinking about it is enough to confound one's reason.

17. – Dispatch from van Haastert informing me that my Dutch godsons are in safety in Rotterdam, after a perilous voyage, through mines, in the North Sea.

A Munich newspaper from September 1 informs us that French prisoners are penned in a sort of camp, at Lechfeld. By way of additional precautions, they are surrounded by an unpassable barrier of barbed wire. The public is allowed to come and feed on the sight of those poor souls. The admission price: 20 pfennigs! Solid German business. It appears that there are countless visitors.

18. – Boredom gnaws at me. We are here in a stinking old house, prey to innumerable fleas, and forced to submit to a hostess, a brigand like Prussia, who responds to every reproach with this: "I am a Breton," which, in my mind, evidently authorizes and even sanctifies all villainies and every depredation. We think she is a drunkard, to top it off.

News. Charles Péguy is dead, killed in action. Funeral oration by Barrès who mourns in him a *great writer!* "Behold the man, having become one of the heroes of French thought!" he said.

19. – *The Figaro* publishes a prophesy from 1600 attributed to a Friar Johannès, wherein there is much talk of the Antichrist, which the translator Péladan, who was himself formerly a prophet, identifies with Wilhelm. It is announced that that antichrist must succumb in the same place where he "forges his arms." Now, Essen and German metallurgy are in Westphalia, province that other prophesies designate as the location of the supreme battle.

I really wish that that prophesy were authentic, but it has the double defect of being too precise and above all of being presented by Péladan.

20. – Yesterday was the anniversary of La Salette. It seems to me that something should have happened. But the newspapers don't mention anything.

21. – (What a shock.) I learn with a sob, the sob of all France, I have to believe it, that the cathedral of Reims no longer exists.[51] The Germans have destroyed it "without military objective," purely for the fun of it, because of that barbarous instinct of children of the demon that encourages them to destroy works of art and above all religious art.

Read *Anna Karenina*, by Tolstoy. – Hugely disgusting.

22. – Read with horror the details of the destruction of the cathedral of Reims. Stories of the sack of Senlis and the bombardment of Maubeuge. Always the same atrocities.

23. – Priests saying mass in red pants.

The Germans are not as guilty as one might believe. They were *forced* to bomb the cathedral. Like brutes, they obeyed their emperor, doubtless, but above all Mgr. Luçon, Cardinal-Archbishop, pro-

---

[51]cathedral of Reims no longer exists: for a discussion of this, in the context of historical symbolism, see Bloy's *Joan of Arc and Germany*, Sunny Lou Publishing, 2021.

fessed enemy of La Salette, who had done everything in his power to bring the wrath down on her church. It is fitting that the bombardment should have taken place *precisely* on September 19.

I go with Jeanne and the children to the faubourg of Redon, to visit the Récollet monks where Véronique is received as a tertiary of Saint Francis. By mysterious Will, the father who received her wrote, not the date of that day, but of Sunday, the 24th, feast day of Our Lady of Mercy, the birthday of our little Pierre whom she is the godmother of. What is more, that entrance into the Third Orders takes place on the day of the wonderful Franciscan feast day of the Discovery of Saint Clare's Relics. We were one and the other ignorant of those two coincidences.

To Raoux. I recount our adventures and our imminent return to Mévoisins. Rapid assessments of the war. "We are going to live the Apocalypse."

24. – Anatole France, in a letter to that scoundrel Gustave Hervé, regarding the Reims cathedral which he *deplores* the destruction of, declares sentimentally that after victory we will have nothing better to do than to offer our fraternal friendship to the Germans. I remember that one day in the past Léon Daudet called him Anatole *Prusse*.

25. – Jardin des Plantes in Rennes rather banal, with the exception of a gigantic oak tree that ought to have been already rather large at the time of Joan of Arc. I

admire that venerable witness of the centuries.

26. – In the *Echo de Paris*, that journal of Right-minded People, almost violent article by M. de Mun indignant over the hypocritical sentimentality of humanitarians who are already speaking of *friendship* with the Germans, and saying that they must "cut it out." What surprises me and delights me is the rage of so peaceable a man going so far as to incriminate his colleague at the Academy, Anatole France.

As for Barrès, in the same journal, he continues his little literature of a crafty pasquinade, "Before the Barbarians." But that has no importance at all.

Read a book published in 1910 (Société des publications littéraries, 24, rue Pierre-Charron). *Adventures of the Franc-Tireurs of Champagne 1870-1871, Captain Lange's Memoirs*. It's the story of a good man having accomplished astonishing feats of arms, at the head of several companions, in his region that is so perfectly inert and trembling that it could be Beauce today, and not receiving any reward for it, after the events, save the worst calumnies, followed by an infamous trial wherein it was all he could do to preserve his liberty and even his life, after having been accused of brigandage by all those whose treason he had upset or punished. Evidently a reserved fate, in the near future, for those who will have generously fought for the fatherland – to begin perhaps with our generalissimo.

27. – The German government having officially declared that the bombardment of the Reims cathedral
had occurred only because of the establishment of a
post of observation in the Basilica, General Joffre immediately responded:

> *The military command at Reims has at
> no time placed an observation post in
> the cathedral.* The systemic bombard-
> ment began on September 19 at THREE
> O'CLOCK in the afternoon (!!!)

Letter by Cardinal Luçon, on return from
Reims, after an absence probably necessitated by his
episcopal duty to fight the Holy Virgin. Confirmation
of the disaster and sublime cry: "My house is
intact!!!" His house is intact. His Eminence, the enemy of La Salette and voluntarily blind, does not see
that his *real* house is in ruins.

28. – Departure from Rennes, after an ignoble scene
with our hostess who stole one of Jeanne's scarfs and
who shamelessly denies her larceny. A cooling down
on finding Termier at the train station, having run to
see us off and who will follow up with our robber.

Relatively facile trip, the trains no longer en-
cumbered. Arrival at Mans where Emile Baumann
and his wife are waiting for us.

29. – A visit to the too-little-known cathedral, which
is full of marvels, although very inferior to that of

Chartres and some others. Weather and the enemies of God, Huguenots, Revolutionaries or Sulpicians, have inexplicably respected the old stained glass windows and old stones. Saw also some old houses.

I did not know Baumann except by his books and by his letters. The hospitality that he shows us is an occasion for some conversation that makes me better appreciate that excellent artist with respect to whom I reproach myself for having sometimes lacked fairness. Very discerning mind and very suffering soul. As poorly recompensed as myself for his literary works, he is forced to live by practicing universitarian pedagogy, although persuaded of the absolute and derisory inutility of that exhausting labor.

Promenade to the Jardin des Plantes for Mans, it also, possesses that object of luxury wherein the only attraction appears to be an abominable wild boar.

30. – Very sweet hours. Baumann, whom I did not know was a musician and even virtuoso in the most honorable sense of that word, plays with Madeleine some Mozart and some Beethoven. He himself, alone, executes on the piano a very beautiful piece by Bach.

The English are very numerous in Mans. We had to pay a visit to their camp. The impression is formidable. All those men, marvelously equipped, have the most beautiful bearing in the world. They continually traverse the city where each corps makes a short sojourn, and it is a powerful comfort to be able to count on such auxiliaries.

Met at our host's house the young Abbot M***, a nurse at the military hospital, whom I do not know, him either, except by correspondence. He is a very small man, very active with a vast face, which would appear comical if not for a surprising sparkle of intelligence attenuated by a visible tenderness of heart.

All the autumn papers will reproduce, with or without commentaries, the unexpected farce by Anatole France writing to the minister of War and asking him to make him a soldier. "Many brave fellows," he said, "find that my style is worth nothing *in times of war*." Did it not suffice to have going for him all the imbeciles in time of peace?

Guy de Cassagnac is dead, killed at the head of his company in the latest combats. You will die otherwise, Anatole.

October

1st. – We must depart. I say goodbye to my friend who sadly goes back to his courses.

Extreme joy to find ourselves at home again, to see again the good faces of the reservists who guard the village. The weather moreover is exceptionally beautiful.

Card from Philippe Raoux informing me that

a son was born to him. He was unable to be informed of it until after three weeks.

Very beautiful letter from Jeanne Boussac:

... Often, when I was in the terrible anguish of having no news about my husband, I thought of you as of a soul who contained the greatest torments and on whom all suffering has been tried, without being able to interrupt his canticle to the Glory of God. I thought of your strength and I tried to look at my suffering with your eyes which change the value of things and discover, in those that one fears, the unknown riches and joys. I forced myself as well to imagine your Journal and to guess how the events of these days came to be inscribed, deprived of everything that is anecdotal and contingent, deprived all that one is so tired of hearing in these days of chatter and general cordiality, reduced finally to their divine weight. Your last letter, it was like a page taken out of your Journal, like a promise of the precious joy that we will have later on reading that seventh volume.

I have also re-read much of Sweating Blood, *but, this time, the magnificent artist of those tales disappeared and I saw only your immense supernatural compassion. Even then,*

in the banging about of terrifying ap-
pearances, you had only souls in view,
the poor souls, numb and blind to their
extenuated body's peril, the "banal"
souls of all those poor people "who
fall without indignation or moaning in
the pitiable arms of invisible cap-
tains." (Sweating Blood, *page 128.*)
What compassion is contained in that
phrase which comes back to me now
non-stop when I pray for those who
fight and die...

From Raoul Gilbert; another note:

The women who take care of the
wounded in the train stations consti-
tute the most annoying groups and the
least edifying that there might be.
They are there in part because of plea-
sure. Each announcement by the bell
is greeted with joyous acclamations.
But the happiness that they appreciate
above all is to be in the midst of men
whose obscene and stupid pleasantries
make them easily swoon. I know, be-
sides, that the placement offices that
provision the train stations with that
personnel are Place Blanche, le Rat
Mort, the Abbey de Thélèmes [sic], the
Café des Princes, le Soufflot, in brief,

all the good houses...[52]

3. – The collective folly of the German people has been well enough exposed by the Abbot Wetterlé in an article on modern Germany. For Germany, completely transformed by Prussia, there is but a single doctrine anymore, a unique faith: *Deutschland über alles.*[53] That appears foolish, monstruous, but that is how it is, and it is unchangeable from now on. All that is beautiful, grand, attractive, becomes or has become specifically German. All the tares, all the vices are fatally of foreign importation. That belief is systematically maintained in the soul of new generations by the grade-school teacher, the middle-school professor, and above all by the universitarian scholar. Yes, Germany is above everything and by the incomparable qualities of the Germanic race, and by a divine predestination, rather similar to that of the Hebrew people in the Old Testament.

There is no room then to be surprised by the excesses committed by German troops. They were so well prepared for it! Assassination, pillage, arson, rape, all is permitted to them because Germany alone has the right, and everything that is beneath heaven belongs to it.

---

[52]*Place Blanche... le Soufflot*: all places where sex could be had for hire. For *le Rat Mort*, see *The End of Lucie Pellegrin*, by Paul Alexis, Snuggly Books, 2020. For the *Abbey de Thélème*, see Rabelais, or Restif de la Bretonne's discussion of it in Note K of *The Pornographer*, Sunny Lou Publishing, 2021.

[53]*Deutschland über alles*: German for "Germany above everything," scil. Germany first.

But as it needs sanction all the same, Germany being profoundly and universally impious has felt the need to mix God in with all its manifestations. The coins, as with the soldier's belt plate, bear the inscription: *Gott mit uns*, God with us. The emperor Wilhelm treats God like his younger brother. He imposes on Him his counsels when, peradventure, he does not give Him orders. God would no longer be perfect if he was not German. The Germans annex everything, even the sky.

Collective *folly*, you said, my dear abbot, to make yourself accepted by your readers. It seems to me that the word *possession* would be more exact, and I believe I have read it in your thought.

Mass for soldiers of the parish. There were *two* villagers in attendance. Perhaps they were foreigners even.

One speaks of re-establishing the rank of marshal in France,[54] which is strange at the very least. That, of course, to recompense General Joffre, who appears to conduct the war in a completely superior fashion. I presume that the day after victory the Socialists will make him pay dearly for that superiority.

4. – Letter from Friar D***, with regards to Reims cathedral.

Who knows, who could affirm, whe-

---

[54]rank of marshal: for a discussion of this same idea, but at the time of Napoleon, see chapter 12, *The Soul of Napoleon*, Sunny Lou Publishing, 2021.

*ther that splendid metropolis, which
one believes to have been bombarded
and destroyed by the Prussians, was
not actually riddled, crushed last September 19 by the Reims diocese and its*
Bulletin, *inserting on October 7, 1911,
and accentuating the point on May 25,
1912, that "the tissue of coarseness
and sottishness" published under the
title of the Secret of La Salette or
Mélanie's Secret, etc. had been placed
on the Index and even condemned?*

5. – To Emile Baumann:

*... How marvelous our encounter was,
dear friend! One must recall at each
instant that it is God who does everything and that he does it absolutely for
all eternity. The immolation of a million men was needed then, in divine
Prescience, while we wait for other
immolations, so that we might meet
each other again one certain day. Necessity of concluding that that was extremely important, and behold what
neither of us knew.*

*It is like that, moreover, for all
that God does. The displacement of an
atom participates in the divine plan
and has an inexpressible importance.
Nothing is indifferent and the least*

*acts possess a redoubtable gravity.
When one is filled with enough Grace
to think on that endlessly, it is easy to
be a saint. One is a saint.*

*For a large number of cen-
turies, the prigs give themselves enormous trouble to make us believe that
sanctity is difficult. Prestige of the demon. Nothing is easier. Goodwill suffices, whatever theologians might say
or ascetic writers determined to dis-
courage Christ's poor sheep.* Quærite
primum regnum Dei et justitiam ejus,
et hæc omnia adjicientur vobis.
Adorable simplicity of the Gospel!

*One is so strong and one sees
so far when one is situated on that luminous peak! It suffices to breath. One
is a thaumaturge because one always
wants the same thing. One is a prophet
because one always says the same
thing, and Prayer, which is none other
than an effusion of loving tears, appears like God's Goodwill.*

*So peace and joy, whatever
happens, as the old Martyrs, men of
extreme simplicity who added nothing
to the Gospel, understood it.*

*Millions of enraged brutes
whom the imbecilic Wilhelm has
launched against us, – what will re-*

> *main of them after several lusters?*
> *Scarcely some lamentable duffers on*
> *an immense dungheap. What do they*
> *care, the dear souls who stand at the*
> *Gates of Paradise?*

I wrote these things at an unusually sweet and luminous moment.

7. – Sudden death of M. de Mun. Great mourning for Right Thinkers.

To Philippe Raoux. For starters, I congratulate him on the birth of his son, whose advent into the world he was unable to learn about until three weeks after the fact:

> *... How strange and bitter the power*
> *that is given to an imperial and*
> *Lutheran abortion in order to distress*
> *God's children like that! I know quite*
> *well that a ferocious imbecile can sti-*
> *fle his conscience, but, all the same, to*
> *condemn millions of men to death un-*
> *justly, to decree mourning, misery,*
> *and despair for two thirds of the Euro-*
> *pean families and, at the same time, to*
> *dedicate himself to its total ruin ag-*
> *gravated by infinite shame, all that*
> *seems difficult to conceive of. It is said*
> *that the cretin no longer sleeps and*
> *that he spends all his time at garden-*
> *ing. Anything goes, and I wonder*

where the demons' bastard is who would consent to taking his place.

You were barely born, my dear friend, when already I was expecting the worst catastrophes. It seems to me that I will finally be quit of them. In the past, armies composed of one hundred or two hundred thousand men were lined up. A one-day battle determined the fate of an empire, and that battle, which was waged over several leagues or square kilometers, took on the name of a city or a village forever. Today we see millions of soldiers from the east and from the west combatting, battles lasting weeks, months, and they take place across fronts so extended that one is forced to give them the names of rivers. Nothing remotely like it has been seen in any century.

It is true that the execrable German empire is condemned. That will cost them horribly dear doubtless, but one wants it to perish. The entire world, one can say, demands extermination of that monster and it is certainly inevitable. All our departments of the North, from Alsace to Pas-de-Calais, and at least half of Belgium, will be a desert, but the Barbarians, pushed back beyond the Rhine by fifteen hundred thousand avengers, will be forced to go and face the Russians who will give them no quarter. Never will a comparable effusion of blood have been seen. An old prophesy that I read in 1870 announces that that prodigious crushing will take place on the plains of Westphalia.

The map of Europe will be changed then, God knows how! The Republic swelled by reconquered Alsace-Lorraine, perhaps also Rhenish Bavaria, puffed up by its triumph and more impenitent *than ever, will be occupied by an internal settling of accounts. The apparent union of Frenchmen, at the present caused by the enormity of the common danger, will disappear in one instant... Mélanie, to whom the Holy Virgin had unveiled the future, said that the Terror would no longer be anything in comparison with what had been shown her. No one believes it. There are* signs *however from now on, and this atrocious war is a rather visible one. You must have noticed the surprising date of the bombardment of Reims, September 19, at* 3 o'clock in the afternoon. *Naturally, none of our Catholics noticed that, to begin with the Cardinal-Archbishop, Mgr. Luçon, Mélanie's particular enemy. That prince of the Church found consolation in the destruction of the*

*Cathedral by confirming, in an un-
precedented letter published by all the
newspapers, that his own house had
been spared. "My house," he wrote,
"is intact."*

Jeanne and Madeleine have been to Main-
tenon this afternoon, to bring tobacco and grapes to
the wounded, and they return gravely affected.

8. – I speak with a young priest about the future that
is reserved for us by our bishops whose type seems
realized by Mgr. Luçon. Like him, they will all be attentive to their houses, built perhaps by the Free Ma-
sons, to be sure to keep them intact, *above all else*.
That result obtained, they will be firmly resolved to
preach to their flocks what they call Christian resignation, that is to say acceptation of the most despicable
of laws. And if someone among them is still reminded
of La Salette, how many of them will pat themselves
on the back for their wisdom of reprobates which
made them contemn Mélanie's Secret and obstinately
disobey their Sovereign!

In *She Who Weeps*, chapter XIV, I speak of
the Holy Virgin's threats concerning the potatoes that
must rot, and I bring out a letter that Jeanne received
in Tréport, September 6, 1906, in which she tells me
how she received in a dream the explanation of certain words: "The potatoes signify the dead." This
year, the potatoes rot, and the deaths are innumerable.
Strangely significative coincidence, after the catastrophe of Reims. There will be others.

9. – Mass of Saint Denis. We were alone. Shame on this country where there are parents of soldiers. The curate had announced that this mass would be for them.

Found this in the *Deutsche Handelswacht* of Hamburg:

All that there is of the lofty and noble in the true culture of the soul and spirit, in the development of mankind, has attained its most complete, its most pure expression in the German people. A German defeat would be the end of true humanity, and if the world wants to see progress, the world must become German. Germany must have domination over the world.

10. – Confirmation of what precedes. Pierre writes to me from Rotterdam:

I possess a small document of immense and incommensurate infamy by the Germans. You know of course their 42-cm canon. In Germany, I do not know where, people can see an example of that diabolical machine, by paying a price of admission. They receive a small piece of paper, a ticket on which it is imprinted what follows (I translate from German):

The ACTIVE BERTHA
or *Krupp's Secret*!

"Krupp's new artillery with which the armored fortifications of Liége have been bombarded. – Canon weight: 113,000 kilogr. Length: 21 meters. Calibre: 42 cm.

"Shell weight: 950 kilogr. Cartridge powder weight: 383 kilogr. One shot costs about 38,000 marks (47,500 fr).

"Length of shell, 1 m. 70 c.; range 40-45 kilom. It pierces at 40 kilom. a steel armored plate of a thickness of 1 m. 90 c.; at 45 kilom., it still pierces a reinforced concrete cover with a thickness of 5 m.

"Its profits are for the benefit of the Red Cross."

I attest to the authenticity of this document. It is too monstrous not to be absolutely true. And then, the spirit of that, the spirit of that sinister joke at the bottom, to turn the profits to the benefit of the Red Cross!

Despite those engines evidently calculated for the destruction of fortresses and cathedrals, it appears all the same that our less ambitious artillery disconcerts a little the German churls' vanity.

Our artillery men in stern costume, – they call them "the black butchers."

Our curate invited one of his parishioners to pray for our soldiers. "I have nobody in the war," he responded.

11. – Other confirmation of the beauty of the German soul.

The *Hamburger Nachrichten* on September 23 published the following letter written by a German officer on the subject of the treatment given to French prisoners:

> *After all the experience that we have had with the French, experience that has given rise to astonishment, disdain, and disgust, I have to say that every German soldier lightly wounded has to have the upper hand over a grievously wounded French one. Treat the French like patients, but above all like prisoners. They are not worthy of any personal sympathy, because they would not be grateful... Forbid our sisters and our nurses to approach them... Be just, but do not be soft. They simulate gratefulness, but, in fact, they are liars and degenerates. Do not forget that the French are not like our soldiers. They are cowards and lay traps for us. We are constrained to*

*make war on a people that is at a very
inferior moral level compared to our
own and whom we contemn. The
French are a fallen people. Also, with
respect to them, once again, justice,
but not gentleness. Those people are
capable of anything.*

Proclamation by Wilhelm to his army of the
east:

*Remember that you are the chosen
people! The Spirit of the Lord has descended on me because I am the emperor of the Germans.*

*I am the instrument of the His
Highness.*

*I am his sword, his representa-
tive.*

*Woe and death to those who
resist my will! Woe and death to those
who do not believe in my mission!
Woe and death to cowards!*

*That all enemies of the Ger-
man people might perish!*

*God demands their destruc-
tion, God who, through my mouth,
commands you to execute his will.*

Extreme stupidity coupled with dementia,
such appears to be Wilhelm's case.

The taking of Anvers is announced.

12. – The Free-Masonic conspiration works. They make a rumor run through the countryside that the curates are paid by the Germans to make war on us, and the government just interdicted nurses to give medals to the wounded.

Yesterday, *Taubes*[55] flew over Paris, killing or wounding many people. They have even tried to set Notre-Dame on fire.

13. – Enormous sadness. I can barely support what is happening. France is for me like a lion eaten alive by vermin.

The text of Millerand's circular is communicated to me, concerning the medals or objects of piety that one must not distribute among the sick or wounded. It really does not conduce to his honor. That poor minister obeys his orders which must particularly disgust him.

14. – The Germans occupy Lille and the Belgian government has been transferred to Le Havre, while waiting for that unfortunate country to be delivered of the horrible villains who have almost totally overrun it. Unprecedented nightmare. Hardly any news. The Germans having gotten past the obstacle at Anvers, the battle now plays out in the north. One has no idea

---

[55] *Taubes*: single-engine Austrian planes designed for the military.

how this will all finish.

The beautiful German soul. Letter from a mother to her son:

> *... We are getting along very fine, but fourteen days ago we had to stop working... We honestly do not know when that will improve, but we must hope that you will soon make your entry into Paris and that* you will bring back to us much jewelry and golden watches *because we are short on money. Exterminate that band of brigands that one calls the French army. Your mother, brothers, sisters, as well as all your friends, send you many a "hallo." We hope you will return to us safely and in one piece,* but once again, do not forget the gold watches. *We are very tranquil, there is nothing better than the German army.*

16. – German horrors. At Dinant. That unfortunate city had 7,500 inhabitants. A thousand of them have been shot, had their throats cut, been mutilated. All those crimes have been committed without the shadow of a motive. At Aerschot the Boches, on the orders of their leaders, shot the mayor and his children. They have buried alive many people among whom the elderly. Before submitting to that appalling punishment, the poor souls had to dig their own grave. At Andenne, another massacre. At Spontin, a village

near Dinant, not one inhabitant has remained alive, not one house has remained standing. Everywhere the cutting of women and children's throat. It is impossible to finish if one had to tell everything.

After Reims, it's the tour of Arras, the marvelous Artesian capital. Its sublime *hotel de ville* is in ruins. The belfry still stands but for how many more days?

17. – To Philippe Raoux:

> *When will this atrocious war end? The Germans' pride and nastiness surprise the world and cannot be equaled, quite happily, except by the mediocrity or sottishness of their leaders. Imagine Napoleon at the head of two million soldiers, maneuvering in so imbecilic a fashion? The end of ends, for those brutes, consists in spreading terror through the abominable means that you know. Result: absolute dishonor, exasperation of the oppressed, universal execration, and the enraged desire for merciless reprisals. Such demoniacal madness is a case of* collective possession, *with no means for exorcism. The vile Priks[56] who call themselves "intellectuals" have called on*

---

[56]Priks: the word in the original French text is Kuistres, which must be cuistres with a "K." Thus priks, for prigs with a "k." (Cuistres means prigs in English.) The "K" for "Krauts" or "Kaiser" probably.

death. They will have accompanied it with indescribable bitterness and despair. "God is with us," they said while setting afire, violating, pillaging, and massacring. Their kaiser sleeps every night with his "old God," the Wodan of his ignoble ancestors. They are right, doubtless, in this sense that they have condemned themselves in the most precise, in the most terrible fashion. "God is with me, in me, on me," says the damned, and it is his infinite torture.

It is with a Christian spirit that the Germans shot women and children. Here is what a priest (?) by the name of Hein, a member of the Reichstag, wrote in the *Gazette de Voss*, according to a correspondent of the Copenhagen *Standard*:

It is true that our soldiers have shot, in France and in Belgium, men, women, and children and that they have destroyed their homes. But whoever considers that as contrary to the teachings of Christian doctrine only shows that he has not the least comprehension of the veritable spirit of Christ!...

18. – Horrible cold and sadness, aggravated by the thought of our departure to prepare for. Our godchildren, the Maritains, having returned from England, wait impatiently for us in Versailles. Pierre writes of-

ten enough. He lives in Rotterdam, in horror of what he learns from Belgian refugees.

19. – I am told of these two abominations which have become extremely banal: a wounded man whose eyes were gouged out by the Prussians, and that *naked* woman crucified on a door. Dreadful symbolism desired by the demon: the French people naked, crucified on the door to heaven.

Beneficial reading of *The Life* by Anne-Catherine Emmerich.[57] The Germans of Westphalia, of that epoch, little resembled those of today. Prussia, then, hadn't yet empoisoned Germany.

24. – Return. Versailles and Bourg-la-Reine.

25. – Apprised of that beautiful expression by Hanotaux: "We (!) go to Bordeaux to organize the victory."

28. – To Termier:

> *Not being a combatant under fire, I am all the same a victim of war together with hundreds of thousands of others. All the economic conditions have changed, or [are] on the verge of changing, and I see myself here, in*

---

[57] *The Life*: presumably *The Life of the Virgin Mary*.

this season, with laughable resources nearly exhausted; having nothing to hope for from my publishers; crushed by universal distress; suffocated with shame and rage at the thought of all the pigs who are going to pollute France, after those brutes who will have trampled it down; tortured finally by the necessity *to achieve my work, my very own work, to bring it to completion and, come what will, the mission that was confided in me, frightening privilege that it is impossible for me to dodge. You know how my dear godchildren have come to me. Pierre van der Meer told me quite often: "Without your books I would not have become a Christian." Assuredly God could have done without me for him and for others, but* he did not want to, *it is evident, and that in a nutshell is what constitutes my mission, my vocation. After that, does God still require that I become the godparent to a multitude, or that 20th-century France should become my goddaughter, and that I should endure incomparable torments for that? That idea is frightening...*

A Boche who does not have a smidgen of hypocrisy, marvelous exception, is the General von Disfurth. Here is what he writes in the Berlin *Tag:*

It is beneath our dignity to defend our troops against unjust accusations from within *and without. Our troops and we ourselves owe no explanations to anyone, we have nothing to excuse, nothing to justify.* All that our soldiers do *to cause trouble to our enemies, to attach victory to their banners, all that will be well done and all that is justified in advance, at least we ought to consider it so. We have no reason to be bothered by the opinion of other countries, even neutral ones. And* if all the monuments, all the works of architecture *that are placed between our cannons and those of the enemy* went to the devil, *that would be perfectly all the same to us. We will regret them perhaps in a calmer time, but at present there is not a word to lose on the topic. Mars is the master of the hour, not Apollo.* The most modest burial mound that rises above the body of one of our warriors is more venerable than all the treasures of art in the world. *They treat us like Barbarians, who cares! We laugh at them. We can ask ourselves, besides, if we haven't any reason to be proud.*

Let's spare ourselves finally and definitively that idle gossip, let's stop talking about the Reims cathedral and all the churches, about all the palaces that will share its fate. We no longer want to hear about it. From Reims, let the news of a second and victorious entry of our troops reach our ears. Everything else is all the same to us.

O sticks, pointlessly shaken by the wind on so large a number of trees, and you, solid cords, that creak in vain in all the water wells of the world, – what do you think of that funny man?

20. – To Baumann. Generalities. La Salette and the hypocritical disobedience of our so-called faithful. *Deus non irridetur... Nisi pœnitentiam habueritis, omnes similiter peribitis...*[58] As for myself, I am a poor old man facing a dark wall.

One does not see an end to this dreadful war. There were the battles of the Marne, of the Aisne; now the Germans make enraged efforts to vanquish us from the side of Dunkirk and Calais, having, they say, a plan to descend on England, for their leaders seem given to insanity and Wilhelm pretends to do better than Napoleon.

---

[58]*Deus... peribitis...*: Latin for "God is not mocked... except ye repent, ye shall all likewise perish..." Galatians 6:7 and Luke 13:3.

November

1st. – In the *Matin*, evidently *disinterested* article in defense of our generous government which "organizes the victory" so well in Bordeaux, while forbidding that anyone should live it up, as some vicious fellows have wanted to do. It suffices to cast one's eyes on a map to see that our ministers could have gone to Bayonne or Perpignan.

2. – Brou comes to see me. He has a terrible job, miserably compensated besides, at the town hall of his arrondissement, in the office of allocations, where he sees march past him from morning to evening the most appalling miseries. One rejoices as best one can for the discomfiture from now on probable of the Germans.[59]

3. – To Termier:

> I would like to be able to tell you something by M. Quinson whose death afflicts you. He is among those whom I have the duty and the intention not to forget. I have known him as one of those miscreants whom God loves, whom God prefers and, persuaded that all that happens in life is adorable, I tell myself that the certainly generous

---

[59]Editor's note: what followed appears to have been censured in the original publication.

death of that man could actually be a mark of predilection, and of predestination. We see things through our own sensibility. God sees them differently and we enter into his eternal profoundness when we bless him while weeping and without trying to understand.

"November 1st, 92nd day of the war," you write to me. Evidently, something other than the One Hundred Days of 1815. But the military world knows nothing and ignores the rest. Nobody, in fact, knows anything, except perhaps Hanotaux[60] who "organizes the victory." Did you read that phenomenal article in the Matin *saying that our governments work themselves to death in Bordeaux where they were thought to be busy having fun? That is consoling. Someone spoke to me yesterday about something no less consoling. The Kaiser, intimate friend of God, as you know, has made a proclamation wherein he declares to the Polish that the Holy Virgin appeared to him to bless him and fortify his courage! This time that swine is decidedly derailed. He has already assuredly spilt the blood of a million soldiers. Blood pud-*

[60]Hanotaux: Gabriel Hanotaux (1853-1944), a French historian and statesman.

ding will be for nought this year. The generalissimo of the Cossacks has promised them blood pudding for Noel, in Berlin itself. It would be difficult to wait until then... I often tell myself whether this war, short or long, with the enormous suffering that results from it, could not be in fact a gymnasium or a military academy for the training of future martyrs.

4. – Dedications to my children in two sumptuous copies of *The Pilgrim of the Absolute*.

To my beloved Véronique: God wanted this book, whose title gives the meaning of my entire life, to appear at the precise moment when catastrophes, foreseen by me for a long time now, should be unleashed. That, as with all that God wants, should hold deep signification. Do not forget that your father is the missionary of the Absolute, the only one among those who speak or write, that he needed to suffer a great deal for that, that he will need to suffer still, and that he has need of his children's prayers.

To my little, beloved Madeleine, that she should pay great attention to what is asked of her. The Divine Will had a hand in her birth at a

*moment when it was necessary for her,
having become a young woman, to be
witness to the most immense events in
all History. This book will remind her
that an extraordinary courage may
soon be demanded of all Christians
and that it is not sufficient merely to
suffer, but that an artist must be joyous amidst torments. It is for that reason, without a doubt, my dear child,
that the gift of music was accorded to
you.*

5. – The successor to Pius X has done nothing thus
far, but his face is not friendly. So one says, alas!
Politician in the manner of Leo XIII, and I tremble.
Partes vulpium erunt.[61]

I pick up again, finally, my *Joan of Arc* inter-
rupted at the end of July.

6. – Received from San Remo the *Giornale d'Italia*
wherein it is said that the "French muse is dead," because there is no one in France who can be found to
sing magnificently during this war. To the sender:

*Your journalist is a dolt and a prattler.
Since when does one* sing *when one
fights. The publishers themselves are
out fighting and have closed shop. It is
true that I do not fight, being too old,*

---

[61]*Partes vulpium erunt*: Psalms 62:11.

but I meditate, quill in hand, when I
am not praying and, when possible, I
will speak, *quite simply.*

7. – I learn that a statue of Joan of Arc, in Reims, in a place where the shells rained down, has been preserved, to this very day.

8. – Saw some friends. Naturally, one speaks about the war, all the more atrocious when one sees it up close and where the heroism on several scores appears incontestable. It seems that our generalissimo needed a rare constancy, a rare firmness, and a sort of inspiration to act efficaciously in spite of the bad will or shameless incapacity of certain leaders.

11. – "I no longer read any newspaper," a priest wrote to me. "The general blindness irritates me. They all go to the slaughterhouse like cattle who are dreaming of rich pastures along the way." I note down this phrase which is unjust if applied to everyone. How many poor folk ignorant of God are devoted nevertheless and give their life with the feelings of martyrs. God takes note of that.

The Germans, faithful to their system of devastation, have destroyed the little village of Ypres and reduced to powder les Halles, delicious monument of the 13th century.

The kaiser, invoking his God, deplores the

loss of Tsing-Tao, conquered by the Japanese. Occasion to pretend, with an impudence difficult to imagine, that the Germans wage a *defensive* war against a world of hatred, envy, and covetousness! Germany, as thus presented by its chief, resembles a hideous and dirty whore who would believe herself the object of universal desire.

12. – "If one spares the German empire," the Abbot Wetterlé writes, "if one grants it an honorable peace after its defeat, all will, in ten years time, begin anew. Those people there will never renounce their dream of universal domination, unless one definitively paralyzes their [ability to] act. They are incurable megalomaniacs, maniacs of brutal force, virtuosos of barbarity. The world will find peace again only when Prussia does not exist or has become the poor and impotent principality of Brandenburg again."

13. – Letter from Henri van Haastert:

> *... I hadn't noticed the coincidence of the first bombardment of Reims with the anniversary of the Apparition of La Salette. That is immensely remarkable! One of the things that has struck me the most in this war is that everywhere, in almost all events, one sees the apparition of the Holy Virgin,* terribilis acies ordinata. *Here's another surprising example.*

You know perhaps that in Montaigu, small village in the Campine region in Belgium, there exists a miraculous statue of Mary and that a church was consecrated to it, to which church, every year, many pilgrims come. It was in the first weeks of the war. Patrols of Uhlans were sent out everywhere ahead of the Prussian army and, one afternoon, behold the Uhlans arriving in Montaigu. Weary after a long ride, they want to stable their horses in the church. They find the door closed. An officer orders it to be staved in. Impossible. Then he has one of those small cannons brought forward, puts it in front of the door, and gives the order to fire. At the moment when the blast was about to go off, the double-entry doors open slowly by themselves, for there was someone inside the church. The officer, unfazed, orders his Uhlans to lead the horses inside. One Uhlan advances with his horse and, as they are crossing the threshold, both fall dead stiff. Then panic seizes the troop and they all turn frantic and run off. As they were quitting the village, all the bells began to ring the Angelus, *without anyone there to pull the cords.*

To Pierre:

Henri, from whom I received a nice letter this morning, tells me of his appetite for suffering. Embrace him for me and tell him to be careful. God does not grant all prayers, but when one asks for suffering from him, it is infallibly granted because it is the law, then also because in that request there is often combined, without our knowing it, a kind of presumption that must be expiated, and, as one is entering then into the Absolute, the effects can be terrible. I know something about it.

16. – Letter from a German medical officer of the 17th reserve division to his aunt who lives in Halberstadt. Remarkable extract:

I have so habituated myself to the war, little by little, that everything appears natural to me now. One is surprised sometimes when one passes by a village that is not set on fire, when one does not have to begin marching at midnight, or when a day passes that one does not see a militiaman shot.

In the evenings, one finds oneself at ease around the table, one eats dark bread with some lard, one drinks red wine which belonged to the curate who was shot, and one rejoices how well they catch fire, the houses from which one had been shot at.

18. – In the trench:

War is nice, one marches, one bombards,
One plays at Robinson. At night, one stands guard
And one sleeps finally, happy and quivering,
Rocked by shells to the sweet sound shivering.
What pleasures still the war procures us!
It is war that earns us the right to take this cure
Of open air and rest, in the great pine trees' shade,
Living off the land like rabbits and pheasants.
And they say we must go home one day maybe,
To live in houses, stand at the window and gape,
Eat at the table, with the wife, not a bomb detonating;
Eh! well, I wish to say, hold on, that's disgusting!

Dedications for a friend:

She Who Weeps. – *She weeps more than ever, the Dolorous One. She weeps tears of blood, but blind and deaf Christians continue to disdain her.*

Life of Mélanie. – *There you are, the flower of Mystery. As for me, poor among the poor, and beggar among beggars, I offer several million francs to him who will show me in all the history of the Church a saint as marvelously privileged.*

Blood of the Poor. – *The Garden of Olives was watered, but it will be*

*turned into fire when the Holy Ghost,
which has fire as its symbol, gives Testimony on earth.*

The Woman Who Was Poor. – *From
page 287 to page 382, approximative
autobiography of the author. Elsewhere still, some exact details. Can
anyone imagine a more dolorous
book?*

19. – A journalist made the celebrated Irish deputy
O'Conner speak like this:

*As long as it has not suffered some ter-
rible defeat, Germany will be unable
to sober up from 1870. That people is
still drunk. That there is the entirety of
the secret psychology, the cause of the
megalomania that, since 1870, works
on it. There are some toned-down and
innocent madnesses; others are homicidal. The German megalomania has
put on a military form, therefore it is
homicidal. And one has seen that mon-
struosity: a new Tablet [of Laws] pro-
mulgated among them, which declares
that war is not only inevitable, but de-
sirable; that it is needed for the physical and moral health of a nation, that
it is a powerful factor in the progress
of humanity. Humanity, for those people, is no longer composed of distinct*

races, each gifted with particular qualities, each having a right to life and to the fulfillment of its destiny. No, no, for them there is only a hierarchy of inferior races, with, at the summit, the German people, German militarism, German Kultur. It would be something to smile on with pity if the appalling Germanic pride had not unleashed such terrible calamities... Those people want world domination, the crushing down of everything that is not them under the Prussian boot... Of course, I hold Wilhelm II largely responsible and as a criminal, but he is not a normal man physically. You have heard him speak of his syncopes and his crises of nerves. The megalomania that his people suffer from is with him in an acute state. His discourses, his letters, his telegrams, his insistence to claim divine right, his familiarities with God, his mania to want to shine at everything – to the point that one day he dares to offer to Lenbach, the great German painter, a poor daub executed by himself and representing a naval battle, – who would dare affirm that all that comes from a sane person? Bismarck said something one day, while speaking about Wilhelm II to Sir Charles Dilke, which he repeated to me: "That man

*will never wage war; he has a bad
case of the nerves."*

Bismarck was mistaken. That
man *waged war precisely because of a
bad case of the nerves. He was unable
to resist the harmful influence of the
hateful camarilla that surrounded him.
The Kaiser has never heard an honest
or disinterested word. Did he have a
single friend in Europe? The hatred
and deaf machinations of his son, the
incapacity of his chancellor, that Bethmann-Hollweg who wanted to play at
being Bismarck; the excitations coming from military circles, all must have
made that poor sire go crazy. I have
never read anything so gripping as the
articles that tell of the Kaiser's promenade, traversing Berlin on the evening
of the declaration of war, to the cheers
of a populace drunk on pride and hatred. He, however, stiff, all alone in
his automobile, very pale, silent, sinister, bending already under the weight
of his cares, of his fears, of his presentiments, – he looked like a ghost...
That man, his punishment had begun
that very minute, looking at him gave
one a terrible feeling.*

*... You ask how the war will
finish. It will finish when vanquished
Germany and the discouraged Kaiser*

accept our conditions. Above all, the return of Alsace and Lorraine to France; the reconstitution of an independent Poland; recognition of the principle of nationalities adopted from now on as the means to resolve all European problems; remaking the map of Europe, taking into account the right of all races to self-government in all independence; formal condemnation of the German theory that one nation can, by force, take possession of the territory of another nation and enslave its inhabitants. Those are the most essential conditions. But those conditions will not be accepted by Germany except in Berlin, and in a conquered Berlin.

Now, here is what Adolf Lasson, famous professor at the university of Berlin, wrote to his Dutch friend:

... A foreigner is an enemy until he can prove the contrary. Nations do not know how to remain neutral with respect to Germany and the German people. Either one considers Germany as the most perfect political creation that History has ever known, or one approves of its destruction, its extermination. A man who is not a German does not know anything about Germany. We are morally and intellectu-

ally superior to everyone, unparal-
leled... Germany has taught the world
how to direct politics with conscience
and war with loyalty.

In this same letter which is barely credible, Wilhelm is characterized as the "delight of mankind" and Bethmann-Hollweg is called "the most eminent man alive today." In another epistle from the same person to his same friend, the following is declared: "In a world of wickedness, *we represent love,* and God is with us."

22. – The masterwork of that celebrated German organization appears to be that of pillage. When the last Germans, not yet exterminated, will have left Belgium, one asks what will remain in that unfortunate country. The Germans are extraordinary house movers. Wherever there is something possessing some value of any kind, furniture or objects of art, not to speak of silverware or jewelry, in Brussels, for example, one sees large moving vans immediately full of tables, commodes, sideboards, tapestries. All that goes to Germany. On the moving vans the names of officers are written in chalk, with their address. One does not count the objects of art that have up and vanished.

Some of the "goods of pillage" have been found on German soldiers fallen at Aerschot and at Haelen. It's their superior military authority that gives those goods to the most commendable soldiers.

"House good to pillage." Those ordinarily begin with the one's with wine cellars.

25. – A gentle professor Ostwald, laureate of the Nobel prize, has found the means of being more surprising even than professor Lasson. That man organizes Europe simply. He has discovered the "organization factor." That consists, in Germany, in "extracting from each individual a maximum output in the sense that is the most favorable to society." If the beast dies, one replaces it. Society above everything. Now, society, that means Germany, and other peoples are individuals, created and placed on earth for Germany's benefit. Pointless to say that professor Ostwald is a pacifist. All the earth having become German, which cannot wait, and the men of all nations having become the slaves of Germany, the war will have no more reason for being given the world will be definitively *organized*.

Some inferior folk will ask maybe where the souls will be situated and what role religion will take. Here is the response by the brilliant Ostwald:

> *That there is a consequence that has been impossible to avoid. The present situation necessarily evokes, in quite a few domains,* atavistic instincts. *I will say however that God the Father is reserved amongst us for the personal usage of the emperor (sic). Once, God was mentioned in a report by the great top staff general; but take note: his*

face has never been seen again.

26. – Letter by Félix Raugel:

My very dear friend, I leave a frightful battle. Miraculously, I have passed through thousands of bullets and shells. It was the battle of Cirey. I thought of you, for I was able to speak of God to all those whom I love and to repeat in manus tuas *many times. How was I able to get out alive? God did not yet want me. Very affectionately yours on this feast day of Saint Cecile, the gentle martyr.*

What music! I should have been killed by one of our 75 whose explosions got to my combat buddy. He had his thigh luxated. I only had my breath cut short. Soon afterwards, a hailstorm of bullets, and two others were killed on the spot... It was 7 o'clock in the morning and the battle didn't finish until 3:30 pm. So one had time to pray, but I wasn't afraid. We rested some days at Baccarat, demolished and burnt town, while waiting for new orders by dear France which is really, despite everything, the chosen nation and which will be saved. I know that your prayers follow me and serve as my shield.

28. – Extremely unexpected letter from Lumbroso's daughter asking for news of me. They love me and they admire me, naturally, while deploring that I could not understand such feelings. Hope for a new autograph for papa's collection. Silence.

The newspapers are filled with the news of a great victory by the Russians, at Lodz, in Poland, enormous catastrophe for Germany, it is said.

December

1st. – My *Joan of Arc* was causing me some anxiety. I could only think about the first three chapters so painfully obtained thus far, and that incertitude was a torment. Then, this morning, sudden visit by René Martineau and his lovely sister-in-law Elisabeth, come expressly to hear me read those chapters. That reading has been for me a revelation and a deliverance. Evidently, I have succeeded a great deal in this difficult work and behold me recomforted.

Admirably generous letter by Philippe Raoux who fights for four months now with great courage, although persuaded as much as I am of the emptiness of that "sacred union" that one speaks of so much and the impossibility of conserving even the illusion of it as soon as the war is over:

> ... *The days will come then when one will think back in all sweetness to the*

days of the world war which will appear almost paradisiacal in comparison with the hell that awaits us...! There will be such accounts to settle afterwards... that this apparent union absolutely will not, I believe, be reconciled with Justice... So what will happen then?

While waiting, France is pushed forward towards glory and will need to accomplish its mission, which is to exterminate that race of philosophers of darkness, of stinking modernists, and of hideous Lutherans...

What a strange encounter that the Pilgrim *should appear at the exact moment when the most gigantic war and the most supernatural one that has ever been seen should be unleashed throughout the universe...*

2. – I write to Termier that we must be on guard against losing our view, "as if we were in the middle of a crowd gone wild that rushes to see an execution."

3. – The incontestable moral superiority of the German army continues to affirm itself by the massacre of our wounded. I'm told of an ambulant medical facility where nearly 150 wounded French citizens

coming from the battle of Ethe (August 22) were located. That facility was installed in the village of Gommery (Belgian Luxembourg). All the rest of the village, moreover, was filled with miserable souls, all the granges were occupied.

Arrival of an enemy detachment. Immediate fusillade, butchery, setting of granges on fire... In the evening, after the departure of those visitors, anywhere from 75 to 80 wounded remained alive out of the 300 at least that the village had. The German troop that committed those atrocities belongs to the *47th regiment of infantry*.

(Episodes of this sort are beyond counting anymore. They have become banality itself. But an implacable inquest, methodically pursued, will make known at least the names of the head assassins who will receive their just reward, one day soon. September 15.)

4. – At the opening of the Reichstag, which just took place, the chancellor Bethmann-Hollweg has had the incommensurable cheek to pretend that Germany did not want the war.

5. – Letter from a young, wounded officer who writes to me from Bordeaux that on leaving for war, August 5, he had slipped a copy of the *Exegesis of Commonplaces* into his sack, with the regret of being unable to bring more of my books with him, and that that one sustained him quite often in the accomplishment of

his rude task. Response:

> *Yes, my dear officer, I have received your letter with pleasure, and it is I who should be thanking you for having taken the trouble to write to me that my books were of some use to you. No one thinks about it. One very gladly avoids expressing gratitude towards a writer that one knows to be miserable, and there are swine up and down the river, have no doubt about it. My 68 years have disqualified me to fight as in '70 – unfortunately.*
>
> *I am not without wounds however, as you know, having read me. Deep wounds that cannot be gotten rid of except in the cemetery. I write, at this moment, a book on* Joan of Arc, *work that I believe will be important and salutary for some souls. If you are a Christian, pray to God that he gives me the opportunity to finish it before I die of cold and misery.*

Extract from the *Lanterne* to confirm Raoux's presentiments and my own:

> *There are some of us in France whom the declaration of war did not cast down at the foot of altars. There are in this country some Republicans whom fear of the Prussian did not push, sweating with anguish, toward holy*

*images, dispensatories of victory...
They hope, these days, to glue back together the pieces of the torn Concor-
dat.*

*To require such a renunciation
(!) from a people who have affirmed
themselves to be free thinkers overly
exceeds the tactical hability and even
the prudence of attack. The adversary
who profits from our desire for patriotic concord in order to traitorously
seize positions that we have conquered
abuses our politic of "pacifism."*

*All the Machiavellis of Roman
diplomacy will not convince us that
the Republic must abjure its* principles
*(!) in order to take up relations again
with the Vatican, which were wisely
and logically broken.*

*Under threats (?) we are invit-
ed to submit. One expects that the un-
tamed free thinkers might understand
that at the end of the day the Country
deserves a mass. Now, that procedure
is of another age and we are no longer
led to believe that the tutelary shadow
of Saint Geneviève has protected
Paris, given also that Joan of Arc, ar-
dently petitioned, could not save the
Reims sanctuary, where her image
shines...*

One feels shame, sometimes, knowing how to read.

6. – Extremely pointless deglutition of the *Démon de Midi*, in two volumes, by Paul Bourget. That academician, who does not seem to know that we are at war and that the times are no longer sentimental knockabout farces, continues not to *write*. 600 pages of commonplaces. His characters, which perhaps he wanted to situate in the Absolute, are puppets made of pinewood and hinges. As soon as they appear, one knows in advance everything they are going to do. The only practically sympathetic character is the Boor, a wily industrialist who achieves cuckoldry and deputation. Pointless to say that everyone in that world there is rich. Catholicism and an itching sensation of sensual desire something fierce, such is the case of the protagonist. The more religious one is, the more exposed to temptation one is. This would not be so stupid if Bourget, who thinks he knows, could understand. But he does not understand, and he lacks all intelligence of the matter. Literarily, several passages about Auvergne rather good in his poor, coddled language. The ladies will be ravished.

9. – A large merchant from Bourg-la-Reine threatens, in the event that I do not immediately settle up with him for a draft made at the end of August, to make me incur a 5% interest rate from that time forward. Merchants, as with proprietors, are subject to a moratorium, being unable to get around it, but they do not wish to immolate themselves for the fatherland.

10. – "I am beginning to believe," Raugel writes to us, "that the absolute gift of oneself must be put above artistic genius."

Read Benedict XV's first Encyclical. Surprising mediocrity. The Pope naturally deplores the horrors of the war, but does not ascribe fault to anyone and thinks that there would be means to work things out and love one another. He sees "the ardor of religious zeal in all ecclesiastical ranks and a more vivid piety of Christian people!" Not a word of La Salette, of course.

12. – Despite the incessant constriction of heart procured by unprecedented events at the end of this year, despite constant threats of poverty, I continue my *Joan of Arc*.

13. – *The Region of Liége Under German Domination*. Title of an article in the *Journal*. The stories of that genre can be multiplied infinitely. Always the same nightmare. The systematic organization of terror by means of the most inexpiable atrocities. It is all that the German genius could come up with. To dishonor itself irrevocably for all time, to make itself execrated everywhere like demons, in the imbecilic believe that one will subdue the entire world by fear. Such is the incredibly inferior level to which Prussian Kultur has plunged the great Christian Germany of ancient times.

Long letter to Termier. I speak to him at first of my *Joan of Arc*:

> *... Dedicated to the somber blue of the Absolute, I can see things only synthetically, and that is terrible when it is a question, as in the present case, of presenting* a synthesis of strategy. *Did you know that Joan of Arc was one of the greatest captains that ever existed and men of that profession who have studied her story have no hesitation comparing her to Bonaparte, yes to Bonaparte on his best days.*

> *The good friends of the Maid want her to be supernaturally gifted to be able to lead soldiers, but they want nothing more than that for her, and sentimental religiosity intervenes soon enough to caricature that great figure. Good devotees to whom images of piety suffice, and who believe they know, would be surprised to learn that Joan of Arc's acts of war were not an expansion of her enthusiasm, but the result, more or less spontaneous, of a powerful and grave thinking.*

> *At the present hour, that's where I'm at, and I assure you that it is extremely difficult, all the more so as one must not forget, for one instant, the saint. When, with a voice that has pierced five centuries and which I still*

> *hear, Joan cried to her men: "Push*
> *forward.* It's yours!*" she expressed*
> *clearly a perfect confidence in God,*
> *but, at the same time, she spoke as a*
> *general who prepared everything and*
> *who knows what she is saying. That*
> *there is what people don't* know *about*
> *her, and it is important to show it...*

I speak also, completely naturally, about the war, about Benedict XV's deplorable Encyclical, and finally about Belgium expiating, through the destruction of its cities, the crime of having been the metropolis of Catholic Pharisaism.

14. – According to the *Times*, the situation in Anvers is terrible. There are 20,000 workers without work, and famine. A single factory functions with incessant activity, having been transformed into a crematorium furnace for German soldiers whom one incinerates by the thousands.

(To be compared with those dreadful funereal trains bringing back into Germany, after the slaughter of the Yser, armies of cadavers arranged *standing up* in the wagons and pressed one against the other to economize space. Edgar Allan Poe could not have come up with those horrors. Witnesses have seen the train tracks marked red with blood for the entire extent of it.)

15. – From Philippe Raoux:

I am surprised that certain people find what is going on to be completely natural, while visibly everything exceeds us and no purely human explanation can suffice. That coalition of the universe against execrated Germany... and all those encounters that will have been necessary to save France in spite of itself!

I am right there with you when you glimpse what sort of light will issue from parliamentary discussions later on. It will be so abominable that they will need, by complete necessity, to persecute in order to deflect the anger. They will want to escape Justice by persecution. Yes, the second act will be terrible and many will find that the first was milder.

16. – Extremely hard day. Poverty strangles us. It would seem that the suffering that has always presided over my work was favorable to it. I have never yet done so copious a job in one single day, since my book has begun.

The *Corriere della Sera* recounts how, in a sermon spoken in Berlin before three thousand people, one P. Samuel said that God was not neutral, that he was on the side of the Germans; that it was not for naught that God had placed Germany at the center of Europe...! Final victory for the Germans is certain.

Frederick the Great, didn't he declare that God is always on the side of the strongest?

When Germany ceases to be the strongest, its Old God will then need to come over to our side.

17. – A beautiful thing happened to Jeanne. Full of sadness as she was thinking that she would be forced to run to the Mont de piété [to pawn something], she opens her drawer and, because it is the anniversary of the death of her mother, she looks sadly at the dried flowers that her sister brought her from Denmark in memory of that death. Without asking for any miracle, she begins to hope for any kind of help. Suddenly, she notices, in the same drawer, a 5-franc bill that she didn't remember having left there. Enough to live on for one day. That thing happens to us quite often.

18. – It appears that the Prussian Wilhelm, dignant offshoot of the Hohenzollern robbers, not content with the annexation of Belgium, which was in the works for a long time, had, at the same time, prepared for the annexation of Switzerland, where the Kaiser himself went, two years ago, to reconnoiter his future lodgings. Today, the *Matin* publishes facsimiles of future postage stamps of the annexed Republic. Those incredible stamps, with the effigy of Germania on them, and bearing in exergue the ordinary *Deutsches Reich*, are, to add insult to injury, struck with an inscription in black letters indicating that the Swiss belong to the German empire from now on.

The Prussian professor Oniken lately wrote that the neutral States are parasites that *grow fat on the substance of great States* and that they ought to have the fate of parasites, that is to say, *to be rubbed out*.

The Vatican observes an absolute neutrality, Cardinal Gasparri, secretary of the Papal States, declares. The "Old God" of Germany is not neutral, it was said the day before yesterday. Jesus Christ's Vicar declares himself *neutral*. It is all mapped out for annexation then. But that declaration is monstrous.

"Often," Raugel writes to us, "I think that it would be a shame to survive. It will be more difficult, after the war, to be saints and heroes."

19. – The heart fails to speak about the destruction of Dinant and the horrible massacre of inoffensive citizens. This abominable history will be retold one day, with many others, and will become part of the infamous epic of the Boches that nothing would be able to efface. I do not want to accept what I read, that episode of the officer having shot 153 innocents, giving the order to machine gun the heaps of bodies, then saying to the women forced by him to watch the execution and insane with grief: "Madames, I have done my duty!"

20. – To Philippe Raoux:

Will you receive this letter by Noel? More than ever that great feast day will be notable. So many dead! So many desolate! And how many survivors will feel themselves closer to those whom they love, however great the distances! I am extremely sad, sadder doubtless than many others who cannot see what I see. But, without being surprised, I do not succeed in coming to terms with this diabolical war. The number of those who consider it as it really is, is actually very small; that is to say a colossal enterprise of brigandage and nothing else. What confounds me is the gentle, almost fraternal treatment accorded to German prisoners, when it has been demonstrated a thousand times that each one of those men is a robber, an arsonist, an assassin!

"Honor to unlucky bravery!" it is said stupidly. By the effect of a nobility of race bordering on absolute stupidity, one comes to be persuaded that this war is like all others before it, and one ends by no longer accusing the German leaders. I read an article yesterday full of good intentions, but particularly outrageous for France, saying that at bottom the German soldier is of another mentality *than the French soldier and that one needed to*

put the responsibility for the huge atrocities that you know on their leaders, by excusing the miserable souls who were forced to obey. That sottishness, come from America, I believe, felt like a slap in the face.

What to think of the cretinism or spinelessness of those who accept that? Imagine yourself a French officer giving to your men the formal order to pillage, to assassinate the wounded or elderly, to rape women, to cut off the hands of small children, to set fire to thatched cottages and churches, etc.? But the last of our troops would spit in his face and tear off his stripes! The truth, the blinding evidence, is that the German, at every level, is an abominable, heinous, and envious scoundrel who will never forgive our millenarian superiority, knowing very well, in spite of all that "Kultur" of prigs and slaves, and feeling it with rage – that he has no reason to exist, no other real subsistence than our crusts of bread, and no other function than to rinse out our chamber pots!

Is it not the height of idiocy to act chivalrously with such swine? One will pull through soon enough anyways. They worry too much! With their affairs going from bad to worse, they will need to leave us, but they will not go before destroying everything, before avenging themselves on the weak and innocent whom they have not yet assassinated, before turning Brussels, Gand, Anvers, Bruges, etc. into piles of ruin, and that will be a prodigious abomination that will make any pity for them impossible. I think that total war then will be put into practice, which I have spoken of somewhere, that is to say a war of extermination, where one no longer takes any prisoners. It is enough to make the blood boil to notice that France has condemned itself to nourishing thousands of wicked men who deserved the worst tortures, while half its children die of misery! When I read your letters, my dear Philippe, I rather guess that you are of my same sentiments.

Filled with these thoughts, I have completed half my book wherein I often speak of the present war in the context of Joan of Arc, a parallel that will give perhaps an illusion of virginity to our Joffre. You will see it in several months, if there is still a means to publish books at that time.

It is not very likely that you have read the first Encyclical by Bene-

dict XV. It is of an unprecedented indigence. The day before yesterday, the Cardinal Secretary of State informed all the universe that the Vatican observes absolute neutrality! *The Vicar of the Son of God declaring himself* NEUTRAL! *I wonder what kind of Pope has been sent to us...*

25. – To an excellent man who presented several objections to me timidly:

... As for La Salette, I think that your objections have been suggested to you by enemies of the Holy Virgin, quite simply. And that, right at the moment when the dangers brought forward 68 years ago by the Mother in tears begin to be realized. The universal ignorance of the fact of La Salette is a very great crime whose responsibility lies with the Episcopacy. From the first day, the bishops have stifled as much as they could of that Revelation. All means have been employed for that act of iniquity which will be punished, you have to believe me, in a terrible manner. Having accepted the mission to disclose it, I am however unable to address myself to those who were the instruments of it. If I had not thought it possible for me to do without the imprimatur, *I would not have obtained*

any *bishop [as censor] for it, my book would never have been published, and the Holy Virgin would have remained without witness. Not belonging, moreover, to any sacerdocy, and not touching on Doctrine, I had no need for that too often pharisaical formality. Not wishing to be, as so many others, a "mute dog," I have carried on regardless then, in all surety of confidence.*

I do not know what you mean by "the original" of the Secret. You have the text before your eyes, at the end of She Who Weeps, *such as it was published, in 1879, with the* imprimatur *of Mgr. Zola, bishop of Lecce, and no other exists, unless it is in the imagination of ignoramuses or impotents.*

As for the "Passion of the Holy Ghost" which troubles you, I can answer you, in several words, that it would be deeply unjust to attribute the value of a doctrinal teaching to a poetic expression. That is a perfidious maneuver practiced many times in the past in my regard. You can offer that response to the malevolent.

26. – To my good friend, Friar D***:

... The times have grown horribly dark, my dear friar. Happy are those who are dead in the Lord! Something that is seen everywhere, and more and more by Christians, is practical atheism *among the greater part of them. You have noticed the most apparent symptom of it: priest-soldiers, proud to be such, that is to say divine law subalterned, held as accessory by the ministers themselves,* being uninterested in public safety *and, by consequence, negligible. From the position of non-Christians, it is the divinization of the Republic, alone capable of saving France.*

When the German danger will have been definitively put behind us, which is probable, our offended Lord and his Mother in tears, not wishing all the same to abandon their beautiful kingdom to swine; yes, in the case of the definitive victory of the allies, what will happen? It is quite simple. God will no longer exist at all, as it will have been demonstrated that one can so easily do without Him. Ah! the gift of prophesy is not necessary for the discernment of that very near future. The government and administration, at every level, are in the hands of the Free Masonry. One groans more or less hypocritically over the destruction of Belgium, destruction that will be, one presumes, entirely complete, and one will be surprised by it, forgetting or not wishing to know that Belgium, for a long time now, was the metropolis of Pharisaical Catholicism. One has Protestant England and Schismatic Russia for allies. Renegade and Garibaldian Italy, which counts hundreds, and perhaps thousands, of altars to Satan, will hardly tarry in joining us, when it sees that we are decidedly the strongest. After victory, it will be necessary to do something for those good friends. And what more agreeable thing could one offer to them than the effective destruction of what remains to us of Christianity? Our bishops, persecutive of Mélanie, will employ themselves with great zeal.

One talks a great deal about the little Belgian children with their hands cut off, Teutonic abomination that one can barely comprehend, and which makes the sweat of death come to the bravest among us. I have just read in the *Journal* a sort of poem: the Kaiser meeting, on the night of Noel, the little baby Jesus with his hands cut off, and I recall all of a sudden those frightening photographs come from Belgian Congo wherein it was seen, several years ago, unfortunate negroes whose hands had been cut off by the colonists!... *Fracturam pro fractura, oculum pro ocu-*

lo, MANUM PRO MANU... [62]

28. – Raugel writes to me that he expects, for 1915, terrible events. "The cannon thunders non-stop. That makes me, for the first time in my life, suffer during the sweet night of Noel. When it came though, peace reigned o'er all the earth."

---

[62]Fracturum... manu: Latin for, "A broken bone for a broken bone, an eye for an eye, a hand for a hand."

1915

January

1st. – "I believe," a religious wrote to me, "that what fans the flames of Paul Bourget's patriotism is the fact that he is 62 years old and that no one will remember the class of 1873."

2. – On the occasion of the New Year, the bloody Show Off has addressed a hypocritical proclamation to his troops and to all of Germany, in which he cannot stop himself from acknowledging that the situation is serious. He speaks of "brilliant battles won," of his vassals who "have heaped honor on themselves," but, at the same time, of the "sacred hearth that we *defend* against criminal attack"... "The growing number of our enemies will not frighten us. Although the situation might be serious, and the task *arduous*, we can look to the future with a firm confidence in the *enlightened* (!) aid of God." What a sinister and glum clown!

3. – Horrible story. One receives a letter from a prisoner saying that he is treated by the Germans with gentleness and kindness. The letter is dictated, of course. But the prisoner inserted a postal stamp for

the so-called collection of the recipient, and behold what is found on the reverse of that stamp: "I tried to escape, and they cut off both my feet!!!"

One begins to suspect that the assassination of the Archduke François-Ferdinand and his wife, pretext for the war against Serbia that soon became a world war, was a simple machination of imperial politics. *One had need of a grievance*. The underbelly of history will not be known except at the Last Judgment when the emperor of demons takes the stand.

4. – To Jean de la Laurencie:

> *Dear friend, my wife, who saw you yesterday, tells me that you attribute to me the power of recomforting you. You have already written to me such things and that always astonishes me. It must be you have no other contemporaries to turn to, to think you have need of me! I too have a real need to rely on someone else! How many times I have tried! How many times I have thought I found columns of granite which turned out to be only ashes or worse still! And I am quite afraid, myself, of being nothing but that for you.*
>
> *The little I have, God gave me so that I might not be for nought, and what use have I made of it? The worst evil is not – to commit crimes, but not*

*to have accomplished the good that
one could have. That is the sin of*
omission, *which is nothing other than
non-love and which nobody accuses
himself of. Someone who observes me
each day at first mass would see me
often weeping. Those tears, which
could be holy, are instead very bitter
tears. I am not thinking, at that time,
of my sins, some of which are enormous. I am thinking of what I could be
able to do and what I have not done,
and I assure you that that is very
dark...*

*Do not tell me that that is the
case with everyone. God had given me
the sense, the need, the instinct – I
don't know how to say it – of the Absolute, as he has given needles to the
porcupine and a trunk to the elephant.
Extremely rare gift that I have felt
since my childhood, more dangerous
and more torturing faculty than genius
even, given that it involves a constant
and furious appetite for what does not
exist on earth and for what infinite
isolation has procured for it. I could
have become a saint, a thaumaturge. I
have become a man of letters.*

*Those phrases or those pages
that one wishes to admire, if one only
knew that they were merely the residue*

*of a supernatural gift that I have odi-
ously frittered away, and which I will
be asked to give a redoubtable account of one day! I have not done what
God wanted from me, that is certain. I
have dreamt, on the contrary, about*
what I wanted from God, *and look at
me now, 68 years old, not having anything but paper in my hands! Ah! well
do I know that you will not believe me,
that you will suppose, – I do not know
what, – some innermost repair of humility. Alas! when one is alone in
God's presence, at the entrance to a
very somber path, one has a discernment of oneself and is poorly posi-
tioned to lie to oneself about it! Real
goodness, a totally pure goodwill, the
simplicity of small children, – what I
call the kiss from the Mouth of Jesus,
– one knows quite that one does not
possess it and that one really has
nothing to give to the poor suffering
hearts that implore secours. That is
my situation, with respect to you, dear
friend. Without a doubt, I can pray for
you, I can suffer with you and* for *you,
trying to bear a little of your burden;
yes, but the drop of water drawn from
the chalice of terrestrial Paradise, – it
is impossible for me to give that to
you. Today, I felt that I had the duty to
tell this to you so that you might not*

count too much on a weak and sor-
rowful creature...

6. – Belgian Catholics complain that Benedict XV,
who exploits his inconceivable neutrality, has not
raised his voice to condemn the German horrors committed in their country. That pope, whose face is anti-
pathic, I really do not know what to think of him. If
he is, as some say, a politician, and nothing but that, it
is something to cause fear. At the moment of his election, the war was in full swing, the danger was frightening for us, for all of Europe, and the victory of the
Marne was not yet to be anticipated. What a magnificent figure he could have cut at the beginning of his
pontificate by throwing a great Interdiction over all
Catholic, and so-called *apostolic,* Austria if it did not
immediately sever ties with heretical and brigand
Germany; by threatening the most redoubtable canon-
ical difficulties for the ecclesiastical dignitaries of
Germany itself, the which have placed themselves
basely, sacrilegiously, at the command of the Kaiser
to encourage the massacre of priests and the profana-
tion of churches in all invaded countries. What a
unique occasion to give back to the Papacy its ancient
prestige!

Dedication to my friend Henri Boutet, for *The
Pilgrim of the Absolute*:

*Pilgrimage without return. One does
not pick up travelers along the way, on
the contrary. There are no wagons-lits
nor wagons-restaurants. One is abso-*

lutely miserable and the terminus is beyond the most distant stars.

7. – A wounded Belgian soldier wrote to me that my books have made him into a Christian, and he thanks me. Response:

> *Dear comrade, your letter touches me greatly. It is a marvelous sensation for a poor writer to learn that his books can be useful to a man who suffers the worst difficulties, having generously made the sacrifice of his life. The epoch is terrible. God sorts out his friends today. Whatever your fatigues and your sufferings, how preferable your situation is to that of many of your companions who do not know what they do nor why they suffer! You are perfectly and holily blessed, have no doubt about it.*

8. – This morning the newspapers publish the first report by the Commission of inquest. Dossier of German crimes. Terrifying.

> In the *Echo of Paris*, from the 6th:
>
> *Ouzouer-sur-Trézée, January 3.*
>
> *Today, in our region, where we have installed (French Red Cross, marquis de Vogüé) three hospitals that hold the*

wounded, Briare, Gien, Ouzouer-sur-Trézée, a solemn Requiem mass in memory of the "soldiers and sailors who have died while in active service for France" has been held.

Mgr. Touchet, Bishop of Orléans, presided over the ceremony... It goes without saying that the place was packed... It has been like that in the countrysides (!?) for four months now. Ever since one chants the canticles at church, everyone comes (!) and is borne along "to the religious cadence"; then, at the exit, one often hums the Marseillaise, and the curate comes and joins in...

Mgr. Touchet has given a very remarkable, "very laic" discourse of superb inspiration. On several occasions, he has spoken of Barrès (!), has cited his articles (!!), and in one of his parenthetical remarks, I found this: "... The *Echo of Paris* which was, since those days of sorrows, the VERITABLE VIATICUM of France." *(!!!)*

Oh! the worthy and holy bishop! The *Echo of Paris*, doubtless, does not know its good fortune to be able to publish that shameful advertisement.

9. – Like me, Cornuau foresees the worst horrors to come after the war, and he sends me copy of some

pages, in that sense, letters by Mélanie which were entrusted to him. But those pages add nothing to what I have known for a long time now. When will Providence deign to send us the Man who would be needed to rid us of the prattlers... the political whores?

Threat, frightening for all of France, of the imminent reopening of Parliament.

13. – One begins to be surprised by England which had promised to send a million combatants and which has sent, thus far, only 200,000, leaving almost all the weight of the war on us.

14. – An earthquake has just caused thirty thousand victims in Italy. (Mélanie's Secret.)

15. – Benedict XV's politics. It appears that the Papal nuncio to the Belgian court, Mgr. Tacci Forcelli, most recently would have offered a dinner to the German authorities, in his nunciature's palace, in Brussels, on the Wavre causeway. The gathering was supposed to have been really Germanic so one had drunk, in chalices stolen from churches, the blood of thus-far sixty or eighty assassinated Belgian priests.

16. – *Joan of Arc and Germany*, such will be the title of my new book, decidedly. Here I am, very near to the end of it.

I cannot avoid, for the conclusion, saying some words about Luther. Reading his last German historian, Father Denifle, exceptionally learned Catholic religious, but heavy like all the mountains on the moon, who shows the heresiarch however in his patriarchal hideousness of German ignominy.

17. – Gospel message of the day: *Deficiente vino*[63]... Where are the priests? Where are the bishops? Where is the Pope[64]

> To Jacques Maritain:
>
> *I suffer for not seeing you, my dear godchildren. Everything becomes so somber! This horrible war fills me with anguish every instant. It is such a demoniacal vision of perfect justice! And Benedict XV, who could do such great things and who declares himself* neutral! *And our Christian contemners of La Salette who admire themselves, believing themselves heroic! And all the cavalry of the Abyss that is on the march!*

19. – German losses: 1,500,000 men in five months, not counting the sick or ill! That is what the newspa-

[63]*Deficiente vino...*: Latin for "And when they wanted wine..." John 2:3.

[64]Editor's note: the remainder of the sentence has been suppressed here, by the original censors.

pers say. They do not mention our own.

In one year, that will be double or triple. The Republic and Napoleon, after twenty years of continual warfare, did not exact so large a number. Those figures make one's head spin.

20. – To a friend who procured the money for my tax contributions:

> *The tax collector is paid, joylessly. I have always been persuaded that the sums forked over to that functionary were like bread thrown into the loo. I still think so, and you seem to be of the same opinion more or less. A day will come when there will be no more tax collectors, nor proprietors, nor even merchants of any kind. That is how I imagine Paradise, where your place is certainly marked next to mine. 1915 will perhaps earn us that happy encounter.*

21. – The newspapers are filled with the story of German dirigibles that have been the cause of some damage in England. Their bombs have assassinated several inoffensive people and destroyed here and there some houses. That farce is assuredly not to the English taste and will not dispose them to kindness.

22. – Letter from Philippe Raoux:

I have received your letter from the 2ⁿᵈ, – I should say your formidable letter, insofar as it strongly moved me. As for me, very humble participant in this operation of extermination, in this apocalyptic war, I have the impression that nobody understands anything about what is going on. When I read you, I am enlightened. I seem to understand, as much as I can understand of the inexpressible mysteriousness of events.

For example, the victory of the Marne, which I do not tire reading about. I am stupefied that one might not be blown away by the supernaturalness of that vision, which history provides no other example of, and the more I learn the facts that preceded it, the more miraculous it appears to me... what I am saying is that it cannot humanly be explained,... nor that sort of statu quo *in which the entire campaign seems to have been brought to a standstill. All that has a strange character to it. Of course, we will win, but too often one forgets that there is an expiation that is only now beginning. It is the Wrath of God, the Indignation of God. Just as you wrote about it to your brother D***, the fact that there are priest-soldiers in the war is the* *supplement of iniquity to be expiated. I confess that I had hardly seen anything but this: the hands the Bishop solemnly consecrated such that they might give Life have failed in their sacred ministry and have administered Death; but the "divine Law subalterned," – that evidently is the extraordinary offense...*

Soon, it will have been six months since the war started, and it seems to me that the real war has not yet begun. There is nothing really to do but to abandon oneself to God in complete confidence and love... but I am afraid that our Chambers, so worthy of esteem, as one knows, have not in gestation many other means at their disposal. At this moment, all calamities are to be feared, and I understand that you expect them in the absolute certainty that you will see them before leaving.

During the course of the Consistory that was held this morning, the Pope spoke at length about the war. After having deplored the massacres and his powerlessness, he declares however that "the highest duty that is incumbent on the Sovereign Pontiff is to proclaim that nobody is permitted, for whatever motive it might be, to lese justice." But he adds that, for all that, it is pointless to engage pontifical authority in the belligerents' litigation itself. If that is the case, one does not see at all how one could practice the high duty in question. Benedict XV supposes a *litigation*. What a strange word? The sack of Rome by Alaric was a litigious case then? He declares further that being the common father of all the faithful, he cannot "adhere to either of the two parties," which is the same as saying that the father of a family, seeing the stronger of his children crush his brothers, must suspend his judgment and abstain from all blame for an indeterminate time.

Finally that extraordinary phrase: "For those who see their country occupied by the enemy, we understand how hard it must be to find yourself under the foreigner's yoke, but we would not want that their ardent desire to recover independence should lead them to get in the way of the *maintenance of public* ORDER!!!"

So, then, unbridled pillage, savage destruction, the raping of women, the massacring or torturing of old people and children, – all that is public order, the German order, and it is appropriate to respect it...

Terram miseriæ et tenebrarum, ubi umbra mortis et nullus ordo, sed sempiternus horror...[65]

24. – An extraordinary secours comes to me. I can pay my proprietor.

25. – To a lady who says she is obsessed by my

---

[65] *Terram... horror...*: Job 10:22.

books:

> *... You ask me if this war has not en-*
> *lightened Catholics about me, if it puts*
> *the clergy at my feet, etc. Here is my*
> *response. Nothing could change the*
> *Catholics you speak of. The war, far*
> *from enlightening them, augments*
> *their blindness and I am, more than*
> *ever, their* bête noire, *having commit-*
> *ted the unpardonable crime of taking*
> *divine law seriously, of being an* abso-
> lute *Catholic, the only one among all*
> *those who speak or write. I will never*
> *be forgiven for that. The punishment is*
> *facile. Prohibition of purchasing my*
> *books, prohibition of reading them*
> *and speaking about them. One knows*
> *the author to be poor. What a victory*
> *if one could make him die of misery!*
> *The conspiration of silence. It is an*
> *immense honor for me to be treated*
> *exactly like Our Lady of La Salette*
> *whom it is highly recommended not to*
> *pay any attention to. The effect of that*
> *chastisement is naturally misery, par-*
> *ticularly today...*

> *You are right to think that La*
> *Salette is unknown. Whose fault is*
> *that, if not the clergy's, who have so*
> *criminally cast her aside and calumni-*
> *ated her for sixty-eight years? The*
> *priest who spoke ill to you about*

Mélanie is a wretch. Supposing even that he is nothing but an imbecile, which is possible, all the same he did the work of the demon by seeking to empoison your soul, and he placed himself in great danger. Pius X, who was a saint with miracles, *profoundly venerated Mélanie. I have made a great effort to make her known. My books will tell you what one should think about that extraordinary creature whom the lowest ecclesiastics dare speak of with an insolence that makes one shudder.*

I send to you a copy of The Pilgrim of the Absolute, *my last book. I recommend the entry that begins on page 227. It is a preface excluded from a recent edition of* The Desperate Man *for reasons of merchandising. Read that, and it will inform you a great deal more about my person than I could do in a long letter. When you come to know all my books, many of which are the direct or indirect story of my life, you will perhaps be astonished that a man could have been singled out for so dreadful an existence. If our correspondence should continue, I will explain that to you. I will tell you also what I think of Lourdes and many other things.*

While waiting, I affirm to you that you are cruelly mistaken and that you deprive yourself of the most precious secours by not taking communion save "rarely." Me, I take communion every day, not because I am more pious than anyone else, but because God requires it and it is a formal precept, whatever your priests might say. The daily bread *that you have the right to ask for is not the bread that bakers sell; it is the Body of Christ, and if you ask for it, why not eat it? Everything that afflicts you would disappear and your prayers would become efficacious. Without quotidian communion, I would have been dead a long time ago...*

27. – Visit to Henri Boutet. He inhabits, behind the hideous Protestant temple, in Bourge-la-Reine, a small, lovely house separated from his atelier by a small garden where the least exotic plants grow as they please. Impression of finding oneself in the company of Balzac, in the company of an old artist of yesteryear, of sixty years ago. Good-naturedness, finesse, talent, and poverty. Those exemplary qualities have become rare. One cannot look them straight in the face without turning one's back disrespectfully on an entire century.

(One will be astonished, one day, by the deluge of inept books that the war will produce.

Monochromatic and monochord brochures in which new commonplaces triumph, which are already legion, which our unfortunate language is afflicted with for eighteen months now. How refreshing to encounter finally a very simple, very humble book: *The Heart of Paris*, by Henri Boutet; book of grievous compassion written by that artist with the broken heart, where the soul of a child appears, whom the Germans would have cut the hands off of, alas! but so French and so generous that it is not possible to read it without emotion! – Publisher: Crès; February, 1916.)

The priest-soldiers. The curate of Ponsault-Combault (Seine-et-Marne) had enrolled in the military almoners of Albert de Mun and he was about to depart when the German wave came to menace the fortresses of Paris. His place having become more useful amidst his parishioners, he stayed. But December 4, he was drafted, *to his great joy*, in the armed service. Here is what he wrote:

> *The priest under the soldier's capote, leading the same life, knowing the same fatigues, subject to the same dangers, finds himself in the best situation to warm hearts, sustain spirits, and exercise his ministry. But his incorporation is made to wait. To think that all my parishioners have departed, the majority of them into the trenches.* And me, at thirty-three years old, I stay back with the women and disabled!... *I am trained in physical*

exercises, having always directed gymnastic clubs. I am a good shooter, *etc.*

The good patriots of the *Lanterne* or the *Guerre sociale* have to admire priests of that ilk. They will know how to compensate them at the right time.

28. – To Termier:

> *Given that you pray for me, remember to ask God to give me the light that seems today refused to everyone.* Domine fac ut videam.[66] *It is the prayer of the blindman of Jericho, my habitual prayer for thirty-five years now. When I die, they will probably be my last words. Never has there been so many blindmen. It suffices to cast one's eyes on a newspaper. It's disconcerting and numbs the mind.*
>
> *You have seen the highest glory awarded to Garibaldi's grandchildren, by whom we are beaten down for two weeks now, ignoble sycophancy for renegade Italy's benefit, proud to have seen the hero of the Freemasonic riffraff march out with Napoleon III like a puppet, in 1859. You see our Catholics represented by the* Echo of

---

[66]*Domine fac ut videam*: Latin for, "God make it so that I might see."

Paris, contemners and blasphemers of La Salette, so content with themselves, so sure of divine benediction! You see finally and above all Benedict XV declaring neutrality, *while his children are massacred by the hundreds of thousands and believing in politics, without having even thought to use the redoubtable arms in his possession!*

As for me, dear friend, I am always at the same point. Knowing that what is happening is only a curtain rise, I wait for the real drama, I wait for Someone. That someone certainly exists, in the most impenetrable obscurity. He is here or there, very far or very near. When he enters onto the scene finally, a prodigious quantity of scales will fall from everyone's eyes, and there will be an enormous clamor in the world. Such is the spectacle that is promised us, my dear Termier, and I really hope to be sitting in the first row, having paid dearly for my place and those of some others.

February

2. – Here is what, to my surprise and joy, a Catholic has just written on the subject of Benedict XV's neutrality:

When the gentle shepherd Abel was assailed by the savage Cain, when the blood of the first man assassinated had reddened the earth and cried to heaven, Adam did not say: "I am the common father. That is why I remain neutral, limiting myself to making vows so that peace might be restored between my children." He curses the murderer. Eve herself curses him. Under that double reprobation, the ancestor of all men of prey, the Nimrods, the Attilas, the Timurs, the Wilhelms, Cain, excommunicated, was plunged into the obscurity of his exile.

Holy Father, not merely thousands of human voices implore you: voices of soiled women, massacred children, tortured priests; but the voices of stones and church bells, the voices of Louvain, Malines, Termonde, and Reims; Holy Father, it is not your neutrality that religion has need of! There used to be popes who, like the magnanimous Gregory VII, had taken up the motto: "I loved justice and I hated iniquity." Those popes would not have hesitated, according to the formula of two Romes, to "speak the Law." Provided you deign to look for it, you will find it, Holy Father! And we, your children in Belgium and France, we are fearless as to the judg-

ment that, granted to the duty of your charge, you will promulgate then with sovereign authority.

3. – To the obsessed lady:

... It happens, and that is a kind of prodigy, that you think or that you feel exactly like I do about everything. Example: I have nothing more to say to you about Lourdes, given, from the very start, before I had time to open my mouth, you made me understand that it is the abominable mercantilism practiced in that place that revolts you, to the point, you tell me, that you are unable to recite an Ave Maria. *As for me, I feel myself capable of the Angelic Salutation wherever I am, but it seems to me that at Lourdes that prayer would leave me like an incendiary bomb against the despicable shops. I have never wanted to go there then, and I am not near consenting to it. As for miracles, I have already asked for this: A Christian full of sanctity making a pilgrimage to Lourdes to ask for the cure for a malady and returning with joy, leprous or paralytic. That there is the miracle I would like to see, the others don't interest me.*

I have thought, quite often, that the innumerable disabled who were healed by Our Lord must have been in the crowd that was asking with rage for his crucifixion: Meditate on that, and an additional idea will come to you perhaps about Lourdes, considering that the people miraculously cured or so-called miraculously cured are very probably the worst enemies of Our Lady of La Salette who had only her Tears to propose to them. You must understand me quite well, given you feel the injustice "with tremendous indignation." But then a part of the vast store of that indignation would need to be reserved for yourself who dare to write to me! that quotidian communion is good only for others, because you are too "indignant." A little common sense, I entreat you. What would you think of a soldier on the front who said to his captain, "I refuse to obey you, because I am too indignant to fight."

As for the suffering that you do not understand, I hope that God will make you understand by placing at the bottom of your heart the certain truth that there are creatures in his image who suffer for you, who carry their load. That, I can tell you with infinite certitude from personal experience. "Each time someone suffers in body or soul, there is someone who pays for it."

You will find that in The Pilgrim of the Absolute, *and I'm not the one who invented it. Among my books, there is* Blood of the Poor, *wherein I do not stop saying it. It's a book that I am particularly fond of. But, fundamentally, what difference does this or that make? I have always written the same thing and it will not take you long to perceive it.*

*I do not fear any incomprehension from you, since I know your annoyance hearing me called "a great pamphleteer and powerful writer." That encourages me to send you a book that would be certainly condemned by the Abbot Bethléem. (*Je M'Accuse...*) Without being otherwise surprised by my cheek, you will notice, once again, the virtuosity with which I pass from canticle to the most violent bawling out, when it is a question of demolishing a villainous person. You will notice above all, I insist on this point, that I always say the same things, in one language or another, no matter what anyone might think and whatever might result, having uniquely in view the glory of God, which is the complete secret of my sorrowful life.*

"What do you want from me?"

> *you cried in your anguish. "It's you*
> *whom I want," said the Holy Ghost,*
> *"and it is because I want you that I*
> *have sent to you that poor man who*
> *has received from me the power to*
> *awaken some souls..."*

4. – Saw Léon Bonhomme. He lives in Saint-Denis, in an environment extremely hostile to religion. He spoke to me about Benedict XV whose obscure and timid conduct scandalizes so many Christians. He has been witness, among his entourage, to the triumph of the impious saying, "There he is, your pope! He is neutral; *in other words, on the side of the strongest.*" What to respond to those miserable wretches? I think the demon could not suscitate a heresiarch as lethal as that pontiff.

6. – Finished *Joan of Arc and Germany*. God alone knows what that book cost me.

To a friend who sent me some money so that I could, on the occasion of Mardi Gras, "disguise my thinking, which would be the source of my fortune":

> *Disguise my thinking! you say. I do*
> *nothing but that, for a long time now,*
> *as I have succeeded in making believe*
> *that I am a monster of violence, when*
> *the opposite is precisely my case.*
> *However, I have not made a fortune.*
> *On the occasion of Mardi Gras, I can*

*try still to be agreeable to you. But I
have so extraordinary a head that it
breaks all the new masks that can be
found for sale. It's discouraging.*

10. – To Philippe Raoux:

*You speak to me of the surprise that
the incomprehensible victory of the
Marne and the surprising immobility
subsequent to it gives you. Here is
what a Dutch Catholic wrote to me:
"Is it not satanic in the highest degree,
that near immobility of six peoples,
armed, boiling with hate, enraged and
gnashing their teeth, furiously desiring
to exterminate one another, and* being
unable to. *God chastises people by
means of the Demon, and to be punished by Satan like God's instrument,
– is that not hell itself?"*

*We are in that strange situa-
tion of being unable to do anything decisive before the Russian triumph. And
then!... With Germany reduced to despair, there will be what I have called*
total *war, that is to say, extermination.
One has barely the ability to conceive
such a horror. Nevertheless, that perfect abomination, would it be anything
other than the curtain rise? It seems to
me that the real apocalyptic drama*

will play out like this: the German monster definitively beaten down and all peoples rushing at the quarry, each wanting to get a bigger piece of the rotting carcass. Say it, my dear Philippe, that we were born to see these things.

As for that which regards France in particular, you were able to notice much better than me the scandalous and inept apotheosis of Garibaldi's progeniture, who have been harassing us for several weeks now. Garibaldi the hero of Lodges and occult societies, because of his hatred for Christianity. What do you think of that sign?

Our Lady of Compassion is always weeping on her Mountain, more forgotten, more disdained than ever. What an account to settle! With that, one prescribes prayers "for peace"! Yes, prayers in contempt of the Mother of God's Tears, prayers in Disobedience of Neutrality! One will see where that gets us.

Printed dedication of *Joan of Arc and Germany:*

*To Thérèse Brou
du Lys,*

Joan of Arc's
Great-Grandniece

This book, my dear child, was written for you. It will remind you, every day, that you have the duty to become a saint and – if God requires it – a martyr, in the example of your marvelous Forebear who gave her life to save France.

You have the incomparable honor and privilege of that ascendancy that makes you much more than a princess, by imposing on you the obligation to practice the highest virtue.

God served first! *responded Joan of Arc to her accusers. Those three words could have been her motto. Make them yours, my dear Thérèse, and be her heir in that way.*

13. – Received the *Corriere della Sera* from Milan. An article marked in red emphasizes that absurdity of prescribing prayers for peace, when no one can pray except for victory.

There would need to be a response. Prayers for peace naturally suppose war. Now, *there is no war*. There is in Belgium, in France, and elsewhere, a formidable invasion of brigands and ferocious animals, which is completely different. There cannot be any question then of peace. It is a matter solely of defending oneself by exterminating the criminals and the ravagers by all means possible. How does the Pope not understand so simple a thing? He is mistaken *infallibly*, that is for sure. It is justice that one must demand. I believe even that one would need to pray for Benedict XV who does not do his duty as the father of a family, the which should, as I have already said, condemn with the greatest vehemence those of his children who take advantage of their strength to crush the weakest. The German or Austrian bishops who bless the assassins and the arsonists ought to be struck inexorably by him. That is suggested by the most elementary common sense.

14. – Words of a priest cited with admiration by the *Journal*:

> *Eh well! as divine mercy has not wanted to prevent such massacres, I am happy, I tell you sincerely, that I should be* allowed *(!) to take part in the ordeal. As for my strong points, it is not a great gift that I am able to offer to the fatherland. I am a stone thrower, I have to confess, and if one made me a sergeant it is not the case that I might have the opportunity to provide the most precious of services.*

> *But at least I would have done my* duty *(!). Yes, me, a minister of the God of peace, I congratulate myself each day for having made war like ev-*

*eryone else... I would have preferred
to remain praying (!!!) while the others combatted.*

Here is, one tells us, what the majority of
Americans think, with the exception of those of German origin.

The insane Kaiser will not win. The
world's good sense *is with the allies.
Wilhelm thinks he is a superior man,
but the devil will explain to him one
day that he is merely a superior instrument of evil.*

Being mindful of God's Wisdom, I think that
the Devil will not grant any superiority to the Kaiser,
even as an instrument. One must be an American to
see in Wilhelm anything else than a blood-thirsty imbecile.

15. – From Lieutenant-Colonel Rousset:

*What is interesting is the cynicism
with which the Teutons not only avow,
but go out of their way to justify the
atrocities that they multiply against
defenseless localities and populations
oppressed by them. An article in the*
Gazette de Cologne *signed by a certain Walter Bloem is, in this regard, a
monument of monstrous conscience:
"We have," he said, "taken it as a
principle that the fault of a single per-*

*son must be expiated by the entire col-
lectivity to which he belongs."*

*The fault? What fault? Can
one qualify, in that way, the act by
which a patriot seeks to serve his
country or simply to protect his family
and hearth? "If the* culpable *party
cannot be designated," Herr Bloem
continues, "then the innocent must pay
in their place. Each time a village is
set fire to, each time hostages are executed, each time inhabitants of a com-
munity are decimated, those are less
the acts of vengeance than warnings
for regions not occupied."*

*It has to do, then, for the Ger-
mans, with seeding terror along their
way. It is evidently a system, but which
makes those who employ it outlaws of
humanity and legitimizes all future
vengeances on the certain day of their
liquidation.*

*As for the rest of it, the timid
editor appears to forget, unless he's
ignorant of it, that in 1813 the King of
Prussia Frederic-Wilhelm III had published a rescript ordering all the inhabitants of his kingdom, called or not
called to arms, to* fight tooth and nail
against *Napoleon's soldiers. Something that, one century ago, was considered by the Prussians a pious act,*

would become a crime then when it is practiced against them? And is it also quite certain that their acts of banditry have always had for an excuse, if they should have so much as one, some general outcry by isolated civilians?

The truth is that the Germans wage an atrocious war, as has never been seen since the invasions of Barbarian hordes. And for all the impossible justifications they might try to find, it will not prevent us from remembering, when the hour strikes, justice and punishment.

16. – To Felix Raugel:

We have just received, with extreme joy, your portrait, which gives us a rather advantageous idea of your physique as a combatant. I will not go so far as to say that you are an irresistible beauty, but I see that the existence of a field mouse has nowise debilitated you, and that is already a great deal for a lion-terrier momentarily deprived of a mane. In return for that precious image, I expedite The Pilgrim of the Absolute *to you, with this letter,*

... Yes, you give them a thrashing little by little (the Boches), well do

I know, and I know also that one will finish by "having" them completely. But, while we wait, they continue their filthy acts and their infamies, and it is extremely hard to think about. The "Religio depopulata" pope, the neutral *pope encourages the crushed, the burnt, the plundered, the violated people of Belgium and France to respect "public order," that is to say to show themselves obedient and affable towards their assassins. Ah! one must have a faith of nine lives! With that, he prescribes prayers* for peace. *Peace with enraged pigs! What else will we see? Impossible to tell you all that I am thinking in a letter that the first man to come along can read. But you will divine easily what may boil in the soul of a Christian who has written* She Who Weeps. *What is happening after six months is only a prelude. The real apocalyptic drama has not begun. It is what Mélanie would say if she were still alive. It pleased God to have us born the spectators of it, and we have nothing better to do than to want it, while blessing it for this privilege.* Nunc dimittis... Sursum corda.

"*Joan of Arc* mit uns!" *In a church in Longwy a statue of Joan of Arc had escaped bombardment. The Boches scratched off the engraved inscription on the plinth and replaced it with this, in German:*

*The Maid of Orleans has always been
the adversary of the English. The
French combat today beside the English. Joan of Arc cannot be with the
French. She is with us.*

17. – To Jeanne Boussac. I write to her what I have
already written to many others, about my book, about
the Pope whom I call Pope Pilate XV, about the continuation of contempt for La Salette, about the consecutive apotheosis awarded to the Garibaldians and
the certitude of a violent persecution after victory –
perhaps before.

I begin to grow furiously weary of always
writing the same things.

18. – All the newspapers talk about is Wilhelm's
project of a maritime blockade of England by German
submarines which would torpedo and sink not only
English ships, but all neutral ships, without any regard for human life.

21. – Eighty-six million Germans and one hundred
thirty million slaves. That is what one of their oracles
wrote in the volume entitled *Grossdeutschland und
Mitteleuropa um das Jahr 1950* (Thorman, Berlin),
page 48:

*In a span of several years, which will
be short, we should see this: The German flag will give shelter to 86 million*

Germans and these latter will govern a territory populated by 130 million Europeans. Over that vast territory, only the Germans will exercise political rights; only they will serve in the navy and in the army; only they will be able to acquire land. They will be, then, as in the middle ages, a race of masters, condescending simply to this, that inferior work ought to be executed by the peoples subjected to their domination.

23. – Some extracts from the official instructions given to German officers, a manual published by the Great General Staff of Berlin. That manual wants, principally, to protect the officers against the excessive sensibility that they might have:

- *The only true humanity consists in the often brutal application of certain severities.*

- *The brutal employment of means of defense (?) and intimidation necessary against inhabitants is not only a right, but even a duty for the army commander.*

- *Can one kill prisoners of war? Response: That is not pretty, but sometimes it can be HANDY!*

- *Can one make use of Sicarii and fire-throwers? Response: It is not very seemly (anstaendig), but the law of war is not delicate (empfindlich).*

- *The elderly, women, and children must not be permitted to leave a city before bombarding it, for their presence constitutes a great advantage.*

- *A war conducted with energy cannot be directed simply against the combatants of the enemy State and the positions that they occupy:* it must also destroy all intellectual and material resources of that State.

Edit it a little and you will have, *in images*, the complete program of future war against the Church of which this despicable war appears to be merely the prefiguration.

24. – A marvelous person, learning that my book cannot be published for nothing, has assumed all the costs. Georges Crès will be the publisher.

27. – Joyful news. We learn of the imminent return of van der Meer, my dear Pierre having obtained a job as a correspondent in Paris for a large Dutch newspaper.

March

1st. – Two dedications to my friend Charles Grolleau:

> Blood of the Poor. – *I have often been treated as a scatalogue. That makes up part of my legend. What would one not say if I had written "Blood of the Rich"?*

> The Pilgrim of the Absolute. – *Must it be confessed to you? I am the hero in one of my stories. That miserable soul was never leaving, because he had missed all the trains. Such is my case. I am the pilgrim of this genre.*

3. – To Cornuau:

> *... You are going to find yourself in the presence of an extraordinary case. A female reader is flushed with enthusiasm. Her letters are unprecedented. Example: "Your thought positively suffocates me... What do you want from me?... What do you want from me?... What do you want from me?... Look closely. It's the Pilgrim of the Absolute! It imposes itself on you, whether you like it or not, it bears down on your soul like a formidable block of granite. It is heavy to bear, very heavy! And nevertheless, my God,*

*act in such a way that it does not pass,
like so many others, – that admiration
that draws me close to you!"*

*What do you think of a soul
that God pursues with such violence,
and what must I think of the prodigious honor he has shown me, having
designated me as the current dog that
brought it to bay?*

4. – *Les Pétroleurs*. Tale of a male nurse:

From the Argonne line, March 1.

*The Germans have just distinguished
themselves by a new act of criminal fe-
rocity in which they surpass themselves. Can a more cowardly and cruel attempt on people's lives be imagined than what a recent communiqué
has announced in these terms: In the
Malancourt woods, between Argonne
and Meuse, the enemy sprayed with a
flammable liquid one of our forward
trenches which, by consequence, had
to be abandoned. The occupants were
grievously burnt.*

*... It was yesterday evening, at
nightfall. Nothing suggested an imminent attack by the Boches. Suddenly,
one our comrades exclaimed: "Wait!
but what is this falling on us then? It*

*would seem to be petrol." Incredulous
at first, it was necessary to gather the
evidence. That liquid was indeed
petrol. The Boches launched it at us
with the aid of a fire pump they had
stolen from some village, or by means
of some special apparatus. The sub-
lieutenant who was in command had
all the pipes put out immediately. Useless precaution, for after several seconds incendiary-grenades began to
rain down on us. The trench burst into
flames after several instants. To im-
prove on their barbarous work, the
bandits, profiting by our disarray, did
not hesitate to draw near the trench
and throw lit torches inside it. Not one
of us escaped that torrent of fire. Our
clothes were drenched with petrol. We
were immediately surrounded by
flames and forced to abandon our position. We fell back then. But, at least,
we waited until the appearance of our
comrades of the second line whose ardor had been augmented tenfold by the
desire to avenge us. The petrol throw-
ers paid dearly for their infamy.*

5. – The combat kit. Peroration of a homily by the
kaiser on exit from a religious service in a church in
Poland!

The advantage that we have over our

*enemies is that they do not have a
word to rally around. They do not
know why they combat; they are ignorant as to why they are killed. They
bear on their shoulders the heavy sack
of a bad conscience, for they have attacked a peace-loving people, while
we, we march against an enemy with
the combat kit that is a pure conscience.*

I do not know what the imbecile means by a
pure conscience, but his is dead and stinks, certainly.

6. – Heard this phrase by a woman whose husband is
at the front and extremely exposed: "Fortunately, *luck*
protects him."

7. – When one does not eat God, one must expect to
be eaten by the dogs. That is the future of apostate
France.

10. – Still the priest-soldiers. *A curate-captain of artillery*. Incredible article published by the *Croix*, for
the edification of its readers. It is a letter:

*... It was a question of retaking a posi-
tion that we could not see, but which
had great importance. That went badly. All of a sudden, a battery of 75 at
full speed, commanded by a big devil*

of a captain, a colossus, buzzcut, clean-shaven, in the American style and who did not have a seemly air.

He grimps up a tree, remains there for three minutes and comes back down. "Gunlayers listen up." He indicates the point of reference, gives the drift: "Bring down by 3, corrective 2,200, 2,500, 2,550, 2,600, 2,650," and he yells: "That's it, they won't give us any f***ing problem now."

And in fact, the two German batteries were knocked out... The French battery packed it back up and was on the road again. The horses are rapidly unhitched, the gunners clean up a bit in a rundown grange. What are they going to do?... Someone has placed a stone on some empty cartridge cases, and the captain of before... is going to say mass. That captain is a curate. He gets dressed in five secs, *and it's* a funny touch *he has, that curate.... Nothing is missing, at mass. There is a sermon, and what a sermon! It's not a curate who delivers it, it's a "poilu" who speaks to other "poilus"...*

To give you an impression of that mass... the sight of that curate who gives the benediction, when only a half-hour earlier, on his order as

> *captain, under his cannon fire, more*
> *than one hundred enemy gunners are*
> *sent* ad patres, *there, I cannot...*

One will notice that the word *curate* is employed here in place of the word priest, which would have been upsetting, even for readers of the *Croix*. That said, I will stop speaking about priest-soldiers. I have really had quite enough of them.

12. – A colleague whom I do not know, Emile Fabre, member of a Committee of contingency for artists, thought of me, who was not asking for anything, and made me keep a sum.

14. – Beautiful musical performance at our home. Trio de Franck performed by Madeleine, Viñes, and the Argentine violoncellist Olivarès. I am extremely proud of my little Madeleine who has become, in so few years, a veritable artist, capable of astonishing her masters.

20. – Russian triumph. Capitulation of Przemysl. I would have preferred that of Thorn or Kœnigsberg.

21. – Zeppelins flew over Paris last night without success. The assassins were unable to harm more than a few people and material damages of little importance were reported only in the north suburbs, at Levallois,

Asnières, Courbevoie, etc. But the emotion was intense in Montmartre. First warning.

My *Joan of Arc and Germany* is being printed with rapidity. Prepared a small legend to be read on the wrapper "*Just out*":

> *One knows that the Germans have recently undertaken to annex Joan of Arc by means of that fathead reasoning that suits them so well: "Joan of Arc, having been the enemy of the English, must be on our side." Léon Bloy's excellent book is a daunting response to that insolence of the Boches.*

22. – I am told that, in a bookstore outside Paris, this was seen: My book *She Who Weeps,* and all around a single copy of it a group of brochures entitled: *To Those Who Weep* (to be read during the war) by Abbot Gamber (?). Is that not admirable? It is evident that the abbot, author of that small probably edifying and sentimental religiosity, has read at least the cover of my book and that he has wanted, by *rectifying* in his manner, with a stolen title, to do me one better and to break my back. I am used to it, being one of the most used contemporary authors there is. One does not name me, of course, but one uses me. I have read at least two books wherein entire pages of mine were reproduced without quotations nor references of any sort. At times of leisure in my 68-year-old trench, I find that rather comical.

23. – To a lady... Japanese, whom I interest passionately:

> ... *To respond to you with suitable au-
> thority, I would need to be your direc-
> tor of conscience. I know this. Howev-
> er, I will try. To speak usefully to a
> woman of your sort, it seems to me
> that I must begin by putting aside all*
> verbal *humility, like an ass who
> throws off his harness so as to trot
> about more joyously.*
>
> *So you have been in love with
> me, to start with, – which does not sur-
> prise me in the least, being one of
> those people whom one must either
> love madly, or execrate; – then, be-
> cause of me, you say, you have fallen
> in love with Our Lady of La Salette.
> And with a lack of profundity that af-
> flicts me, you declare that "that hardly
> resembles a supernatural attraction."
> What does it take then for you? A
> dozen years ago, a young man whom I
> do not know wrote to me some rather
> curious letters, calling himself an old
> maid whom my books consoled, and I
> was taken in by it for a spell. But re-
> calling that adventure, I ask myself on
> re-reading your letter if you aren't a
> young woman.*

For example. You speak of Renan who was your "apostle," because you found his book "well written"!

I am too generous to insist, but in the future I will ask you no longer to mention that individual. I have a strong stomach and I can support a pile of filth, but that name, on paper, no, it's beyond my forces.

A pious priest, of evident superior intelligence, has told you that you were "a woman loved by Our Lady of La Salette and that your love for her was a sign of predestination," which is totally incontestable. You cry out about that like a little pensioner to whom the good nuns would have taught what they so stupidly call humility *and you recount to me a pile of horrors or nonsense to prove to me that you are unworthy of everything. I am too old a fox to fall for those stupidities and I absolutely maintain that you are a* predestined *person. I know it and I see it. Ah! oh, do you believe then that God is summonable and that his Grace depends on our actions? Ten thousand years before your birth, it was known by Him that you would love his sorrowful Mother. You were made for that, and the rest is* nothing.

You say to me, in the moon-

light, that you are completely committed – O how presumptuous! – and that you have had all sorts of curiosities. If that were true, which I do not dare hope, you would be with the Good Thief and Mary Magdalene, who were the first chosen. Jesus Christ cherishes sinners and detests good folk. Fill up on that thought which is a thousand times more fortifying than all the prattle contained in books of piety.

The religious whom you have spoken to me about as if he were a saint appears to me to have been sent to you by the devil. When one speaks to me of a saint, I ask immediately where his miracles are. Now the miracle of that man has been that of exposing you to despair and the entire effort of your zeal has been the killing counsel of taking communion but once a year *and praying as little as possible. I understand that after that you might have thought yourself damned...*

25. – Some Teutonic aphorisms:

In anticipation of my death, I make this confession that I despise the German nation because of its immense stupidity and that I blush to belong to it. – SCHOPENHAUER.

What harm would there be in this, that for a greater good, one tells a big, fat lie? – LUTHER.

I do not know who might answer this question: Is it permitted to deceive men?... I am going to look into the matter. – FREDRICK THE GREAT.

Law is the game of the weak; law is the monotony of the world. – SCHILLER.

27. – Letter from Raugel written "on the ground, under fire":

Yesterday, France's cannons performed, from 6 o'clock in the morning to 11 o'clock, a continual symphony of four beats per second. One is crazy, deaf, and enraged...

28. – Found this in a letter by Mélanie:

The great must be brought low, and the little people become smaller.

29. – Found phrase: "Barrès is the *literary man* of the territory."

31. – All our thoughts go out to our dear godchildren of Holland whom we can see coming from one moment to the next. But our thoughts are accompanied

with anguish. They could have gone to London, can they now come to France?...

Has one ever seen, before there were German sailors and a kaiser with a name of Hohenzollern to command them, has one even imagined a scene like that which has just unfolded on the Channel? A steamship filled with innocent travelers, merchants belonging to neutral countries and without arms, passengers, women and children, sunk at high sea, before the crew could lower the lifeboats! All that human cargo thrown overboard amidst clamors of fear; arms that grasp at all the debris; faces convulsed by the most grievous agony; heart-rending adjurations; sobs, imprecations, death rattles suffocated by the waves – and continually circling around that death scene, the criminal vessel, the murderous submarine, rising to the surface, with all its crew on the platform, to look on at the success of its work!

And among the forty men who are there, officers or sailors, not a single one who might have a look of pity, not one who gives a hint of a gesture to offer help!

They look on... and they laugh.

April

1st. – Return of our godchildren finally. We have so desired this moment that we do not succeed in realizing our joy.

4. – Easter Sunday. Peculiarity that has perhaps a mysterious meaning. This year, Holy Friday has taken, in a way, the place of Easter Sunday. The day before yesterday, magnificent sun all day long. Today, rain, fog, and cold.

5. – To an afflicted friend:

> *I am particularly touched by this, that on feeling despondent you immediately thought to share it with me, as if I had the power to console you. My compassion, I assure you, is real, having myself passed through the worst passages of sorrow, but I cannot offer you anything other than the prayers of a poor, old man who loves you and who blesses you. The suffering of souls is universal and infinite at this moment. All that I am able to say to one or another, being situated in the Absolute of the Faith, comes down to this: Cry, if God gives you tears, but have pity on yourselves, while gently accepting what is required of you. There is nothing better than to want what God wants. It is the only consolation, and I have found only that over the course of my frightful life.*
>
> *Consider, dear friend, the inex-*

pressible distress, the extraordinary deprivation of the powerful who have wanted that war of demons, and compare their future fate to that of their innumerable victims. One is always on the good side when one is with those who suffer persecution and injustice. One is well placed then to have compassion for oneself, and one is rocked with an infinite tenderness in the arms of the Consoler of the afflicted.

6. – Response to a stranger who overtaxes me with letters devoid of simplicity. She says she is ignorant and asks me rather ridiculously for spiritual assistance:

I inform you that I am in my 69th year and that I prepare myself for death. I have little time then to correspond with a person that I do not know. Besides, all that I could tell you, you will find in my books. You say you are ignorant, and you beg me to instruct you. Here is my advice. Take several sous and go buy the catechism for little children and learn it. Then, go find a priest who will reconcile you with God. The most mediocre among them have that power. If you reject this advice, I will be forced to think that you are not sincere and that curiosity alone brings you to read me and to

*write to me. In that case, how could
you interest me?*

8. – Does one wish to know what proud and insane
Germany pretends to? One should read these two
short, but significative extracts of works by two
pangermanists, more famous than all others, extracts
reproduced by the *Bulletin des Armées*:

> *So that nobody might be ignorant of it,
> we proclaim that our continental na-
> tion has the right to the sea, not only
> the North Sea, but even the Mediter-
> ranean and the Atlantic. We will ab-
> sorb then, one after the other, all
> provinces that we are neighbors to.
> We will annex successively Denmark,
> Holland, Belgium, Franche-Compté,
> the north of Switzerland, Livonia, then
> Trieste and Venice; finally the north of
> the Gaulic region, Somme and Loire.*

> – General VON KLAUSEWITZE

> *We will annex Denmark, Holland, Bel-
> gium, Switzerland, Livonia, Trieste
> and Venice, and the north of France,
> from Somme to Loire. This plan which
> we expose fearlessly is not the work of
> a fool; this empire that we wish to
> found will not be a utopia; we have
> from now on, in our hands, the means
> to accomplish it.*

– General BRONSART VON
SCHELLENDORF

Fundamentally, those cherished fellows wish
to annex all of Europe to begin with, and, a little later,
the entire world. Why not? That would be the restora-
tion of Paradise on earth.

10. – To Termier:

> *I would like to be able, as of today, to
> send you a copy of my book, but it
> cannot appear before the 4th or 5th of
> May. May God bless it! The extraordi-
> nary circumstance and even a little
> miraculous that allowed me to publish
> it at a moment when no book is being
> published gives me great hope. It will
> be perhaps the only book of the sea-
> son, which I would encourage you to
> admire. Prodigious effect of the apoc-
> alyptic war! The victim of the conspir-
> ation of silence, for so many years, be-
> come finally the only voice that might
> make itself heard! Then the to-be-
> hoped-for success will coincide with
> our silver anniversary, O Termier!
> which will take place, the Tuesday of
> Pentecost, May 25.*

> *It is true, I hasten to say it, that
> that is too wonderful to be believed.
> However... I do, each day, what I have
> never done. I pray to obtain success,*

considering that I would have in that way, beyond material security, the notoriety that is indispensable for me. God knows that I have a job to accomplish and that that job is not accomplished. Those who have read Salvation Through the Jews *know it also and often reproach me for keeping to myself what was, more than thirty years ago, entrusted to me for others.*

But what could I do before having conquered sufficient authority? If Joan of Arc *gives me that authority, and that independence, with what joy would I forget our contemporaries and their imbecilic thoughts in order to give myself entirely to the Word of God, in solitude, while some empires crumble around me, as the ancient Fathers did!...*

It has become banal to talk about the war. Besides, you know as much if not more about it than I do. So many things are hidden from us! But we know in general and in a certain fashion that all goes very well. The English are our heroically disinterested brothers. The Russians also. One can even expect that the latter, the Cossacks principally, will surprise the world by their gentleness, already proverbial. The chevaleresque Italians will certainly talk about them, when they have stopped keeping pace with them. As for our parliamentarians and politicians, they will keep at the sacred union *and will try it out in good time.*

The future is magnificent, Faith is reborn everywhere and Christianity has never been so flourishing. We will have multiple proofs of it soon enough after the war. Our bishops, besides, are they not completely sublime? There you have it, dear friend, all that a solitary, whose optimism you know, can tell you...

12. – Extremely touching letter from Félix Raugel, written on Easter Sunday, after mass in the forest, to the sound of cannons, at several hundred meters from the line of fire:

A chaos of giant rocks, in the hollow of a small cave. The altar, a simple oak plank, two little wax candles. At the bottom of the ravine, officers and chasseurs piously attending, heads uncovered. Vibrant and short speech by the almoner. Easter communions. For liturgical chanting and its bells, nothing but the small sound of raindrops and the formidable voice of the cannons. Precious moment, sublime hour, immense peace, unforgettable memo-

ry!

To a friend:

... The stupidest thing in the opinion of bourgeoisie, which is not the Last Judgment, is to do something for the Love of God, and that is the case here. The excellent man who told you that and whom you desperately try to make an admirer of my books, told you, on the same occasion, that he was preparing against me a small dossier that he was going to read to you. I do not ask you to share it with me. Everything that he can read to you or say to you, I know it by heart for forty years now. It is from that same material that I made two volumes of the Exegesis of Commonplaces.

My wife was very touched by what you wrote to her. You know her already by my books. Believe me when I tell you that I'm not exaggerating. She married me, 25 years ago, uniquely because she saw in me the most miserable man in the world. That alone must demonstrate to you at what stage her soul is.

14. – To Ventura Garcia Calderon, Spanish journalist who made me promise a response to his inquiry on

the occasion of the 3rd centenary of the publication of *Don Quichotte*, which they wish to celebrate in Spain:

> *Monsieur, I can only repeat what I declared to you in Bourg-la-Reine, when you honored me by your visit. I do not like* Don Quichotte. *That too famous book amused me when I was 16 or 18 years old. Later, it annoyed me and revolted me. I cannot suffer that great things should be turned into derision, and chivalry is assuredly one of those great things, one of the most beautiful that man has ever seen.*

> *It is possible that Cervantes did not wish to vilify it, as some of your compatriots suppose – even though that is difficult to believe – and that he only pretended to ridicule certain extravagances of his time the very memory of which no longer exist for three centuries now. But his book lives on, and it's an ineffaceable stain.*

> *If there was nothing but the poor knight with the Sad Face, one could lend some credence to his madness, but Sancho is intolerable. The brutal appetite continually, systematically, victoriously opposed to the Dream; the belly always getting the better of Enthusiasm, and the coarse laughter of the multitude in the dolor-*

ous face of Poetry, that is what cannot be supported.

Such, I believe, is the sentiment of a rather large number of French people, at this moment above all when the role of Sancho is played by loutish Germany. I hope you will accept this very sincere response by a writer who takes glory in ignoring the protocolar attentions.

16. – To a priest-soldier who sent me his portrait:

... I'm so sorry to see you with a rifle. Priests should never be armed. It's the effect of a sacrilegious aberration and you should feel it deeply. You have been forced, as so many others, to obey the law of mobilization, but no authority has the right to constrain you to use your weapons. I hope that God will spare you from finding your-self in such situations.

17. – Having received at church certain impressions, I endeavor to put them down on paper:

DE PARADISO TERRESTRI[67]

"Quod oculus non vidit, *etc. Things that the eye has not seen, the ear has*

---

[67]De paradiso terrestri: Latin for "About Earthly Paradise."

not heard, and which have not arisen in the heart of man – things that God has prepared for those who love him."

What is Saint Paul talking about here? Assuredly, it is not about the earthly Paradise that always exists according to Tradition, and which is, according to the unanimous testimony of ancient Fathers, the vestibule of celestial Paradise where the Just and the Saints would not be admitted except at the unimaginable end of time.

The Holy Ghost affirms by the mouth of Saint Paul, citing the sublime chapter 64 of Isaiah, the absolute *impossibility of conceiving what God reserves for his friends in celestial Paradise at the end of ends. It is not a question here then of earthly Paradise, which is possible, not to comprehend, but to conceive of, insofar as earthly, as the Liturgy itself says something about it:*

Piissime Domine Jesu Christe qui redemisti nos pretiosissimo sanguine tuo, miserere animæ hujus... et eam introducere digneris ad SEMPER VIRENTIA ET AMŒNA LOCA PARADISI.

Such are the last words of that agonizing Christian's Commendation of the soul.

*Without a doubt, our concep-
tion of earthly Paradise is immensely
rudimentary, but possible nonetheless,
because the testimony of our senses is
invoked. Not to mention the sense of
smell that appears to be the most
earthly and that which brings us clos-
est to animality, it is not necessary to
be a poet to imagine a perfume capable of making one die of voluptuousness. The other senses, sight, hearing,
above all, cannot procure, even in this
inferior world, the delights that the already so precarious notion of time or
space seem to abolish. It suffices to
suppose a prodigious, supernatural
excess of our sensations, an excess accompanied in us by an unlimited power of susception, in order for us to
form an idea, after a fashion, of earthly Paradise.*

*By consequence, however
miraculously beautiful and delectable
that paradise might be, it is earthly
and therefore accessible to our imagination in a manner. It is the Garden of
Voluptuousness, it is the Holy Ghost
that tells us that. Adam and Eve, infallibly illuminated, must have known
quite well that that place was not their
final end, and the serpent did not surprise them when he said:* Eritis sicut
dii. *To speak in a human way, he had*

only to seduce them, but that was certainly not the work of the duration of a lightning flash.

When we want to think of the Infinite, the phantasmagoria of astronomic quantities are presented to our mind. The frightful figures by which one forces oneself in vain to measure the distances of the stars, what are they in comparison to the columns of millions of centuries needed perhaps by the Tempter? For the age *of our first parents was only able to begin at the moment when, their ceasing to be immortal, time began for them.*

Adam and Eve, seduced finally, wanted too soon to be gods, that is to say to take possession of celestial Paradise before having sufficiently cultivated *the earthly one, in whatever sense one wants to understand this expression, and it is what one calls Original Sin. But the testament endures. Eritis sicut Dii, the testament and the heritage, the House of the Father that no one can know. All images of artists or poets refer exclusively to the terrestrial Paradise, the only one that might be* imagined.

18. – *If my Emperor saw me!* 190,000 imprints of that

pious exhortation by German pastors have been distributed on the front to the Kaiser's troops, we are
told. Authentic or fabricated, that piece is so German
in its stupidity that it is worth being conserved:

> *You are billeted in enemy territory, or
> still in reserve in your fatherland.
> Death and danger are distant for the
> moment. You obtain permission. Be-
> hold your master. It is at that moment
> that* sin, impurity, *come around solic-
> iting you. Darkness protects you. You
> can abandon yourself, with impunity,
> to the ardor of your blood.*

> *Comrade, brother, stop!*

> *Be strong! It is the occasion to
> demonstrate that you are really a man,
> master of your debasing desires. Think
> on the malediction of impurity. What
> assisted in 1870 the fall of Metz, the
> fortress bristling with arms, impreg-
> nable? And in that Japanese war, that
> of Port Arthur? The weakness of the*
> senses *and its consequences:* sexual
> maladies. *Think, in such instants of
> passion: "If my emperor saw me!"*

19. – Prepared several dedications for *Joan of Arc
and Germany* which is about to appear:

To Termier:

God served first! *said Joan of Arc.*
"The Boches served first," you are
compelled to say, while expediting
your shells, my gentle colonel. It is the
difference of the times. But the sense is
the same, as it is necessary to destroy
that wall of scum who obfuscate God's
throne.

To Alfred Vallette:

Who saw me "smile," that he might be
witness to the tears of love that flow
sometimes under the mask *of the pam-*
phleteer.

To Henri Boutet:

This here, dear friend, is a book that
defies all illustration. *It is the super-*
natural constant. Don't you think that
it would need, at one and the same
time, the childlike soul of a primitive
and a Michelangelo's genius?

To Ricardo Viñes:

Behold a warrior who tears into your
Almogavars a little, who were, without
my wishing to offend you, terrible ras-
cals. I imagine that El Cid, himself,
compared by Hugo to the Pic du Midi,
would have bowed down before that
hill of glory and angelic purity.

To Raïssa Maritain:

That incomparable face of the saint, visible only to God's good friends who have received the grace to see above *time.*

To Christine van der Meer:

You will find here, blessed companion of my Pierre, something to content your artist's soul and your soul of an elect of Jesus Christ. I ask only for a small tear for the author.

To Georges Crès:

I don't know if this book will make you rich, but I am sure that it will content your heart and that you will be happy to have assisted me in offering this testimony to the great Saint of France.

To René Martineau:

If Joan of Arc is the "soul of France," as I have said, then in some way she acts similarly in each of us, and it is for that reason, doubtless, that it is difficult not to weep when thinking about her.

To Carlos Olivarès:

People have often spoken about my books, but nobody has said that I am a poet, nothing but a poet, that I see men and things as a comic or tragic poet, and that all my books can be ex-

plained in that way. I let you in on that secret.

To Abbot X.:

Don't you think that Joan of Arc*'s burning at the stake is a prophetic image of France's now-near future, such as Our Lords have been preparing for us for sixty-nine years now?*

To Brou:

This book which he desired so much and which I could not have written without him.

To Emile Baumann:

Here, as with The Soul of Napoleon, *I dreamt of putting my poor soul in Joan of Arc's place, persuaded that it is by that means that one can really write history.*

To Edmond Barthèlemy:

History seen through tears.

To André Baron:

While waiting for France to mount the funeral pyre in turn.

To Cornuau:

This book of sadness and glory, which is a form of predication for Our Lady of La Salette.

To Friar D***:

God served first! *That cry by Joan of Arc would it not be the real watchword of all my books?*

To Emile Fabre:

"He who loves greatness and who loves the abandoned, when he passes by the abandoned, he will recognize the greatness, if greatness is there," said Hello.

To Louis Hénault:

Today, as in the 15th century, history is a torch taken out for a stroll amongst the ruins.

To Vincent d'Indy:

The history of all the centuries, is it anything else than an ocean of horrible darkness, illuminated here and there by some bright figures?

To Jean de la Laurencie:

Human acts, human tears, and the incomprehensible Will of God, history is filled with it.

To Father Louis M***:

While waiting for the kingdom of the Paraclete, which will put an end to the idle gossip and commonplaces.

To Jacques Maritain:

My dear godson in eremo. *For him, I confide this book to the faithful raven that carried, each day, the Eucharist to the Patriarch of Solitaries.*

To Pierre van der Meer:

Time and history being nothing more than dreams, it seems to me that I could have been one of that warrioress' companions, and I have quite often thought that I would finish like her in a blaze.

To a soldier-priest:

While praying to him to disarm in order to read me.

To Uncle Louis:

There are some who have gotten themselves killed by the Boches. The author has killed himself to write this book which will augment perhaps the courage of some. One does what one can.

To Raoux:

While waiting for inexpressible and miraculous events that this monstrous war has been only the prelude to.

To Raugel:

The impotent author who would like to be near him in order to take part in the marvelous dreams of Christians who offer their life every day.

To Georges Rouault:

While waiting for the joyful massacres and the sweet exterminations[68]

To a young priest:

Received the surprising compilation on earthly Paradise, liber totius consolationis, as you said. Profitable reading, no doubt about it, but painful and long. Ecclesiastical authors, in general, ignore concision. Whether they write in Latin or in any other sublunar language, their prolixity is frightening and their references infinite. I am far from having read all of it. However, I have had the joy of seeing that I have not deceived myself in my presentiments on the subject of an earthly Paradise. (See my Exegesis of Commonplaces, 2nd series. Conclusion.) Here attached is a draft that you may keep. I have copied it with care. It is a kind of note for future work. I recommend you to Our Lady of Transfixion and the Good Thief.

---

[68]Editor's note: possibly a suppressed passage by the original censors.

A number of Belgian refugees are hospitalized in a building next to Saint-Sulpice. One lady who visited them noticed a little girl of twelve years, whose hands were obstinately kept, in spite of the elevated temperature in the room, in a miserable little muff.

"Blow my nose, mama," she said all of the sudden to her mother.

"How's that!" said the lady, "such a big girl and she cannot blow her own nose?"

"She has no hands," responded the mother softly, as if to excuse her daughter.

The visitor stood for a moment unable to understand.

"Was it... the Germans?... No, that cannot be possible!"

The mother lowered her head and burst into tears.

22. – Interesting letter by Philippe Raoux. He is, like me, without illusions for the future, for that imbecilic and impious "sacred union" that suppresses God. He speaks to me about wounded soldiers, threatened to be sent back immediately to the front if they go see the almoner, and about a male nurse punished for having brought the almoner to a moribund.

"Perhaps," he says, "some beautiful thing, more beautiful than others, might take place at the front... some magnificent act... as in the luminous time of the Middle Ages."

At that moment, and as if in response to my friend's wish, this comes before my eyes:

> GET UP, DEAD MEN, ON YOUR FEET! *It's the sublime cry of a wounded soldier in a surprised trench full of the dead and dying. On that call to action, like something out of the Middle Ages, the agonizing, interrupted in their agony, get up and defend themselves so terribly that the invaders are pushed back, exterminated, and the position is retaken. (The recitation of this marvelous and almost supernatural episode was reproduced by a large number of newspapers.)*

28. – I'm told of a lady who declaims *Blood of the Poor* "with the voice of a dove." My friends know that I read that and other things with a totally different kind of voice and I cannot imagine very well the cooing of that lady. It is true that the prophet Jeremiah speaks somewhere about "the anger of the Dove," symbol of the Holy Ghost, but I do not see the immediate application here.

29. – Pierre, who spends his time gathering information, is profoundly disenchanted. What he sees and what he hears demonstrates to him that all is lost and that God alone can do something today.

30. – From Lieutenant-Colonel Rousset:

The enemy seems determined to renounce procuring victory for himself by honorable means. If what has just happened in Maucourt, in Tracy-le-Mont, near Souain, is not a simple psychological crisis consequent to some return fit of anger, it can only be the demonstration of a military powerlessness in which one sees oneself incapable of triumphing.

What does it mean then that handful of men – eighty, we are told – who went on the attack with, for weapons, scissors, Brownings, and knives? What is that pharmaceutical apparatus of tubes of ether, stupefying smoke, and firework bombs? Has one ever seen an army still making a military show of it and conserving so little confidence in itself, that it should have recourse to like means?...

Really, the Kaiser's soldiers give us strange spectacles. But if they think they are intimidating us thereby, they are mistaken. On the contrary, there is nothing better than those expedients borrowed from the most vulgar banditry to convince us of their moral decline and the anguish that so completely troubles their disappointed mind.

May

1st. – Preliminary note to a citation of my book in the *Mercure de France*:

> *I had undertaken, before the war, a study on Joan of Arc. The introduction to that study, which was bound to be purely historical, was written, last July, and here it is...*
>
> *It was three months later only that I was able to pick up that work again, but then to the sound of cannons and my ears filled with the enormous clamor of the immolated. It was inevitable that my vision of the past should be in a way confounded with the haunting vision of the actual deluge. There were, besides, many points of similarity!*
>
> *That is why I have entitled my book* Joan of Arc and Germany.

3. – Trip to Bures, with my godson Pierre, just like before. Everything is changed, however. That delicious valley still makes one think of Paradise, but something enormously anguishing weighs on us.

There is no longer any peace to be hoped for in this world.

4. – "*The Pilgrim of the Absolute*," I said to someone. "That title resembles a mysterious invocation. As soon as the book came out, the monstruous war was unleashed, like a response to all the demons."

5. – Long letter from an unknown Polish person whom I have little desire to know. He has the tact of sending me a stamp for a response. He calls himself Lutoslawski, calls me his "dear friend," and gives me some scientific advice worthy of a German professor. He calls himself a Catholic and the inventor of an infallible recipe for effecting conversions. That letter is nothing but pride and sottishness.

7. – Response to the Pole:

> *Sir, you have the goodness to wish to make me profit by your experience "much more ample than mine," you say, and you generously inundate me with your counsels, embellished here and there by some expressions of heavy irony that an prickly rhinoceros could find insulting. Being an idiot by birth, incapable by consequence of understanding anything of no matter what* psychology *and saturated with*

contempt for modern science that I be-
lieve is come from the devil, I am sor-
ry to say that I cannot appreciate your
charitable intentions. My sixty-nine
years salute you.

Reading Vertot (*Chevaliers de Malte*[69]). The hideous sight of contemporary things forces me to take refuge in the Middle Ages.

Brou tells me a nice story, however. Frédéric Cousot, the poor writer whom we knew in Montmartre, is a civil prisoner in Germany, having voluntarily switched places, heroically, with a poor father of a family.

8. – My book has just come out and already its insuccess is announced. I am too different from the rest of the world. There is nothing to do about it. People willingly acknowledge that I am an astonishing Writer but never *write* that. I could write the most beautiful book in the world, the *Divine Comedy*, the Gospel even, just more silence. A horrible sadness grips me.

There is talk of the catastrophe of the *Lusitania*, immense English commercial vessel torpedoed without prior warning by the Germans and sunk in several minutes. 1,500 dead, it is said, among whom a large number of women and small children. The German sailors were already accustomed to that sort of abomination, but they had not, until now, effected so

---

[69]*Chavaliers de Malte:* French for the *Knights of Malta*.

sumptuous a horror. (We have learnt since that Berlin celebrated on the news of it, and that the perpetrators were magnificently praised and recompensed by the Kaiser who himself awaits his recompense...)

9. – The *Gazette de Cologne*, May 6, announces that the bishop of Metz (!), Mgr. Benzler, has given his clergy the command to remove statues of Joan of Arc from all the churches in his diocese. That violet pig would be completely at ease in the archbishopric of Reims, when his emperor has conquered all of France.

10. – Another exquisite day in Bures. But what new things to say in this permanent nightmare of a war that obsesses us and empoisons all joy.

14. – A poor chap of Lyon, another giver of counsels, writes to me that I ought to write a small popular book for 25 sous to propagate La Salette, taking care to "renounce my style from the great days."

16. – Admirable liturgy. The feast day of Joan of Arc has been fixed for Sunday in the Octave of the Ascension, and I read with a rush of emotion the last words of the Gospel on this occurrent Sunday: *Hæc locutus sum vobis, ut cum venerit hora eorum, reminiscamini quia ego dixi vobis*. To be compared to Joan of Arc warning Cauchon: "Write it down, so that, when the

time comes, one will remember what I said."

20. – Raoux speaks to me about Italy, which evidently will, after so many months of hesitation, be forced to take part in the immense war, but "which would want to limit the spiral of cataclysms that that *desired* intervention will trigger... on Rome and on the Church?... As vile and as miserable as François-Joseph is, he still represents nonetheless the Holy Roman Empire and protects against the anti-clerical explosion... transalpine and cisalpine?... And who knows if we should not tremble for that support *ex diabolo!* What leucoma do we have on our eyes that that satanic hymn (by d'Annunzio) to Garibaldi, which jolts Italy, should be joyously welcomed by us?"

21. – To Philippe Raoux:

> *... Joan of Arc's statue is covered with flowers by the same people whose only dream is to destroy the Church. Absolutely no one wants anything to do with God, our bishops themselves having disqualified him. It is quite simple then:* God retires. *It is clear for us that if God suddenly withheld the little stones from his benediction, the disintegrated granite and flint would immediately turn to dust. What will that mean for modern societies?*

22. – Pilgrims extremely in love with my books come to visit me, saying that they are in accord with me on all points, but that, nevertheless, they cannot understand my continued admiration for Napoleon. I have tried to tell them that I admire Napoleon as one of the finest works of God, but they cannot conceive that, and it is strange. It's as if someone said to me: "We see the noblest sentiments in you, but it is impossible for us to conceive that you really have a soul."

23. – Pentecost Sunday. The Italy of Garibaldi and d'Annunzio have declared war on Austria, by consequence on Germany, to the infallible applause of Maurice Barrès! That event for the feast day of the Holy Ghost!!!?

24. – Pentecost Monday. *Altissimus dedit vocem suam et apparuerunt fontes aquarum.* Two streams of tears!

25. – Pentecost Tuesday. Silver anniversary. It is exactly twenty-five years since we got married, that we suffer together, one supporting the other, nearly everything that can be suffered. This morning, at Saint-Lambert, at the very altar of the Virgin, where our marriage was celebrated, the good Abbot Cornuau blessed us for the trials that are still to come. In 1890, the marriage of two poor people; in 1915, the *silver*

anniversary of two poor people. That is the one thing has not changed. We don't recognize anything here anymore. Vaugirard, which was almost a suburb, has become one of the quarters of the immense City always menaced with the dreadful destruction that the Sorrowful Mother announced. But what difference does it make? Everyone's life, and ours in particular, is it not but a dream?

Crowd at Bourg-la-Reine. Children, godchildren, friends, kind letters from those who are absent. It is nevertheless marvelous that the old refractory, condemned by all councils of literature, should be able to group together so large a number of affections! What victory and what hope for a future life – after a return to dust!

27. – The sales of my *Joan of Arc* are null or nearly. No more publicity than several lines by Gustave Téry, which seems rather to have killed my book. That news, although expected, crushes me a bit. God does not want this kind of victory for me.

29. – Benedict XV again. Here's what the too-famous Clémenceau, nicknamed Death Head, wrote today in *l'Homme Enchaîné*. Is it not dismaying to think that the Vicar of Jesus Christ can be *justly* reprimanded by such a man!

> ... *These are Christians, Roman Catholics even, who are being massacred; it is Catholic Belgian that is being*

drowned in blood by the sons of Luther allied with the very Catholic Emperor, qualified as such to indicate his path to the divine Spirit itself, when he intervenes in a sovereignly fashion into the Conclave's decisions. And in all that horrible mêlée, the Pope who (for earthly reasons) cannot even say what is just or unjust today, proposes to impose on it morally tomorrow.

For it is justice that we seek, Holy Father, an earthly justice that we have been reduced to attempt to conquer by arms, for our inability to obtain it, however mediocre it might be, in the peace of your Christianity. It is one of your more cherished sons who has unleashed this war, claiming to submit a neighboring people to servitude. And here You are speaking in the name of Heaven, you dare – for fear of losing your earthly support – neither to blame nor to approve!

What! This is the bearer of supreme truth who, for six months now, locks himself away in silence, when the supreme Arbiter of worlds, by his voice, can speak! And that, at the precise moment when a universal massacre that the Pope possesses the means to make stop, not by protocols of arbitrage when the combatants are at the end of their strength, but today, by the authority received from on High. That arbitrage, do not ask for it, Supreme Pontiff. Seize it. Tell where just law, and the enemy of humankind, under the high sentence of power that is invested in you, stand. The Church proclaimed you Pope. Be it. We await only that miracle to line up under your law.

June

2. – To Edmond Barthèlemy. I expose to him the need I would have of an article in the *Mercure* so as to break the universal silence. "After Napoleon, it's Joan of Arc who asks that of you."

4. – Am I about to lose my mind? For some time now I am tormented by a sort of grievous oppression. Brusquely I lose my breath, I am forced to stop if walking, and I suffer. It is especially in the first hours of the day that that illness makes itself felt.

5. – In *The Little Bollandistes*, a history of Saint Boniface:

Formerly, the priests were made of

gold and served from chalices made of
wood; today, they are made of wood,
and serve from chalices made of gold.

And now, here is something we have not seen before in our tormented existence: fire at home. Without warning, one of our rooms all of a sudden is seen to be filled with flames which we succeed fortunately in extinguishing. But the damage is considerable for the poor people that we are. Divers objects of some value are irremediably destroyed. A window and a door have been burnt. It is true that we possess an insurance policy, but will we be reimbursed?

The partially-consumed table was covered with papers reduced to ashes. Among those burnt papers, I have found *The Life of the Holy Virgin* by Anne-Catherine Emmerich. That book alone has been inexplicably spared.

In the midst of action, I was not lacking in sangfroid, I was able to render myself useful, but soon afterwords, insupportable palpitations of the heart. The illness that I have been suffering from for several days now would declare itself finally.

7. – The Insurance Company sends a representative. I would have thought the affair quite simple. Constatation, evaluation of damages, then compensation. I was unaware that there were litigious points involved. Incapable of understanding a thing, in poor health, and, moreover, inept at any discussion, I would have stepped away if a friend had not been present, fortunately, who knew how to step in for me.

9. – Appearance of a doctor looking rather like a country veterinarian. I have rarely seen a face so devoid of intelligence. He interrogates me, listens to my heart, and stands stupid, finding absolutely nothing to say to me. He leaves finally, leaving me a prescription that goes immediately into the wastebasket.

11. – Rough day. I was expected at my godchildren's house in Versailles. It was a great celebration for us. I arrive only to take immediately to bed until the moment of departure. My return is very nearly like that of a man in the throes of death. Obscurely, I imagine that I *pay* in this way for someone or something.

12. – Visit by a highly-recommended female doctor. The look of this person is satisfactory. She examines me attentively and with a good deal of grace. Lungs fine, etc., perfect health if not for the heart. It appears that I have abused that organ. The actual malaise, painful as it might be, is banal.

However, she prescribes an extremely disagreeable diet. I would be completely recovered and *restored* by dying of hunger and thirst. We will resign ourselves to it.

13. – A prescription more painful than others prevents me from attending mass.

17. – To a friend who wrote me a recomforting letter:

> *I was just beginning to rebel. I was left hypnotized stupidly by an astute physician who had undertaken my extermination by famine. In less than eight days, I have arrived at a complete exhaustion. Immediately after having seen your letter, I pounced on a slice of bread, a large glass of wine, and my strength has come back to me. In honor then to your Burgundian common sense. I will continue with this new treatment.*
>
> *It is true that that will change nothing as to the scenes of abomination and ignominy that make me despair and gnaw at my old Gallo-Roman heart. It is probable also that that will not make any noticeable dent in the sale of my* Joan of Arc, *but I will be stronger to support everything, and who knows?... God may have need of me perhaps in the coming days.*

18. – Second visit by the female doctor who notes that I no longer have a fever and accepts my transgressions rather well. From my side, I concede the abstinence of meat and fish and we end by coming to an understanding.

19. – Letter by Armand, Jeanne's relative:

> *Will you tell Léon Bloy for me that his*
> Ungrateful Beggar *is an admirable*
> *book? If I tell you that he makes me*
> *think of Beethoven's late period, I*
> *would, I believe, have indicated in*
> *what esteem I hold him.*

I pull along until evening, very painfully, reading alternately the first book of *Kings* and *The Pioneers* by Fenimore.

21. – I am doing better, but the oppression, the impossibility of any effort without suffocation, that still continues.

22. – A young woman writes to me that she is tormented by religious doubts and that she counts on me to dissipate them. I suspect she is tormented principally by the desire for an autograph.

> To Jean de la Laurencie:

> *God, calling me to the exceptional*
> *path, has wanted me to be deprived of*
> *everything, except friends, and what*
> *friends! I cannot tell you what emotion*
> *and recomfort your letter gave to me*
> *yesterday. It is not easy to express,*
> *and I strongly feel that literary re-*

courses are no help.

Yes, my friend, I am very certain that something else remains for me to do, that a task was entrusted to me that nobody else can accomplish, and that the necessary strength will be given to me. I suffer for several days now, all the more as my illness cruelly deprives me of what I found at church each morning, but my soul is not demoralized. I wait with a marvelous and inalterable confidence. The monstrous events that we are witnesses to for nearly a year now, I have also expected them for more than thirty-five years, and I see very clearly the inevitable cataclysms that will follow. La Salette's threats must be done. The time for penance has passed for Nineveh. Regardless of the prattle by simpletons or clever folks, there is no longer any faith, that is too certain; there is no longer any flock and there are no longer any pastors. *Such is my vision and here it is eleven months almost that I live with a continually constricted heart. But God knows the remedy, and he knows how to apply it to me when he is pleased to use his creature. Do not be afflicted for me, my very dear friend, my portion is certainly excellent and we will be consoled together, very fully.*

23. – To Philippe Raoux:

How fortifying and sweet your friend-
ship is to me! I am depressed not only
for the malady and the horror of injus-
tice, but also for the feeling of a com-
plete impotence that makes me a
wreck when so many others are com-
batting. Have you understood that for
eleven months now this feeling gnaws
at me? The diabolical iniquity of Ger-
many which is not worthy even of the
Vicar of Jesus Christ, and the Chris-
tian world's appalling blindness which
does not see itself chastised, finally
and above all the vision, so clear to
me, of the infinite abominations that
infallibly will follow this cursed war,
whatever the outcome might be. Ah! I
would like to be able to fight, me too,
and risk my life each day, I would suf-
fer less. But I cannot even go down-
stairs to go to church. When I was fit
enough for that, I did what I could, my
book on Joan of Arc, which nobody
wants and which would reach tens of
thousands of souls if it was signed by
Maurice Barrès.

As you advise me, I accept that
extreme bitterness "in the Sacred
Heart," warned moreover by the fact
that the strange illness that physically

torments me announced itself on June 11, feast day of my friend Saint Barnabas, and feast day, this year, of the Sacred Heart.

I am not too distressed for you. I believe you are protected, "quietly protected," as you yourself put it.

We will see each other again, if not in the joy, at least in the peace of a victory of love. A long time ago, a very long time ago, when I was young and strong, I was also told to be patient because God kept me in reserve for his service, much much later, in very hard times.

24. – Read, a little late, an interview of Benedict XV by a journalist of the *Liberté*. If that document, published three days ago, is veridical as is probable, it is a frightening scandal, an appalling denial of justice. It is the bankruptcy of the Papacy! Immense joy for the enemies of the Church.

25. – Some friends, Barthèlemy, Vallette, Marguillier, had arranged to approach the minister of War. It is known that Millerand is a fervent admirer of my books. It was a question of suggesting to that minister the noble and assuredly very un-banal idea of distributing *Joan of Arc and Germany* to military libraries and hospitals. A signature would have suf-

ficed. The moment appeared rather well chosen, the State wishing to compensate publishers for the suppression of deluxe books intended as *literary awards* to students. The highly foreseen response was a bureaucratic and protocolar flat-out refusal, deploring the present insufficiency of available funds, etc. I think that Millerand was completely unaware of the proposal.

Benedict XV's inertia. Silence of bishops showing no energy except against the Holy Virgin and the Revelation of La Salette. Universal indifference or hypocrisy. *God retires*. Robespierre II, will he wait for the end of the war?

Someone tells me that in the latest conflicts in Flanders a certain advantage already obtained was supposed to have been followed up by a victorious march on Lille. That serious blow to the war effort was lacking because of the cowardice of troops from the Midi who had taken flight at the moment of attack (?).

26. – To break the horrible boredom that is consuming me, I undertake to revise my notes of 1913, in view of the seventh and present volume of this Journal begun in 1892.

27. – Visit by a friend who is a provisional nurse in Val-de-Grâce, while waiting to get dispatched to the front. Our assessments of the war, whose end seems so distant, and on the hideous political attitude of

non-combatants, ministers, deputies, and other vermin, are not of a nature to cheer us up.

29. – Someone sends me a copy of a serialized col-
umn by M. Paul Souday in yesterday's issue of *The
Times,* wherein my *Joan of Arc* is mentioned. I am
still, for that gentleman, the "truculent and entertaining pamphleteer." He gives, by way of proof of that,
the fact that I condemn Charles VII, La Trémouille,
and Regnault de Chartres, individuals whom he seems
to esteem. He reproaches me for having attacked Cauchon, but only just. His visible intention is to appear
equitable by honoring me with a mention, but in such
a way that that mention should be absolutely useless
to me. He's a poor fellow who practices his profession.

30. – Letter from a Ch. Meunier (Maison du Livre)
offering to collaborate with me on a collection of literary morsels for a publication destined to serve as an
aid to wounded artists. That would earn me one hundred francs.

> *Sir, I am surprised by your proposi-
> tion. People neglect me so voluntarily!
> On the other hand, for a large number
> of years there has been a tradition of
> refusing everything I produce, whatev-
> er it might be. So, what's the point?
> What's more, I am ill at this moment
> and hardly capable of working, being
> a wounded artist myself, and how! But*

out of respect for your letter which you had the goodness to write in your own hand without recurring to the machine, I offer to you the conclusion from my most recent book, Joan of Arc and Germany, *a page that garners, I believe, the unpublished, chevaleresque, and ritualistic conspiration of silence by which I have been assassinated these last thirty years, that work having been stifled since it came out. I add that the mediocre wage of one hundred francs you mentioned is extremely worth consideration by a writer who is ill, almost without resources, and who accomplishes difficultly his sixty-ninth year.*

To Termier:

I would have been, yesterday, quite unable to write to you, so great was my weakness. I was only able to languish dolorously all day long while forcing myself to think of Saint Peter, whose shadow alone could heal, and thinking of you. It was, I think, the extreme point of descent before reascending, which seems to begin today.

The day before, I received from M. R*** a very fine letter, although a bit embarrassing. That letter was accompanied by a money order drawn from "household savings," the expe-

diter making me observe judiciously that my books, which he loves for a long time now, would not have been of much help to him if he was not poor.

He did not speak to me about the war, nor about you, which seems strange. It is impossible for me not to think about it, and you know that that is a big deal in my deplorable physical state... You greatly exaggerate my "contempt and my vilification" with respect to polytechnicians. Before knowing you, I knew nothing about them, but I had never had such sentiments against them. Besides, all that is already a long time ago.

Incapable presently of any invention, I have taken it upon myself to put some order to the more important notes of my Journal, from 1913 to 1915, in view of the 7th volume. The material is copious. But I have not yet written a single line. That will be my occupation at Mévoisins.

I understand you quite well when you speak of the task that remains for me to do. I think on it every day, and I believe even that it will be part of my most important work. I hope that God will give me the strength and the inspiration.

July

1ˢᵗ. – Finally, a little justice, the admirable article by Edmond Barthèlemy in the *Mercure de France*:

> Joan of Arc and Germany, *by Léon Bloy (Georges Crès & Co., 3.50). – There is nothing but the simplest and most comprehensive intuitions of the heart in the title of the recent book by Léon Bloy:* Joan of Arc and Germany. *To evoke the most extraordinary, the most exalting of memories from our History at the hour of greatest perils that have fallen on France – that there is,* par excellence, *I just said it, a spontaneous feeling of the heart. And that's just fine. Encouragement and consolation are offered with a profound candor, full of sagacity because it is appropriate in an extraordinary epoch like this one, where, in the moral order, all has been profoundly simplified. It is a very good, very sweet, very comforting book. It should be read in the trenches, where names like Joan of Arc have taken on a sublime* actuality. *In the trenches, and everywhere in France. There is, in this book, a precious accent for many hearts, in days like our own. I have seen women weeping at the words of adoration with which the Christian*

and Catholic Léon Bloy erects, before the iron Cross, the poor wooden cross that Joan of Arc kissed on her pyre,"the Cross of indigents and vagabonds, the sweet Cross of old roads winding through the country-side, the welcoming Cross of the poverty-stricken, of the extremely run down, their feet bleeding, their hearts tearful, those who have been bitten by serpents in the desert and who heal from their wounds while looking on the Cross of misery and glory!" And it is also, I will say even, the tone of some Saint Jerome, in some 5ᵗʰ century, letting fall, on the civilizations horribly blood-soaked by the Barbarian's lance[70], the words of a melancholic spirituality.

The first pages of the book were composed when the war broke out. Léon Bloy took up the book again in the middle of November, after the unparalleled days of the summer and autumn of 1914. It is, without a doubt, with an imagination profoundly shaken by those events that he picked up the pen again. Shaken? Let's just say rather that he found his way again! This 20ᵗʰ century complemented that 15ᵗʰ century: Léon Bloy had only to remain himself in his medium as a writer

---

[70]lance: "framée" in the French original.

in order to be up to the common hor-
ror of these two epochs, and to the
compassion as well, the "great com-
passion" that is contained in them. To
the pity principally, I might empha-
size. This book on Joan of Arc is a
huge network of biographical data
where the irradiated translucidities of
a burning Love are set like resplen-
dent pieces of stained glass in an iron
framework. At the heart of this book
burns a writer's heart, made fervent
by suffering. And the fervor is discov-
ered to be all the brighter here as the
suffering has increased, grown larger.
There is, in that heart, founded in the
same source of tenderness, its own
misfortune, the misfortune of Joan of
Arc, and the misfortune of France.

 From which results a very
moving, and so clear, reading. So clear.
Like all Léon Bloy's books, moreover.
The events have only confirmed the
writer in his manner of feeling and ex-
pressing himself. But he was always,
in his other books, what we see him to
be in this one. He has always had, for
want of extraordinary events like those
of today, his own reasons, the events
of his soul. The intensity of emotion
with him has always carried so irre-
sistibly the clarity of expression. Bloy
is a seer of the moral world. Emotion

and form, the one in its profundity, the other in its lucidity, announce the unparalleled energy of his intuition, of what must be called his practical sense of the Invisible, which is the only reality. I will pay no attention here to the theological Mystic, where the Catholic Bloy will rest like a great poet: one would have to go through his work to collect, in this respect, a crowd of thoughts, images, original to the point of being strange, brilliant to the point of fulgurating: dazzling breaches giving a view onto the Christian beyond, stained glass windows of clear light for the church that is Bloy's work. In that sphere of the Invisible, I will pause only at what is sentiment, the life of the heart. Ah! it is here, I have to say, that it is so delicious to listen to Bloy express himself with that same clarity. *I have always thought that the author of "The Woman Who Was Poor," in all that he has written, addresses himself above all to our hearts. Women are the best judges of this, and I have seen them, I have seen mothers of families, whom his books have attracted. This writer, who does not flatter women, inspires confidence in them. They are advised of a loyalty that is in him, they feel the rectitude and the authority that is in his thought.*

They know that there is a gentleness in him, which they can trust. Life, of course, has made it such that that gentleness has not proceeded without many bursts of anger. But who wants to count, at the foot of the statue finally extricated from its mass, the pieces of marble or basalt glanced off under the mallet? Ah! well do I know: Bloy had administered them, those rough blows of the mallet, which were able to lead one astray sometimes, and risked breaking, with the envelope *that* emprisoned *it, the statue itself. But his work, for all that, is still full of meaning, a meaning of great gentleness, if you want to reflect on it.*

*   I return to* Joan of Arc. *It is at this moment, – as with Napoleon, Napoleon whom Bloy sang in an astonishing book that I wrote about in its time, – the most* practical *subject in the history of France. When similar subjects are treated of, at a like hour, by writers like Bloy, one immediately senses a reality that one didn't possess a clear perception of in ordinary times: one senses the reality of the world of the soul, the only positive reality that is the common foundation from which forces in action come out into the light of the immediate. With respect to Joan of Arc and to all that*

his evocation of her contains that is invigorating, we feel how much the world is led by ideas. Belief leads it.

Some *have written rationalistic histories of Joan of Arc. I know what these extremely laborious things are, writings full of science and art. Sometimes even, the concern to "explain" everything, the skepticism, is not without tenderness for the heroine. I have found one of my own articles on an important work inspired by that same humanly affectionate skepticism. The tone of that article, written years ago, is very negative, and one will accuse me then of improvising my ideas on the occasion of the present book by Bloy. The fact of the matter is that I must have felt that that was not at all the proper way in which to speak about Joan of Arc. And I feel it more than ever today, in the times we live in. Similar attempts at rationalistic history, despite all their effort, all their art, all that they possess of affection in their humanly comprehensive skepticism remain, at the end of the day, for all practical purposes, arid, fallow land: not a flower of feeling and not an upsurge of action issues from them. They can do nothing for the vital instinct that, from the back of the trenches, from the ambulances, from everywhere where one fights and suffers, cries out to us: To live above all; they cannot do the thousandth part of what the instinctive pages of Bloy could do in that respect.*

Let nobody be fooled: those pages are written very close *to our heart. The subject of* Joan of Arc, *so extraordinary, so outside everything, is, because of that, brought near to us,* humanized, *rendered practical in a word, more than all the scientific, rational, "humaine" exegeses in the world could ever do. Read the chapter entitled "The Tears." Faced with a story like that of Joan of Arc, faced also with a story like that of present-day France, all is resolved in them, all is concentrated, feeling, mind, in that dew of the heart. I have just spoken my mind. Now I let Léon Bloy speak his:*

> *Tears, to be honest, cloud the view already so uncertain, but clairvoyance of the heart can replace it with an advantage, and a magnificent divination can illuminate the poor historian. And then, at a certain depth determined by the deposit of the illustrious dead, one is really forced to encounter universal Solidarity which is concealed to us by the social lie, and which their dust denounces with so much eloquence! That, above all, is what makes one weep!*

One feels oneself to be on an equal footing in that excessive misery of all men. The dazzling effect of Heroism or Beauty has disappeared. Whether it has to do with Charlemagne, Napoleon, or Joan of Arc, one sees in them only one's neighbors or friends, very humble brothers in the immense herd of coheirs of the Expulsion. Chants of glory, cries of enthusiasm, popular acclamations no longer exist; they never existed except in a dream that has evaporated. There is nothing left but tears of penitence, compassion, love, or despair, luminous or somber rivers that flow towards unknown gulfs.

That means that human destiny is not well understood, or felt, except from the heart's point of view; that if suffering is at the bottom of that destiny, we are all in this together; and that great souls, great men, in whom, by a necessity and a glory of their nature, universal suffering meets, are like the mystical place of the concentricity of all souls. All that is left for those mother souls is their tears, but their tears, that is to say the wherewithal to fecundate the earth. Léon Bloy, who has just collected Joan of Arc's tears, will be counted among the very perfect servants of the Saint of France.

– *Edmond Barthèlemy*

To the Japanese lady spoken about here on

March 23:

I am not happy with you. I had written to you, on the day of Saint John the Baptist, a letter that I believe to be very important. It was an extraordinary gift that I gave to you as to a person whom I would love very particularly. I made the most serious confidences to you in the hope of elevating you, of enlarging your heart...

Yes, doubtless, you were touched in a certain way and well do I see that I have not written to you in vain. But, at the same time, I see too clearly that you do not realize at all the supernatural life, as you say that you take communion every day only to obey me! What misery! *You leave the church saying to yourself: "I am going to send it all packing... Why does God love us?... I find that ridiculous..." I am ashamed to reproduce such phrases. Is that you talking? No, right? It's a fantastic and unbearable little girl that has taken your place for a moment.*

Do you know actually what prayer means? Note that I am not speaking to you now about quotidian communion which is a necessity for Christians just like eating is, even without appetite, in order to nourish the body. One takes communion, not to obey some man, but Jesus, who said that it was necessary to eat Him in order to gain eternal Life. No one can understand that, but everyone knows or can know that that Aliment acts on its own, in mysterious fashion, in the soul of the obedient, and that one day, after twenty years even, one will discover suddenly that one is prodigiously far from the beginning of that practice and that one is no longer the same creature at all.

I want to speak with you only about Prayer. What commonplaces! – "Remember me in your prayers, dear sir or dear madame." – "Do not forget me in your prayers, etc., etc..." One acquits oneself by mumbling some Pater *or* Ave *from the ends of one's lips and one thinks to have done something. Has no one ever taught you that* real *prayer must be* supernatural*, that is to say in direct union with Jesus Christ, that is to say even in a spirit of immolation and oblation of oneself? Such and such a person has asked me to pray for her, and I promised to do it, but I know very well that there is only one way to do it. It is to* pay *in her stead. Otherwise, I would have done nothing, and I will have obtained absolutely nothing.*

*I beg you, do not be mediocre.
Do not speak about heroism or impossibility. What I have told you is the
simplest thing in the world, and the
most consoling there is. I know quite
well what I am telling you!...*

2. – To Barthèlemy:

*My dear friend, it is a convalescent,
very feeble still, who writes to you.
You will pardon him for not being able
to send a long letter to you. But I
wanted to tell you immediately that
your article was infinitely sweet and
consoling to me. A little justice finally!
What sweetness for an old artist to
whom justice has almost always been
scandalously refused!*

Have you read, in the Times, *a
serialized column by one Paul Souday,
an authority it appears? That gentleman saw in me a "truculent pamphleteer." He was indignant with my contempt for Joan of Arc's enemies, and it
is just barely if he pardoned me for
having been disrespectful to Cauchon.
But my style made him think of* Péguy
(!) and that militated in my favor.

*After that, you can understand
that I must have read you with a sort*

of drunkenness, and I entreat you to inscribe me in alphabetical order, that is in the first row, among your – insolvable – debtors; debtors for their succored souls! It is something in advance of Paradise...

3. – To Félix Raugel:

I have been rather ill of late. Great physical malaise added to everything that gnaws away at me for as long as twelve months now. It is impossible for me to take my stand against the abomination of Germany, to say nothing of so many French things that seriously displease me with a perfect horror. So well do I sense that there is nothing more for the rare faithful than the acceptation of a rigorous martyrdom. No more pope, no more bishops, almost no more priests. Souls are shuddering and abandoned. Ah! my dear combatant, would that I were still strong and able!... And menaced, as always, by poverty, I must be witness to the ignominious indifference of all those whom the war does not touch and above all to the whorish joy of shopkeepers who take advantage of it by raising the price of their merchandise, afraid to see it end. I envy you really, my dear Félix, when you speak to me of masses

> *at dawn in the hollow of a rock, with the distant sound, or very close, of cannons. What vivifying and magnificent poetry! The rest of us, for how long will we still have mass? God knows, God whose name has been replaced by the words "fatherland" and "republic."*

4. – I learn that my dear Philippe Raoux has just been given honorable mention in the army.

6. – Baptism of a little girl of refugee friends whom we have accepted to be godfather and godmother to, Jeanne and I. Naturally, one is touched and we rejoice in that huge event of a soul becoming a Christian. But how would it be possible to rejoice enough? One does not understand anything, other than that one is at the edge of a gulf of light.

8. – It is the ever-redoubted moment of our annual holidays. Horrible work of packing. A Franciscan monk wrote to me from Cairo:

> *What will become of the Holy Land if war breaks out between Italy and Turkey? Misery upon misery. It is really an abomination of desolation,* in loco sancto.

9. – Versailles, Saint-Piat, Mévoisins... without too much fatigue.

11. – My health seems to have returned. Re-read the 3rd volume of *1815* by Henry Houssaye. Bath of contempt for the politics of that period, so similar to contemporary politics.

13. – Unpublished material for the publisher Meunier who did not want the printed material I offered him on June 30.

WE ARE NOT IN A STATE OF WAR

For Félix Raugel.

My dear Félix, I write to you from a corner of Beauce where I had hoped to find refuge against the profitable patriotism of the shopkeepers of Paris and its suburbs which has decreed the famishing persecution of war prices. You are not aware of this on the front where the only thing you have to fear is projectiles or the Boche gasses less redoubtable perhaps and less foul than the schemes of our grocers and our butchers. I had told myself that my garden would nourish me at least a little, and I soon had to renounce that illusion. My poor vegetable garden, invaded by moles or sewer rats, is dev-

astated, turned topsy-turvy like your
battlefields. Such is the law of the
times, trenches everywhere. As if people were not enough, the animals have
to get into the mix.

A man of prayer, you recall,
doubtless, the Gospel of the 9th Sunday
after Pentecost, August 2, 1914, unforgettable day of mobilization: "The enemies encircled you with their trenches..." and here we are ten months later
and nobody can say when that will
end. Would that I could fight next to
you! I am 69 years old, I am an old
man, very worn out. The hope of demolishing some of the atrocious ras-
cals that are sullying our France is
denied me. What is left for me to do
then?

To write good books, you tell
me. Who would read them? My Joan of
Arc and Germany does not sell. Our
heroes train themselves by devouring
The Three Musketeers and The Count
of Monte Christo. Several intellectuals
snap up Barrès or Aristide Bruant.
There are even some artillery men
who have brought Bergson with them,
and I know a fearless lawyer who had
stuffed two or three volumes of Niet-
zsche into his sack. Who could I interest, knowing only how to speak of

God? In that sense, I am infinitely more foreign than a Fuegian or a Kamchatkan. God, that's the dusty hypothesis at the back of the attic of contemporary thought, and we are, you and me, my poor friend, strange dreamers standing on a very dangerously worm-eaten ladder. We think however that we know something that everyone else does not know and we still think it.

From the beginning of this prodigious war that no other war resembles, we have told ourselves that it was the probable commencement of the Miracle of the End, announced in 1846, by Someone who cannot be deceived, and that the ignoble dream of Barbarians ought to be considered as a preamble quite simply, something like the curtain rise. And the unfolding of events could only confirm us in that thinking.

In fact, how to attribute the Definitive to the inept German farce, however horrible and bloody it might be? It is really too mediocre, too shamefully imbecilic, too disgusting! To pounce like some formidably armed brutes on peoples unprepared for war, to cut the throats of thousands of defenseless beings, and to soil them

*and torture them, to set fire to their
houses, to pillage, to devastate to their
hearts' content the most beautiful
countries in the world, to destroy age-
old masterpieces while sniggering like
crazy apes, while filling themselves up
on the idea that it is in that way one
will make the entire earth tremble, it
is, in truth, too idiotic, and one cannot
represent to himself a buffoon of can-
nibals so sumptuously cretinous as to
imagine that!*

*Such is nonetheless the unique
concept of Prussian Germany, and all
its intellectuals prostrated before a
lamentable stage ham.*

*I have spoken just now of the
war, and I am ashamed to have written that word. The truth, which would
need to be shouted aloud everywhere,
is that we are not at war. We defend
ourselves, as best we can, our soil, our
towns, our homes, our women and our
children against the most gigantic enterprise of burglary and murder that
has ever been seen. To say that we are
in a state of war with Germany is as
absurd as supposing that a miserable
man who is clung onto by a hideous
Maenad filled with all sorts of demons
of lust, and defending himself against
her with rage, is in a state of marriage*

with that possessed woman.

If I had the honor of a military command, I would never consent to recognize a German for a soldier and I would not have enough rope to hand the prisoners. The uniform of those scoundrels offends our intelligence of chevaleresque warriors and constantly makes us forget that we are in the presence of some colossal farce of despicable domestics dressed up as men of war. We treat with consideration, with honor even, the abominable villains whom our galley-slaves would not want for companions. Frederick II the so-called Great, who was himself a bandit, declared on his deathbed that he was tired of ruling over slaves, and the repugnant Schopenhauer was not consoled by belonging to so stupid a nation. Extreme servitude and extreme stupidity, that is what we have before us. How many years, and how many rivers of blood will it take before we wash the filth of that rabble from our poor France?

But, once again, the Definitive does not belong, and cannot belong, to such instruments of the demon. In fulfilling the prophesies that you know as well as I do, Europe is already on fire and the rest of the world is not too far from flaring up. The blind even, and the deafest, sense the unknown storm building, that no experience could have foreseen. But a scout was needed for this nameless cataclysm, and the basest of all peoples was designated for that office by the supernatural Disdain of Him whom nobody mentions. When the real Drama will have begun, the real inanity of the German colossus will be so manifest that it will become difficult to think still on it in the infinite trembling of new torments. One will know then that it was nothing, really nothing, and the memory of that stinking empire will not have the power even to procure nausea in the agonists.

There you have it, my dear Félix, all that can be written to you by an old prophet, little listened to, who has ceased, for a very long time now, to gain credit among the prattlers of men, and who hopes for absolutely nothing in this world if not the imminent coming of God in the terrible magnificence of his Glory or in the unrevealable terrors of his Anger.

15. – From Pierre:

This morning, July 14, I attended – it was my duty as a correspondent – the ceremony of the transfer of Rouget de

*l'Isle's[71] ashes to Les Invalides. Am I
not "Marseillais" enough to be mad
with enthusiasm? It was so poor, so
pitiable, so ashen colored! Behind the
coffin, Poincaré was walking, who had
the look of a sub-prefect, then all the
ministers, then all the band of Parliament; it was grotesque. And me, I was
thinking of the transfer of the Emper-
or's ashes, as you recount it in* The
Soul of Napoleon. *That was so much
more significative.*

16. – I am made to read, in the *Croix*, a scandalous
letter by Mgr. de Cabrières, cardinal and archbishop,
to another prince of the Church, to explain to him his
pastoral indignation against the Holy Virgin who was
not afraid, sixty years ago, to confide in a little shepherdess, while speaking disrespectfully to her about
the clergy. The *apparent* object of that letter is the
condemnation of a extremely imbecilic booklet that
certainly did not merit such publicity, but which appeared to his Eminence a plausible pretext to outrage,
once again, the Mother of God, at the same time as an
occasion to console or re-assure the archbishop of
Reims whose chastisement has already begun.

18. – A priest-nurse in Chartres has told us how diffi-

[71]Rouget de l'Isle: Claude Joseph Rouget de l'Isle (1760 – 1836),
a French army officer during the French Revolution. He is
credited with having written the words and music of the French
national anthem, the *Marseillais*.

cult his situation is. He is with a dozen other priests,
under orders of a Free Mason who does not hide from
them his aversion and vexes them as much as he can.
As for the convalescents whom they are forced to
serve, they are horrible brutes who know only how to
blaspheme and speak filth. In this way, France is converted.

19. – Reading of Houssaye, *1815*, 3rd volume ("Crucified France: Prussian Terror"). The Germans of one
hundred years ago were exactly what they are today.
That reading is dreadful.

20. – Our poor curate is given infinite difficulties to
prepare, without any assistance, for a 1st class funeral
service for a miserable man who never consented to
live Christianly and whose avarice was surprising
even here. According to the custom of honest rela-
tives whom the fear of restitutions *in extremis* gnaw
away at, the priest was not called to the deathbed until
it was too late.

21. – "According to letters that come to me from the
front," a friend wrote to me, "the men's spirit becomes, in many places, frankly poor. It is difficult to
envisage the *outcome* without anxiety."

        That would be terrible, in fact. If the military
dike that separates us from the Germans should be
broken, what a deluge of two million ferocious ani-

mals!

22. – A countryman takes us out for a ride in his vehicle for several kilometers. Excursion promised to Madeleine, whose feast day is today. Why have the most lovely landscapes become so sad looking?

24. – Letter from Raugel from a hospital in Montpellier. He was wounded in the foot and will limp from now on, but the war is over for him. His letter is extremely gentle and Christian.

I write to him of our sorrowful feelings attenuated by the thought that his wound does not deprive him of any of his members. I encourage him to be persuaded that he has been mercifully spared given he could have died or lost half his person. I assure him that all those horrors, seen from afar even, have had a big influence on the illness that I am still convalescent of. Finally, I announce to him that I am working on a new book in my solitude. "The hours appear to me less heavy, and I succeed sometimes in dissipating the phantoms, by seeking the traces of what Jesus wrote with his finger, two thousand years ago, on my heart of mud, when one accused the adulterous woman before him."

Germany calls its combatants: *Das Menschenmaterial* (human materiel). That ignoble word says everything.

25. – To Uncle Louis:

> *... I won't be telling you anything new by telling you that we are in a complete solitude here. The countryside is strangely depopulated by the war. One sees only some old people stagnating in the most fetid impiety. Except for the curate, an excellent man whose face proclaims the most honorable simplicity, that leaves us nobody to speak with, I do not know how or why. Boredom would crush me if I were not working. Remains to be seen whether the new book can ever be published. Not to mention whether there will ever be bookstores and readers again. But I'm disinterested in that, content to know that there is God and that we will see his acts on an abominable world that refuses to know him.*

26. – Letter from a poor, wounded Belgian. He recounts to me how he was deceived and conned hideously by a priest in whom he had placed unlimited trust. That holy man having squeezed him for everything he had, persuaded him to enlist, making him believe that in his absence he himself would watch over his mother and sister, deprived of support, with an extreme solicitude. Soon after his departure, the poor women were left to scrape by on public charity.

One would like to know in what batch of massacred Belgian priests did that ecclesiastic cull the crown of *martyrdom*.

27. – A superior officer who appears informed provides for my "meditations of a solitary" the two numbers here below that are *more or less official*. Since the beginning of the war, the number of French *killed* approaches 500,000. The number of Germans *killed* is between 1,500,000 and 1,600,000. One does not mention the Austrians, Russians, English, Serbs, and Turks. By multiplying the number of killed by 3, one arrives sensibly at the number of men who are definitively out of combat (killed, seriously wounded, or prisoners). The French army would have thereby lost 1,500,000 men then; the German army 4,500,000! It is manifest then that the Germans wear down more quickly than we do, as, having an army nearly double our size, they submit to triple the losses.

Conclusion. The war will last a long time still, six months at least, perhaps a year, unless God should intervene by some thunderbolt.

Letter from Abbot X*** entreating me to attest that in such and such epoch he wrote to me to protest against the publication of *The Life of Mélanie* without *imprimatur*. It appears that that attestation is necessary for him, for one wants to refer my publication, elements of which he had furnished to me, to the Index.

I respond at first that I went without the imprimatur, certain that I would not have found a single bishop to give it to me, having no need for it besides, given that I do not belong to the ecclesiastical world. If I had waited for approbation, *The Life of Mélanie* would have never seen the light of day.

To finish:

You mention an individual (the bishop of Moulins) who wants to refer me to the Index. Ridiculous threat and particularly late in coming, after three years. *If I had the honor of knowing him, I would tell him three things: 1ˢᵗ, that I absolutely don't give a damn about the Index which for me represents merely a* guichet *behind which one dishonors the Church; 2ⁿᵈ, that a mention of my book in the almost always imbecilic catalog of that Congregation would be precious publicity for me, unhoped for; 3ʳᵈ, that the malicious instigator of that profitable interdiction would belong from then on to my* fangs. *One knows what that means.*

28. – To Termier who proposed his optimism to me:

Yes, I know that you are an optimist. I am one too. Only, there are two types: the optimist of Mercy and the optimist of Justice which will certainly meet each other in the Absolute, but after what a journey! You hope for mercy before the end of the chastisement. Doubtless, it is to be hoped for by such and such friends of God, but, for others, what derision that would be! What triumph for the impious bishops or archbishops, for the Echo of Paris, *for the multitude of honest men who "have nothing to reproach themselves for," and what a failure for La Salette!*

My conception of things is such that I am forced to rejoice over the worst misfortunes whose spectacle or anticipation tortures me, because I know them to be necessary, that is to say, wanted by God and, by consequence, adorable; because it is a thousand times clear to me that the announced cataclysms are the indispensable prodromes of the Kingdom of God in terra *that we have the duty to ask for unceasingly; because finally, in several weeks, 69 years ago the Tears and the Words of Mary were scorned, as they are today more than ever, and that can no longer be supported nor pardoned.*

Every Frenchman who is not a brute or a rascal has to desire Germany's punition, that is to say, short of an unfortunately impossible extermination, the infinite humiliation and putting down of that execrable nation.

Germany's impunity would be the demonstration of God's inexistence. It ought then to be punished in the most terrible way. According to known figures, this unprecedented war that only Germany wanted would have cost France, after one year, nearly two million victims, in combatants alone. The twenty years of war under the Republic and the Empire were less costly. It's enough to make one's head spin. But if the most abject of all peoples received the power to cause us so much suffering, what to think of the infidelity that was able to bring such an expiation upon us, and how to believe that that expiation could end, even after the crushing of our present enemies, if the monstrous infidelity continued? Now, that is precisely what can be seen by everyone, except the men of the Croix *and the* Echo of Paris who were born blind. *Such are, dear friend, my meditations of a solitary.*

It is through you that I learned of Boussac's new wound, fortunately not grave, and whom I will write to. Three days earlier I had received a letter from Raugel evacuated to Montpellier where they treat him for serious wounds. He hopes to keep his right leg, deeply affected, but he will remain lame. How many others!

That's all I hear about these days, the dead or crippled.

30. – Letter by Pierre having returned from Reims where he had been bombarded:

Here (in Paris) nothing new, nothing salient. One waits. There is nothing but the gentlemen politicians of the republic who act, who would really like to become the Dantons, the Robespierres, etc. It's amusing and sinister.

It's disgusting for its baseness and even more repugnant when one has seen the front. I have seen, or to say it better, I have heard war. For it is diabolically invisible.

Arrived in auto, July 20, in the morning, from Epernay, at the Mountain of Reims which dominates the plain where the city lies, the staff officer of the division that occupies that sector made us descend to show us that part of the immense battlefield. One still does not see anything of the war. It's a very beautiful and very peaceful landscape. In the distance, the city, the towers of the cathedral. Fields of wheat off in the distance, vineyards. And all that is empty, deserted. Not a living being in sight.

But very far away, to the east or north of Reims, the officer points out white lines to us; they are the French and German trenches where the troops face each other since September, from the time that the bandits were chased out of Reims. Nothing has changed. The first German trench is at a distance of 1200 meters from the last houses of the city. I saw them rather close up. It's unimaginable. No soldiers in sight. Only the sound of cannons can be heard, German cannons.

We entered the city under the violent bombardment indicated in the following day's communiqué. I heard the sinister whistling of shells, then their explosion, hard, cruel, formidable. I saw some explode one hundred meters away from us. But one did not realize the danger. It's very strange to be present, for the first time, at an intense bombardment. That day, more than 300 shells, in the duration of one hour, had been fired on the city.

We ate lunch tranquilly in a hotel, the only one in that empty city. For there were no more than 20,000 poor folk remaining out of a population of 120,000. That is what is revolting above all. The Germans pointlessly *bombard the ruins and a cathedral.*

There are no troops in Reims. The French soldiers are stationed in the surrounding villages and woods.

When one enters into that great, deserted, and devastated city, the impression is agonizing. Weeds grow in the streets. Here and there an old woman, old men, a soldier, children. Other than that, a profound silence. Nothing but the whistling of shells, then their explosion. How stupid and vile it all is!

Several quarters of the city are nothing but an immense mass of rubble. One feels sad enough to cry, and with sorrow and with impotent rage. Is it not dreadful to think that the Germans bombard Reims for eleven months now, from the forts of Brimont and Berru, and that they have fortified them in an inexpugnable manner!

But the Cathedral... It is there, the towers, the nave, the transept. Only its beautiful adornment, its statues, its pinnacles, its stone lacework and all its stain glass windows, have been ripped off, destroyed. It has become a skeleton. The stain glass are shattered. One has the impression of being next to a dead person, next to a cadaver. The day when I visited it, another two shells had fallen on it.

In spite of all that, it is solid like a fortress, the architect told us who guided us. How filthy and stupid it is to persist like that on that house of God! I understand even better now the diabolism in this war.

There you have it, in a few words, my visit to Reims. It's nothing but one point on the occidental front. And there is still the Russian front and the Italian front!

There is nothing but La Salette to make us understand a little about what is happening. But what massacres all over Europe. The tally of the dead, wounded, or prisoners is frightening. Entire populations have been wiped out. Dieu agit. *There is no way to deny it.*

August

7. – Letter from Raoux temporarily at ease. He just spent four days in Lyon, where he had the joy of seeing again his entire family and seeing his son Jean *for the first time*. He feels, like me, everyone's indifference, and the France that is left behind has not given him the impression of a country that undergoes a formidable expiation. He is profoundly disgusted.

Another letter no less disenchanted from another engineer who wrote to me in July. There is no
confidence in the English, any more than in the
Americans, and I think there is no mood to lend credit
to anyone, whoever it might be. It gives me this[72]

A Bavarian curate is asked how it can be that
he (and his country's clergy) could accept so easily
the Lutheran domination of the Prussians: "Before
1871, I had a salary of 400 marks, now I have 4,000."

11. – Madeleine is very happy. Brou gave her a violin
of superior quality, that he had fabricated himself, and
it is an extreme subject of surprise for us and for others. Brou is prodigious. He seems to have discovered
ancient secrets, and he could, it seems, make his fortune as a maker of stringed instruments.

17. – The newspapers mention the plan of a colossal
wooden statue of Hindenburg, in Berlin. Every German would be invited – by paying, of course, – to
plant a nail in that statue. That idea, barely intelligible, is strangely significative of that people. It's not
even an idea of barbarians. It is the lowest stage of
idolatry among the savages of Polynesia.

20. – My dear godson Jacques Maritain came and visited here one night and one day. It is the first visit I
have received in my solitude. How sweet and recomforting! The curate who comes to lunch informs him

---

[72]Editor's note: what follows appears to have been censored in
the original publication.

very amply on the state of the country, really appalling from the religious point of view.

24. – An important naval victory by the Russians in the gulf of Riga is announced. A considerable part of the German fleet has been wiped out. Refreshing news. The attention of the world is fixed, for some time now, on the dreadful, disproportionate war on the eastern front, where it seems that the fate of Germany must be decided. But what to believe and what to conjecture?

28. – It is horribly grievous for me to write the present volume! I have not stopped, moreover, feeling ill, and how difficult it is for me to reconcile my personal tribulations with these immense events!

29. – Visit by Termier. That excellent and marvelous friend has come from very far away to spend three hours with me, and his departure fills me with melancholy. He is, with regard to La Salette, very respectfully disposed, but he has some difficulty believing that the Secret should be perfectly identical to the Mother of God's Word, supposing that the imagination of Mélanie could have intervened.

For example, he finds it enormous and disconcerting that the name of Germany should not be mentioned even. To that, I respond unhesitatingly that the Holy Virgin, speaking in a completely divine manner, in view of *definitive* Events, did not have to mention Germany, which would have, then, *ceased to exist*, and which, consequently, already no longer existed for Her.

Unexpected response that makes an impression on my auditor.

September

2. – To Baumann. I speak to him of the unique Joy, that of suffering for God, and of our ineptitude to write for the multitude who do not know our language and who will never know it. "As for me, I write for the divine Three Persons."

8. – Mary's Nativity. It's the great pilgrimage of Chartres. Mass by our curate at Notre-Dame-sous-Terre. I wanted to honor Mary, I certainly wanted to with all my heart, but the crowd, the jostling, the impossibility of reading my missal in that dark and suffocating crypt, all that was too painful for me and I do not know if I could have prayed. I have always had a horror of crowds, and multitudinous pilgrimages cannot suit me.

The improbable farce of the statue of Hindenburg and his nails comes to be realized. Yesterday its inauguration took place.

That statue is, said the Journal*, at the*

very least, remarkable for its weight: 26,000 kilograms.

It was erected next to the col-umn of Victory, where are found al-ready the effigies of other German captains whose features are repro-duced, however, in marble or bronze.

One knows for what reasons Hindenburg had the honor of wood. By means of a small monetary contri-bution, each person can plant a nail, as a sign of respect, anywhere into Hindenburg's body. There are two million of those nails.

After an imbecilic discourse, Bethmann-Hollweg invited the Kai-ser's sister to come and plant a nail. Mme. Hindenburg advanced in turn and, without blinking, buried a nail into her husband's body. Applause. The Hindenburg demoiselles did as their mama did. They were equally ap-plauded. Some other individuals acted in the same way when their turn came. Then it was the multitude's turn. By 7 o'clock in the evening, the unfortunate marshall had been transpierced 20,000 times.

10. – A dear friend visits us... I can say no more. There are creatures whom God has formed expressly to send them, at useful times, to those of his friends

who are afflicted by sadness. They have, without knowing it, the mission of presenting to them the dolorous mirror on which Jesus' Face is imprinted, and it is a supreme consolation reserved only for some.

13. – *Adjuro te, per Deum vivum!* Jesus had remained silent under the most flagrant outrages. That expression by the Great Priest constrained him to speak. Would that not be an all powerful prayer?

From a young man who said he had been received by me, some years ago. He asks me to pray for a person who died in the war, André S***, who was one of my faithful readers. Become sergeant of infantry, a place of shelter in the trenches was baptized by him *Villa Marchenoir*, because a copy of *The Soul of Napoleon* was found there, which he could read with as much joy as astonishment. He had written down his impressions in a letter that his friend copied for me: "I bless heaven which has procured this joy, perhaps the last, but, assuredly, one of the most intense in my life."

That letter is dated November 28, 1914. January 10, André S*** was dead.

16. – Once again, the curate speaks to me about his parishioners' huge poverty of soul. Supernatural life absolutely impossible and unable to be found in the countryside.

18. – A little beggar woman from Paris, whom Jeanne had taken into our service, hoping to transform her, hightails it after having robbed us of the little money we possessed. All that happens in life is adorable.

Letter from Raoux on return from his second furlough. Same impressions of disgust as six weeks ago. "I had not mentioned the backstory of some fortifying impressions... One has the air of being very far away from the front, and not a few honest women pass for having forgotten that they were married. The number of stories on that subject is considerable. According to most people, we are far from doing penance and many are making a fortune."

19. – A card from Pierre informs us of the birth of his third child, Jean-François, born the morning of the 17th, feast day of the Stigmata of Saint Francis of Assisi, and having to be baptized today, anniversary of the Apparition of Our Lady of La Salette.

This time, I am not the godparent, but all the same I must rejoice over the growth of my spiritual family.

22. – Here I am ill again and the relapse appears grave. It's the definitive *adieu*, I fear, to everything youthful and strong that might still remain in me.

27. – Extraordinary news. Victories in Artois, and in Champagne. 20,000 prisoners. Figure that one must

double by the number of German dead and wounded. Would it be the beginning of the deliverance?

October

3. – In the *Figaro*:

The German "Song of the Sword."

I do not pay enough attention to the literature that rages, at this moment in time, on the other side of the Rhine.

One of our friends mailed to us, from Switzerland, a small volume printed in Leipzig and a copy of which can no longer be found in Berlin, where it was on sale recently and subsequently removed after several hours.

The work entitled *The Song of the Sword*, as brief as it is, is edifying in the highest degree. It reflects in its literature the "chosen nation's" feelings of immense pride and the colossal infatuation that it has. Here are some extracts:

> *It was not up to me to be just nor to have pity. It sufficed that I should be indescribably holy by my Vocation and that I should blind with so many tears the eyes of mortals, the proudest of whom had come away humbly groping towards heaven.*
>
> *I have killed old men who re-*

sembled palaces of Sorrow, I have lopped the breasts off of women who were believers, and I have pierced small children who looked at me with the eyes of dying lions.

Each day, I have galloped on the pale Horse along the avenue of cypresses that goes "from the uterus to the sepulture," and I have made a fountain of blood of all the children of man who found themselves within my reach...

Clearly, I have the right to be proud, being the messenger of the All Powerful Lord...

One can imagine my shock on re-reading thus my poem, "Lamentation of the Sword," from twenty years ago, wherein the despair of the noble sword in the hands of churls is expressed, a poem in prose transcribed *word for word*, under a new title; and it is easy to imagine my stupor on seeing that the ingenious Boche, in order to finish his small volume dignantly, had again *borrowed* from me, two formidable lines from the preface to *Sweating Blood*, without any other change than the name of Germany substituted for the name of France:

"*Germany* is eminently the first among peoples..., etc."

Of course, it would be ridiculous to complain. The Boche heaps honors on me.

7. – The weather has become horrible, and I cannot get the care I need in this desert. I must, starting to-morrow, return to Bourg-la-Reine.

Conclusion

Now, may God's will be done! I will stop here, having had the joy, after so many months of incertitude and anguish, of being able to note an important military success that our politicians were unable to hamper and that seems to presage finally the definitive expulsion of the German brutes.

The immense effort realized in France, after a year, will it be judged, with Mercy at bay, sufficiently expiatory? At the far end of a lake filled with blood, do we need to fear a bridge over the Abyss, a bridge of the Devil to go *beyond* the Abyss? No one wants pastors any longer, and the pastors have condemned themselves as well. He who should be speaking louder than the cannons is silent.

Scarcely two months ago, there was discussion of an appeal by Benedict XV in favor of peace. Silence would be better, the very silence of death. By the effect of the most inconceivable injustice, the Holy Father would have addressed *identical* objurgations or implorations to all the sovereigns and all the peoples, making them all equally liable and responsible for the monstrous iniquity of the aggressors! The oppressed, the spoliated, the tortured, the assassinated, on the same bench as the criminals at the court of assizes of the Vicar of Jesus Christ!

In ancient times, when there was a Pope, he would have stood up from the very first day, speaking to the wicked perpetrators like the prophet Nathan to David:

"*Tu es ille vir qui fecit hoc.*"[73] Wilhelm, you are the guilty one! François-Joseph, you are the guilty one! I am cutting you off, both of you, from my flock, I release your people and abandon you to the vengeance of men, while waiting for God's anger that I summon on your impious heads."

How miserably incredulous the Christian world has become, the œcumenical force of such a *nominative* sentence would have been incalculable. One would have had the illusion at least of a renewal of the supernatural Life and the consequences could have been infinite. But we are far from the popes Gregory and Innocent and their ilk. All grandeur is exiled to the back shelves of History, and if God wants to act manifestly, he will need to act *by Himself,* victoriously, as he did two thousand years ago, when he rose from the dead.

I wait for the Cossacks and the Holy Ghost.

---

[73] *Tu es... hoc*: Latin for "You are the man who did this."

Appendix

EXTRACTS FROM GERMAN SERMONS published by the English newspaper *The Standard*.

> *We do not hate our enemies. We follow God's commandments that enjoin us to love them. But we consider it an act of love when we kill them, make them suffer, burn their houses, invade their territories. Divine love is spread out across the world, but men must suffer for their safety. Parents love their children, but they castigate them. The masters love their pupils, but they punish them. Germany loves other nations, but it castigates them for their own good.*

> *— RHEINOLD SEEBEEG, Professor of Theology, Berlin.*

> *Just as the Almighty had his Son crucified in order to accomplish the work of redemption, so Germany is destined to crucify humanity in order to assure its safety, and humanity must be saved by blood and fire and by the sword. German warriors do not spill the blood of other nations with a joyous heart; it is for them a sacred duty that they would not know how to neglect*

without committing a sin. Our adored emperor hates the horrors of war. For many years, he has worked to maintain peace in the world. Germany has never employed its force to threaten the independence of a nation. It is precisely because of our purity that we have been chosen as the instruments of the Almighty, to punish the envious, chastise the wicked, and strike sinning peoples with the sword. Germany's divine mission, my brothers, is to crucify humanity. By consequence, German soldiers' duty is to strike pitiably; Germany must kill, it must burn, it must destroy. Half measures would be impious. This must be a war without pity. The wicked, the friends and allies of Satan, must be eradicated like bad weeds. Satan, himself, who has come into the world under the form of a great power (Germany), must be crushed. Germany has the divine task of fulfilling the destruction of those who personify evil. When the work is finished, the fire and sword will not have acted in vain, that will be the redemption of mankind. The reign of justice will be established on earth and the German empire, its creator, will remain its protector.

– Pastor Pilippi (Berlin).

Heaven has blessed the Germans and has designated them as the chosen people. We wage this war in the conviction that we execute divine designs, by destroying our enemies and establishing our domination. Germany defends Christianity. Its enemies are those of the true religion [sic]. *It is that consciousness of our mission that permits us to rejoice and to be happy, with a love full of gratitude, when our engines of war beat down the sons of Satan, and when our marvelous submariners, instruments of divine vengeance, send to the bottom of the sea thousands of the non-elect. We must fight the wicked by all means possible; their cries of grief must not move our deaf German ears. There can be no compromise with hell, nor pity for the servants of Satan. In other words, no quarter for the English, the French, the Russians, and all peoples who have given themselves over to the devil, and who have been, by consequence, condemned to perish by divine sentence.*

– Pastor LŒBEL (LEIPZIG)

May 25, 1911, [sic] Mme. Léon Bloy received an important letter signed Joseph Lefèvre, organist, without return address.

All inquiries having been in vain, no response could be made, and the sender, if he is still alive, is asked to make himself known.

Index

Other Books by the Publisher

Fanchette's Pretty Little Foot
by Restif de La Bretonne

Je M'Accuse...
by Léon Bloy

My Hospitals & My Prisons
by Paul Verlaine

Salvation Through the Jews
by Léon Bloy

Words of a Demolitions Contractor
by Léon Bloy

Cellulely
by Paul Verlaine

Flowers of Bitumen
by Émile Goudeau

Songs for Her & Odes in Her Honor
by Paul Verlaine

On Huysmans' Tomb
by Léon Bloy

Ten Years a Bohemian
by Émile Goudeau

The Soul of Napoleon
by Léon Bloy

www.ingramcontent.com/pod-product-compliance
Lightning Source LLC
Chambersburg PA
CBHW021657120626
46545CB00004B/1289